STEPHEN BENZ was born in the United States, and during the past twenty years has travelled, studied and lived in Central America. His previous book, *Guatemalan Journey*, concerns his experiences living in Guatemala, where he taught at the national university. In 1997 he was the winner of two SATW Lowell Thomas Travel Journalism awards. Stephen Benz currently lives in Miami.

Green Dreams

Travels in Central America

Stephen Benz

LONELY PLANET PUBLICATIONS
Melbourne • Oakland • London • Paris

Green Dreams: Travels in Central America

Published by Lonely Planet Publications

    Head Office: PO Box 617, Hawthorn, Vic 3122, Australia
    Branches: 150 Linden Street, Oakland, CA 94607, USA
                    10a Spring Place, London NW5 3BH, UK
                    71 bis rue du Cardinal Lemoine, 75005 Paris, France

Published 1998

Printed by SNP Printing Pte Ltd, Singapore

Author photograph by Cheryl Benz

Maps by Jenny Jones

Designed by Margaret Jung

Edited by Janet Austin

National Library of Australia Cataloguing in Publication Data

Benz, Stephen, 1958–.
Green dreams: travels in Central America.

ISBN 0 86442 523 6.

1. Ecotourism – Central America. 2. Central America – Description and travel. I. Title.

917.2

Text © Stephen Benz 1998
Maps © Lonely Planet 1998

Contents

The Ruta Maya: Guatemala, 1997

The Ruta Maya: Chiapas, 1997

The Ruta Maya: Yucatán, 1997

To Cheryl, for putting up with my rambling.

Acknowledgments

A version of Chapter 1 was originally published in *Grand Tour* under the title 'Green Dreams'.

The author wishes to thank the National Endowment for the Humanities (USA) for support. Thanks also go to Michelle de Kretser and Janet Austin at Lonely Planet for patience and suggestions. Thanks, too, to travel companions over the years, especially my wife Cheryl. Finally, thanks to Warren Zevon for musical inspiration.

Note: With the exception of Merle Greene Robertson and Peter Harrison, the characters in this narrative have been given pseudonyms.

Prologue

GREEN dreams begin like this: in the capital, things are not going well for you. Not at all. A botched deal in a cantina ends in a protracted argument, unexpected gunfire, a narrow escape down an alley patrolled by starved curs and querulous whores. A black market fleecing reduces your resources to near nil. A misbegotten attempt to earn some much-needed money through freelancing ends when all your contacts – a government minister, a mercenary, a rebel commando, a drug lord – either prove belatedly recalcitrant or want cash up front, cash you don't have. At a roadblock, an expired visa brings you under a soldier's scrutiny, and only the production of a 'Press Pass' (your old library card) wins a weary wave of dismissal and a warning to 'comply with your visa obligations as a stranger'. But for you, compliance requires paying some bureaucrat a hefty bribe and you'll probably face deportation anyway. In the weeks to come, you skulk around the city streets avoiding the Uzi-bearing gendarmes on patrol.

The capital is a hard-luck place, and you've had enough. You're bored with the expat circles and their endless rounds of drinking and whoring. You need to head somewhere remote, somewhere well removed from civilisation, somewhere without pavement or pollution or civic authority. You begin to think of the jungle, the empty mangrove coast, a place of green weather. You listen to the stories the adventurers tell, and you think, I could go there too, hell yes, why not?

In the jungle – so you think – you will find an untamed paradise, and mystery and life at its most primal. In the jungle, there will be pumas on the prowl and flocks of toucans bursting from the verdure and the taste of strange fruit on your tongue and the primitive villages of Stone Age tribes. In your shabby *pensión* in the capital you wake to a white carcinogenic haze and find yourself dreaming of endangered species, sacred waterfalls, mangrove swamps, virgin wildlands, remote jungle dwellers.

Green dreams are made of these.

You learn that there's a bus you can take to the end of the road, and then a river boat that penetrates still further into *tierra incógnita*, and then uncharted tribal trails that will lead you to where no gringo has ever gone. One day, you find yourself boarding that bus, and the long journey begins.

Amazonia, 1982

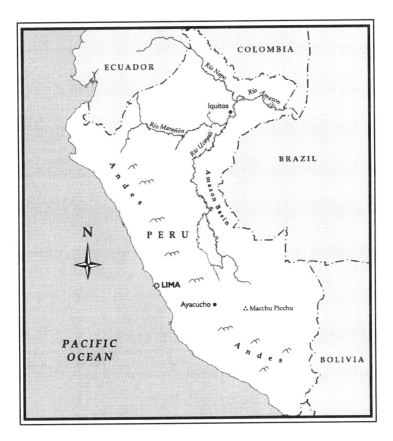

CHAPTER 1

The frontier of ecotourism

THE Maoist guerrillas of the Shining Path forced me to become an ecotourist. I was in Lima, Peru, preparing for an overland journey to rebel territory high in the Andes near the town of Ayacucho. Along with a party of other foreign journalists, I intended to interview villagers and government officials in the troubled region. We thought that we would be safe enough in Ayacucho, that the Shining Path had no interest in pursuing foreigners. We thought wrong. Just when everything was in order and we were about to depart the capital, news of a guerrilla attack filtered down from the Andes. According to unconfirmed reports, three Germans hiking in the mountains were surprised by a guerrilla patrol, captured, robbed and executed. The Peruvian government warned foreigners that the area might be dangerous. The US Embassy issued a traveller's advisory. I changed my mind about travelling to Ayacucho.

I had come to Peru hoping to make it as a reporter, but after six months my fledgling career in journalism was not faring so well. Selling stories as a stringer had proven to be more difficult than I had anticipated. For a while, it hadn't mattered. I was doing what I wanted to be doing, what I had dreamed about doing for years. While in college, I had spent a semester studying in San José, Costa Rica, living with a Costa Rican family and travelling around the country, mostly to its beaches. Enamoured with Latin America, I headed south again after my graduation from university. I ended up in Peru on the advice of a professor who had a contact in Lima, an editor of a newsletter that published stories on peace and justice issues. The contact didn't work out, but after meeting some stringers at a bar in Lima, I decided to stay in the country for a while. I thought I might sell some stories on the events transpiring in the mountains, and then try to land a job as a foreign correspondent for a news magazine – a naive plan as it turned out, but it seemed plausible enough when I listened to the stringers. They all had the idea that Peru was the next Hot Spot, that the Shining Path rebellion would evolve into a major story, bigger than Nicaragua, and way bigger than El Salvador was at the time. 'Salvador's a grain of sand,' one stringer told me. 'But Peru's the whole goddamn beach. Imagine a country this size, this critical, going communist. I mean, Peru's like the most indicative country in South America. Talk about your dominoes – if Peru goes, the whole continent just might turn red.'

The stringers were playing a hunch. 'Stick around, cover a few stories, make some contacts,' they told me. 'Then when the shit hits the fan here, you'll have a rep as someone who knows the place. Editors will want your stories. When they drop in, the parachute boys will come to you for the dope.'

They talked me into it, and I stayed on. But transforming myself into an expert on Peruvian guerrillas was not so simple. Stories were hard to come by – the more so because my Spanish was as yet minimal – and I didn't seem to have a sense for what the editors wanted. When I did work up an article, the editors back in the States showed no interest. Some were hostile. I managed to get through to a New York editor by telephone one day and began to read him a story on Lima's slums. He cut me off halfway into the second paragraph. 'Hold it right there, pretty boy,' he shouted. 'Who you trying to be, Shakespeare? Enough with the purple poetry, already, and enough with the Mother Teresa bleeding heart crap. Call me when you have some news and you learn how to write it.'

After a couple of months, running low on funds and having failed to publish a single story, I was getting discouraged. Part of the problem was Lima itself – a grey, squalid city that was beginning to depress me. The foreign correspondent's life was not as glamorous as I had imagined. We sat in cantinas and hotel bars waiting for news to come down from the Andes. We read the newspapers trying to decipher the abstruse language of official pronouncements. Now and then, someone managed an interview with a minister's secretary or a junior official at the American embassy. But mostly we drank and listened to rumour and passed rumours along and waited for the Big Story.

I had really been looking forward to the Ayacucho excursion. It meant a chance to get out of the capital, to get closer to the action – though the Shining Path guerrillas had a mysterious modus operandi that kept everyone guessing, and the 'action' at any given moment was difficult to substantiate. When the travelling party fell apart and we returned to the cantinas and the rumour routine, I reached the point of exasperation.

'You just need to break into print,' one old hand counselled. 'Then you'll feel better.'

But how was I to do that, without a story?

Well, the stringers suggested, I could try what many another novice had done when news was unobtainable: travel pieces. It was the old stand-by of the profession, they said. The stringer's pot-boiler. You went somewhere unusual, gathered a bunch of information on prices, hotels, food, wrote a few nice descriptions and wired it off to a Sunday travel editor somewhere. Not much money, but a quick and easy by-line, and it paid enough cash to keep you going for a spell without having to resort to the even older stand-by of giving English lessons. Write about Peru's tourist attractions, was their wry advice.

'You mean like hiking the Inca Trail?' I asked.

'Yeah, except that's been done to death.'

'The Nazca Lines?'

'Done, too. And anything Inca's way overdone. You need to find something new and unusual.'

I read through the guidebooks, looking for some alternative, and learned that Iquitos, Peru's port on the Amazon River, served as a base for a number of tour operators who led expeditions to jungle camps. The Amazon held a certain fascination, no question; it was a feral, impenetrable land about as far from civilisation as one could get. I found the idea of a tour through the jungle irresistible.

I didn't know it at the time, but I was about to get in on an emerging trend in Latin American tourism. As problems arose at the traditional tourist sites – guerrillas in the Andean highlands, rampant crime in Rio – countries like Peru and Brazil were beginning to exploit the rapidly developing first-world interest in ecology and the rainforest. Contemporary travellers, these countries learned, wanted fewer tours of monuments and city sights, and more adventures in something approximating wild nature. In Latin America, home to fifty-eight per cent of the world's remaining tropical rainforest, ecotourism was on its way to becoming a billion-dollar business. In the decade to follow, the number of ecotourists to the region would triple, growing twice as fast as the number of conventional tourists. But in 1982, the numbers were still small, and the ecotourism infrastructure was tenuous at best.

My introduction to the burgeoning phenomenon began with a rather lax flight from Lima to Iquitos. Take-off was delayed six hours while the airline looked for a plane to make the one-hour flight. Apparently, all their functioning planes were off flying other routes, and no one knew when they might return to Lima. At last one showed up, but the boarding agent announced with alacrity that although this was indeed the plane, it had to make one more flight – when it got back to Lima, it would be all ours. Eventually, the plane returned, and after some perfunctory tinkering by mechanics, the passengers boarded.

One hour later, we circled over the giant broccoli patch of the Amazon. The airport came into view, its tentative runways hacked out of the jungle. Somehow, in landing the plane, the pilot managed to hit an animal. A tapir, someone said. A stray dog, declared another. We sat in the sweltering plane for another hour while airport workers got the wheels unclogged. All told it had taken eight hours to fly the thousand kilometres from Lima to Iquitos, but no one complained. The same trip by road and river would have taken at least seven days.

Even though Iquitos was at that time a city of 180,000 (its population is now around 400,000), it had a jungle frontier feel to it. Smuggling was big business, conducted openly on the quays in the floating slum called Belén. One whole block of the city was filled with 'Indian doctors' – vendors who sold jungle herbs from blankets and mats spread out on the muddy streets. Using fuzzy, over-amplified microphones, they advertised their cures for cancer and 'blood difficulties' and 'evil airs'. Giant lizards roamed the embankments leading down to the river, and caiman skins hung in store windows. The vast sky was filled with continental-sized thunderheads that hourly unleashed a torrent on the already drenched and dripping city. Now and then fishermen staggered through the street, hauling huge fish weighing well over a hundred kilograms by draping them over their backs.

Like other Amazon cities, Iquitos – the last port on the 6440-kilometre river – had seen great wealth come and go with the rubber boom and bust. I passed a decaying opera house where Sarah Bernhardt had once sung in the glory days of old Iquitos. A sign pointed to some iron structures – supposedly built by the famed Eiffel – that had now gone rust red in the heat and humidity. Down by the port you could see the half-swamped boats used by Werner Herzog during the filming of *Fitzcarraldo*, a disastrous attempt to make a movie about a disastrous attempt to extract wealth from the jungle. That seemed the quintessential drama of the place: people came, tried to make their pile from the land, then staggered out of the jungle barely alive. Now the latest hope for a bonanza was ecotourism.

I visited the offices of several tour operators. Most promised me the same thing: they swore I would 'encounter the animals and investigate much plants', as one brochure put it. *See more monkeys* was the mantra of the day. Guaranteed: many, many jungle animals, and for monkeys we're the best. After a while,

17

the insistence of these promises and guarantees made me suspicious. I collected the brochures and said I'd let them know.

'All right, my friend, but you want monkeys you go with us. Anaconda, too. Indians.'

❂

I took the brochures back to my hotel room. There were two basic choices for tours – soft and hard. The soft tour category included lodges, inns and safari camps – outfits that tried to combine ecotourism with comfortable travel. Evidently, the idea was to see Amazonia without experiencing the hardships of the place. The brochures promised that air-conditioned boats with names like *Amazon Queen* and *Amazon Explorer* would escort you to your lodge.

The lodges themselves featured hot showers and swimming pools, and buffet lunches prepared by chefs who specialised in 'regional and international dishes'. You were invited to 'socialise in the mosquito-screened dining room', spend time in the fully serviced bar (one lodge boasted a twenty-four-hour bar) and sleep peacefully in 'quaint palm-thatched sleeping quarters'. Photos showed boardwalks and covered walkways leading into the jungle, monkeys approaching guests for a hand-out, a boatload of photographer-tourists zooming in on a lagoon of wading birds. This version of ecotourism reminded me of a Disneyland ride: a slick production lacking substance, too cosy, too neatly packaged, too safe.

The hard tours differed primarily in terminology. Their brochures appealed to 'adventurers' looking for 'challenging expeditions'. The adventurers would stay at 'base camp' rather than lodges, and go on treks rather than hikes or walks. Participants were not tourists or even ecotourists but 'workshop members' learning about 'the complex symbiotic relationships that exist in the rainforest'. The brochures referred to 'rainforest' rather than jungle, 'rich biodiversity' rather than plants and animals, 'native communities' rather than Indian villages. They assured the reader that 'your contact with the cultures and environment will be authentic'.

The frequency with which this assurance was repeated sugg
that authenticity was a paramount concern for patrons of the hard
tours.

The operators were also at pains to stress their belief 'that
tourism, conducted in a conscientious manner, has tremendous
potential for a positive effect upon ecosystems and peoples that
we visit'. Most promoted some sort of code of ethics, stressing
'responsibility, awareness, and respect'. Through such a code, the
operators claimed to 'actively foster the concept of ecotourism
among our travellers'. Some operators took the concept to the
extreme and suggested that by becoming part of the Amazon
ecosystem, you could 'also reconnect with your higher self'. This
New Age dimension of ecotourism promoted the Amazon as an
escape from the stresses of civilisation, a place where the ecotourist could 'unwind in a pristine setting' and 'sense the power
of our own connections with others and the environment'. One
operator invited New Agers on a 'Personal Growth Eco-Journey'
featuring 'mini-workshops using music, movement and creative
exercises to recharge', thereby allowing you to travel 'through
your inner paths to discover your uniqueness'. One of the eco-
journey's highlights was 'a night hike around the lodge to observe
various types of glowing mushrooms'.

Despite the promises of authenticity, however, the hard-tour
operators didn't sound too different from the soft tours when it
came to assuring that the basic comfort levels first-world travellers are used to would be provided; for instance, the brochures
promised English-speaking guides and 'a local staff to handle
camp chores'. And while the testimonial letters frequently
included in their promotional materials enthused about adventures in the wild, they also revealed a preoccupation with some
degree of comfort. In between raptures over biodiversity, one testimonial spoke of 'roadside stops to pick up cookies . . . thereby
ensuring our survival until the next scheduled meal'. In other letters, the writers marvelled at termite nests, bromeliads, lianas and
iguanas – as well as the 'delicious treats whipped up by the head
chef' or the 'absolutely comfortable base camp'.

If the hard tours sounded at least a little better than the soft tours, they also presented a major drawback: their cost. The operators were charging a thousand dollars and more just for the ground portion of the expedition. With the inclusion of airfare from the States, adventure travellers could expect to spend well over two thousand dollars for a week's vacation. Apparently there were enough people willing to pay that kind of money to keep these operators in business. I wasn't one of them.

After an evening's study, I didn't much like my options. I tossed the brochures aside and went out to find a drink.

❂

That night in a bar above the Iquitos quays, I fell into conversation with a grizzled Australian called Mick – one of those macho men you meet in seedy backwaters and outposts of progress the world over, the kind of traveller who's always on the road and always travelling the hard way. No matter where you've been, he's been further and under far more strenuous circumstances than you could ever dream of. And he relishes the opportunity to tell you all about it.

Mick listened with evident derision to my story of missing out on hiking the Inca Road – hell, he'd hiked the same road with guerrillas hailing him with bullets – then scoffed outright when I mentioned the local tours.

'Bloody waste of money, that,' he said. '*Lodges*, for Chrissakes, they got anacondas in a pen, tame spider monkeys in trees that've been trimmed for easy photographs. There's no jungle, no *real* jungle, within eighty kilometres of those places. They shake the goddamn trees to get the parrots to fly for your videos.'

What about the more 'challenging' expeditions?

Mick hooted. 'Expeditions, my arse. It's all a sham. Just picnics for rich boys with designer gear who think they're reincarnations of Stanley and Livingstone. Some bloody expedition. You want the real thing, go down to the docks at dawn and hire a fisherman to take you as far downriver as you can get.'

Swayed by Mick's goading, I decided to forgo the package tours and give his way a try. But on the day I went down to the docks, I didn't find any fishermen. Instead, I found a mob waiting to board the river taxis. Whenever one sputtered up to the dock, the crowd surged forward in an attempt to capsize it. No one seemed to have any idea where I would find a fisherman with a boat to hire. The question apparently amused one group enough for them to engage in an animated discussion of my problem. Their eventual solution: better just to go to the market and buy a fish. Much cheaper that way.

Then a taxi arrived, and the pushing and shoving began anew. My advisers boarded the lilting craft, and I was left alone on the docks in the blistering sun to watch the chaos of the river traffic. Just then, a fat man in an embroidered shirt hallooed me. He waddled down the dock and asked me what I was doing. When I explained, he brightened. 'Your lucky day!' he announced. 'I have precisely such an opportunity for you!'

I should have been leery, but by that point I was frustrated and ready to give up. With no other possibility in the offing, I followed the fat man – his name was González – up the embankment to an office where a secretary was busy with the telephone. Two gringos sat waiting. On the wall was a large map of the Peruvian Amazon.

'Welcome to my agency office!' Señor González said. 'Here are two *amigos* also wish to travel far on our river!'

The two gringos proved to be Bruce and Heather – forty-something Canadians dressed for the jungle in khaki outfits, hiking boots and Panama hats – near-perfect parodies of the models in safari outfitters' catalogues.

'Excellent, excellent!' González said. 'We have an expedition party!' He spoke furtively to his secretary. She shrugged in response and continued to dial the phone.

Bruce and Heather explained that they too had been checking out the various Amazon river trips. They had wanted to go on one of the hard tours, but reservations were required and the trip was booked. They flat-out refused to go to the lodges – 'Too touristy,'

Heather said. Somehow they had come across Señor González's 'agency office' (which, now that I looked at it, didn't appear to be much like an agency: no filing cabinets, no brochures, no sign on the window; nothing but a secretary, a malfunctioning telephone, a bare desk and the map on the wall). The Canadians were in the process of negotiating a deal. They needed another person to make the trip cost effective, and that's where I came in.

New to the tourism business, Señor González was building his own lodge. He showed us Polaroids of the site where he had hacked down trees in order to begin construction. At the moment there was only one structure completed – the bar. Despite his all too obvious bulk, he claimed to be an experienced jungle traveller with good connections up and down the river. He was hoping to open the 'first-class lodge' soon, but for the time being he was taking adventuresome gringos way downriver, past all the other lodges. With a gesture at the map, he indicated the village of Francisco de Orellana at the confluence of the Amazon and the Napo. There, he said, we could stay in the village of his wife's uncle, right in the middle of the real jungle.

All we needed was a boat engine, which the secretary was attempting to procure. Again he whispered something to her; again she shrugged and dialled.

Bruce and Heather were all for it – it sounded just like what they wanted and if I went along and shared the cost, the trip wouldn't be too expensive. I considered the barren office, the constantly dialling secretary, the pudgy mustachioed smile of Señor González. The prospects didn't seem promising, but the alternative was either a Disneyesque ferry trip to a jungle lodge or a so-called expedition costing thousands. All right, I thought, why the hell not?

✪

Early the next morning, I made my way through the steamy Iquitos streets to the quays. The river was enveloped in mist when I arrived, large ocean-going vessels looming here and there while fishermen paddled their canoes and cast their nets into the rainbow swirls of oily water. I had carefully packed everything I thought I might need into a small backpack. Bruce and Heather were already waiting on the docks. Lying at their feet were two huge backpacks on aluminium frames. They had a camping outfitter's entire warehouse with them – tent, sleeping bags, bedrolls, cooking and eating utensils, water canisters.

Neither Señor González nor a boat had made an appearance. The mist slowly lifted from the river and the fishermen came in with their toxic catch. The river taxis loaded up – hundreds of people piling in each small craft – and headed downriver, churning and wobbling through the wakes of the larger boats. Still no González.

My fellow ecotourists were from Toronto; Bruce was in television news production, while Heather was a marketing executive. They just loved South America, and had been visiting the continent for years – every vacation they got. Iguazu, Machu Picchu, Patagonia, they'd done it all. Just the year before, they'd flown over Angel Falls and spent three days hiking on Venezuela's Gran Sabana. Spectacular, shouldn't miss it, they said. They had looked forward to adding the Amazon to their list for so long, they just couldn't believe they were really here. 'It's like a dream for us,' Bruce said.

We checked our watches. No González. Now even the brightly painted lodge ferries were passing by, their decks lined with camera-toting tourists on their way to their Amazon adventure. Bruce and Heather were not terribly upset by the delay. In South America, you just went with the flow, Bruce explained, took things as they were. That's what the place was all about. 'Anyway, it sure beats that,' he said, pointing to a large lodge ferry chugging past.

An hour and a half behind schedule, Señor González sauntered down the dock, sweating profusely and apologising for the delay. But where was the boat? González pointed to a small fishing canoe lying upside down on the bank, its paint peeling in the sun. He explained the cause of the delay: he had been searching for a motor to borrow. But there was no problem now; at any moment the motor would be delivered.

By now I was getting concerned. I found it hard to believe that we were relying on an overweight man who had showed up at the docks in leather dress shoes and whose boat was obviously better suited for trolling Walden Pond than for negotiating the currents of the world's largest river. The lodge ferries were starting to look a little more attractive.

González took off his shoes, rolled up his slacks, and set about attending to the boat, uprighting it and getting it into the water. At last the motor arrived, strapped to the head and back of a teenage boy who came trotting down the rotted stairway to the quay. When the boat was finally outfitted with the motor and González brought it alongside the dock, it was all too obvious that we had a new problem: just one of the Canadians' enormous backpacks seemed big enough to swamp the little canoe.

But no one else appeared bothered by this problem. The Canadians handed down their packs, González crammed them into the hull, and we all stepped in until the boat had almost no draught at all. After some tinkering with the engine, González got the boat launched amidst a blue cloud of exhaust. Up on the riverbank, some shoeshine boys waved to us and blew sarcastic kisses.

We settled in on tiny, warped wooden benches, squeezed together by the backpacks, knees to our chins. It was difficult to imagine a more uncomfortable way to travel 160 kilometres on the river. I figured that we might be ten long, cramped hours in making the journey; given the load that the small boat had to haul, I didn't see us doing much more than fifteen kilometres an hour.

I was wrong. González swung us around into the current, and after experimenting a bit with the rudder while we puttered through the city section of the river, he suddenly opened her up and let her rip. We were roaring downriver faster than I thought possible in such a boat. The bow was raised above the surface, spray blasting my face, as we bounced over every ripple and crest to catch up with and then race past the taxis, the cargo boats, and the lodge ferries. Keeping balanced was nearly impossible. I glanced back. Bruce and Heather were huddled together, still smiling as if this were a joyride. Equipped for every contingency, they had already pulled out their ponchos to ward off the spray, while I quickly got soaked. González, perched on the back seat, looking cocky as a teenage hot-rodder, kept his hand on the tiller, making slight adjustments for obstacles – logs, boards, branches, semi-submerged shanties – that I never saw until we were already past them.

Each wide bend in the river held new possibilities for disaster: flotsam, barges, beasts. I imagined schools of piranhas waiting for us to spill over. Bruce tried to take pictures but the spray and speed made it impossible. We were going too fast to appreciate any scenery. The river's banks spun into a green blur of trees and tangled growth, interrupted now and then by a rotting dock, a shack, three or four people watching us fly past. I prayed for engine failure, but the ancient Evinrude held together, its grating whine preventing conversation. I had expected a ten-hour trip, but we covered the 160 kilometres in a little over four hours, averaging forty kilometres per hour in a vessel that should have been fitted with oars, not an engine.

At last we made a wide turn into the Napo River, a large tributary that flows into Peru from Ecuador's mountains. At the confluence, fresh-water dolphins hopped over the waves of the competing currents. A few kilometres up the Napo we came to our destination, the jungle village of Francisco de Orellana. As we scrambled up the bank with our gear, I expected to find a primitive village, and maybe some naked tribesmen; instead, we found ourselves confronting a soldier, who demanded our passports.

We were hustled into the Francisco de Orellana Migration Post – a cinder-block hut with a palm-thatched roof – where a gendarme of the Peruvian Army submitted our passports to an intense scrutiny, making sure that 1) our photos and our faces matched; 2) we had the proper entry stamp for Peru; and 3) the entry stamps were not forged. We were then released to the care of Señor González's wife's uncle, and told to report back every twenty-four hours during our stay in Francisco de Orellana.

The uncle – a poorly clad old man with but three or four teeth left – had not been forewarned of our visit, of course, and stared in disbelief at the apparition of three gringos on his doorstep. There followed a bustle of activity (relatively speaking in Amazonian terms) to find space for three people in the village's huts. This flurry proved unnecessary: while the whole village was busy cleaning out a place for us, Bruce and Heather erected their five-person dome tent in a grassy spot near a bean patch. González appeared mortified at this development – a breach in etiquette, apparently, an insult to the hosts – and attempted to dissuade the Canadians; but they cheerily insisted that there was no problem, the tent was just fine for them, no trouble at all. See, nice and comfortable, they said, unzipping the flap to show him the cots and mosquito nets they had set up.

❂

Later that day, González took us on a brief foray into the rainforest. According to the US National Academy of Sciences, a typical six-square-kilometre tract of Amazon forest contains 400 species of birds, 125 species of mammals, 100 species of reptiles, sixty species of amphibians, 150 species of butterflies. I saw none of them, except a sheath of skin shed from a snake that González believed to be deadly. There were birds, to be sure; at least, we heard them, for the density of vegetation prevented sightings. As for animals, González explained that in the dry season they retreated into the depths of the jungle, and were rarely seen. Besides, in the middle of the day, we weren't going to be seeing any nocturnal creatures. Without animals to gaze at, the highlight of the walk proved to be a photo opportunity at a monument by the river that commemorated the arrival of Francisco de Orellana at the Napo–Amazon confluence in 1542. Orellana went on to navigate the river to the Atlantic, the first European to do so. After showing us the monument, González took us to the clearing where, he claimed, he was building his jungle camp. The hut for the bar was built, but as there were no bottles yet, we had no reason to stay long.

As dusk fell, the mosquitoes emerged – a fanatic, frantic, evil force that seemed starved for white flesh. The Canadians doused themselves with ointments and sprays, then donned nylon windbreakers and denim jeans for added protection. They even had mosquito netting to hang from their hats and cover their faces. They popped malaria pills by the hour and told me all about dengue fever and how you bleed from the ears while your bones feel like they're breaking into pieces. Having completely forgotten such basic protection, I kept slapping and waving at the whining, whirring air around my head. I rubbed my ears, expecting to find blood. Meanwhile, the villagers walked around shirtless and in shorts, apparently impervious to bites and stings.

When bedtime came, Bruce and Heather slithered under their mosquito net. I lay in the hut belonging to González's wife's uncle, cowering beneath the sardonic buzz of the feasting horde while González snored.

❂

We were supposed to go fishing before dawn with the uncle. I was only too happy to leave the cot where I had passed a sleepless night fending off the airborne attack. Bruce and Heather, snug and protected in their tent, balked at the fishing expedition when the moment came, and González continued his profound snoring, leaving me to go alone with the old man.

At the riverbank, a short distance from the monument to Orellana, we hauled a canoe into the water, sheet lightning shivering on the horizon. The old man paddled us out into the dark water, all the while whispering something I couldn't understand. I had no idea whether he was speaking to me, to himself, to God or to the darkness. His paddle made insect-like splashes in the still waters. Then the old man stood up, the boat gently rocking with the movement. Cradling a wadded-up net against his belly, he peered first to one side of the boat, then to the other. Finally, he selected a sector of the river and heaved the net like a medicine ball out onto the black water, where it slapped down and sank. He passed me a cord and indicated that I should haul it in. Soon we dragged the net to the side of the boat. The old man hauled part of the net into the boat and examined the catch. Twenty or so silvery fish flopped at our feet, but he was disgusted with the catch. Growling with disdain, he picked up one of the fish and lobbed it toward me.

'Piranha,' he said – it was the first word he had spoken that I could understand. I nearly fell out of the boat trying to jump back. The old man cackled. '*Desayuno,*' he said. Breakfast.

'You can eat piranha?' I asked.

'Why not?' he said. 'Better you eat it before it eats you.' To him, this idea was very funny. He cackled again while sorting through the throbbing fish until he found the biggest one. '*Gordo,*' he said and again tossed the fish at my feet.

We tried throwing the net several times, coming up with nothing but river wrack, bottles and more piranhas. At the first light of dawn, the old man paddled us back in.

The old man's wife fried the fattest piranha whole in a pan over a wood fire. In its death throes, the fish had bared its jagged razor teeth, so that even dead and fried it looked malicious. It didn't taste good – dry, bitter and full of tiny bones. Piranha was just too much trouble to eat. I understood why the old man was so disappointed with his catch.

The Canadians came out of their tent looking fresh and eager to get going in their clean safari outfits. They were amused by the fish and took several pictures of it, then went off to eat the freeze-dried meals they had brought from Canada, which were now coming to a boil on their camp stove. When González finally came into the hut, he frowned at the fish and announced that we needed *real* food. Guns were produced, and a hunting party was arranged. We set off for the river, González, the old man, the Canadians, and I, followed by every child and dog in the village. We passed the pile of fish the old man had discarded as rejects. Turkey buzzards were now busy pecking out the eyes. Bruce took a picture.

Outboard motor roaring, we took off at turbo speed down the Napo to the confluence, where the Amazon flow swirled debris over the merging waters and dolphins continued to hop over the waves. The boat bounced along, deftly avoiding logs, and then turned up a wide lake-like bowl off the river's main branch. There, González cut the engine and we puttered along the banks, peering into the dense thicket. Blue morpho butterflies flitted in the trees above us.

'What are we looking for?' I asked González.

'Stork,' he whispered.

A few minutes later, the old man muttered and pointed across the water to an islet. There, on the branch of a half-submerged tree, was our prey. We drew closer and González aimed his gun. For several seconds the boat drifted on the rippling waves until González steadied his wobbly bulk. The bird rubbed its feathers with its beak, then lifted its head and gazed at us for a long moment before its suspicion was aroused. Spreading its wings wide for flight, the stork released the branch and had just lifted into the air when González fired. The bird flipped and plunged with a shriek to the water.

'Quick! Before the caiman!' González shouted.

We roared toward the islet and spun a circle around the bobbing carcass. The old man scooped up the bird and brought it dripping into the boat. The Canadians were clapping and yelling, Bravo, bravo! Bruce snapped several photos, and I was given the honour of holding the bird. The old man handed it to me, and I took it by its limp, slick neck. Alive, it had been a silky white. Dead and wet, the stork had turned a pallid grey, the colour of ashes, with a red rosette burned in its breast.

Back in Francisco de Orellana, the old man's wife prepared stork stew, and the afternoon was dedicated to a big feast, with the gringos as guests of honour. There were toasts with sugarcane alcohol and photos and pledges of eternal friendship. The drinking and singing and laughing went on long into the evening and then night. Thunder crashed and torrents of rain fell. Someone killed a scorpion. Pigs passed through the hut, eating up the remains of the feast. A hundred winged things beat against the hurricane lamps and against our faces. Bruce and Heather doused themselves in repellent and donned their protective gear.

Late in the proceedings, another tourist attraction arrived: tens of thousands of ants on the march. They emerged through the walls of the hut like a Hitchcock special effect and stormed the hut, ensnaring and chomping and carrying off whatever they came across. A baby was lifted from the floor. We jumped up on chairs and the table while the army passed. It took ten minutes at least – crumbs, cockroaches, beetles, spiders, even tiny toads caught in the creatures' pincers.

When it was safe to climb down, we said our good nights and went off to bed. But I for one found it hard to sleep.

✪

The trip back to Iquitos was much slower because our boat had to fight against the Amazon's current. González opened the engine and kept it at full throttle. We still passed the slow-moving river taxis, but now we were easily overtaken by the lodge cruisers. As we neared Iquitos, more and more of them left us behind, the tourists staring at us from the railings as they passed.

In Iquitos, the Canadians made a fateful suggestion. They wanted to see Belén, the waterfront slum section of the city where smuggling was openly conducted and the dwellings were built on sticks. Their guidebook suggested that the sight was interesting and picturesque. González was only too happy to take us past the suburb before dropping us off. With a sudden jerk, he veered the boat back out into the middle of the river and sped off in an arc around the port area. Now there were boats everywhere, most significantly bigger than our puny craft. Defying the laws of maritime physics, we darted between barges, trawlers and tourist ferries.

As the stilted slum came into view, a long, sleek powerboat emerged from a thicket of shacks – a drug runner for sure, I thought. The boat glided into the open river, then shot forward, prow high, arcing beautifully over the water on a course that brought it directly in our line. Instead of aiming toward the shore, González kept the rudder straight as the powerboat surged toward us. I glanced back at him, his hair blasted back off his forehead, teeth gritted and a mad grin on his face. González had found the ultimate macho game: playing chicken with a thundering fighter jet-on-water, driven no doubt by some murderous crazy who would just as soon split us in two as spit on us. No way González would back down from that challenge. He even angled the canoe a little to put us squarely on a collision course with the powerboat.

'He's an idiot!' I shouted.

The Canadians smiled and nodded.

When we were within a hundred metres, I saw that it would be close, very close, but we would side-swipe the powerboat with maybe twenty metres to spare. The drug runner bulleted past us, and I caught a glimpse of sunglasses and flashes of gold. Then I saw the wake: a gorgeous white-capped crest splitting the water like a seam. We churned right into it. The bow slapped the wave and popped straight up, and for one wonderful moment we were airborne and shooting up toward the billowing clouds of the Amazonian sky. All our gear – backpacks, gas cans, benches, oars – flew up and out of the boat, and soon we followed, hurtling upwards like salmon hopping up river rapids. From the pike position I saw supine gulls, topsy-turvy palms, fishermen casting nets up to the river's surface, the upside-down turrets of a naval destroyer, plumes of smoke descending from the jungle town. Then came a rush of white bubbles, pressure in my nasal cavities, a blue-green-black aqueous turmoil. I flailed, kicked, gagged and burst to the surface in time to hear Bruce scream, 'Piranha!'

But there were no piranhas, only Heather's nails scratching Bruce's legs as she scrambled to the surface. For a moment we trod water, not knowing what else to do. Now that we were splashing in it, we noticed that the water was black and oily, the surface reflecting rainbows in the bright equatorial light. Our skin was stained a yellowish brown.

González dog-paddled around and found the submerged hull of the canoe for us to cling to. When Bruce caught his breath, he launched into a long tirade, in English, which he seemed to expect me to translate. 'Tell him,' he yelled, 'that he's a frigging idiot.

Tell him we want our money back. Tell him we publish guide-books and we'll give him a bad review!' I said nothing, but González understood the tone. He kept nodding obsequiously and repeating, *sí, sí, cómo no* – of course.

We tried flagging down passing boats with no luck. After ten minutes, I decided to try the one-kilometre swim to shore. Bruce and Heather followed, leaving González alone in the water with the boat; it was the last I saw of him. We ended up wading ashore in Belén, trash and faeces floating around us in the black water. Before we could climb onto the rotting quay, a crowd gathered to watch the apparition of three gringos emerging from the water. Some of the onlookers couldn't keep from giggling. No doubt we were a sight – soaked, stained, stinking. I'd lost a shoe; Bruce had lost his photographer's vest.

The three of us led a procession through the muddy streets of Belén, everyone eager to see what the crazy gringos would do next. Bruce and Heather wanted me to join them in confronting González at his office, but I'd had enough. Anyway, I suspected the 'agency' wouldn't be open for some time to come. My flight left the next morning; I just wanted to clean up and go home.

But the showers in the hotel weren't functioning. No water, I was told. No water all night. What can I do then? I asked.

'Bathe in the river,' said the factotum, and he let loose with a cackle that prompted a response from the roosters wandering through the lobby.

The next morning there was still no water. I dressed in the cleanest clothes I had left and took a taxi to the airport. The flight to Lima was delayed, and I stood off to the side of the gate, try-ing not to frighten people with my river odour. A large group of tourists fresh from a package tour of the jungle waited for their flight to Miami. They compared souvenirs: Indian blowguns and animal pelts and mounted piranha jaws. They were happy and I was miserable. They were smartly dressed in designer khaki and I was filthy and scruffy. They had souvenirs and I had the begrimed clothes on my back. I stank of sewage and scum and looked like hell.

But then I thought of Mick and the macho traveller's code – the only worthy journey is an ordeal, the best trip is the worst one – and I suddenly felt very superior to the soft tourists surrounding me. If they should chance to talk to me, they'd hear a real adventure tale. Me, I'd fished for piranha, I'd hunted stork. Hell, I'd scarfed down my stork. And I'd swum the Amazon like Weismuller at his Tarzan best. I'd taken a dive in the River of Rivers, submerged myself in its primordial slime, yes indeed. I stood there in the airport, smug and contented, and wished Mick were there to hear me crow. Oh, how I'd crow.

The Mosquitia, 1983

Interlude

B Y the end of 1982, the rebellion in Peru, though vigorous in spurts, didn't seem to be advancing. Not seriously enough, at any rate, for the stringers whose livelihood depended on action dramatic enough to focus world attention on the place. At the time, Peru had intense competition from other hot spots: Lebanon was exploding, El Salvador heating up and Angola ready to boil over. A low-intensity conflict in Peru didn't attract the attention of newspaper editors when other powder kegs were igniting.

Come 1983, a new story was emerging in Central America that very much interested editors, involving as it did the President of the United States and the CIA. Ronald Reagan's obsession with destroying Nicaragua's Sandinista government led to the funding of the Contras, a band of rebels who hoped to overthrow the country's ruling regime. With the US directly involved, and with the Russians and Cubans sending support to the Sandinistas, Nicaragua was can't-miss material. Trying to interpret the bizarre antics of a crackpot guerrilla group high in the Andes seemed like a waste of time when the superpowers were posturing in Central America.

Honduras, where the Contras were based, was now the place to be. The correspondents left Lima to set up shop in Tegucigalpa, where they filed reports on Contra activities. I followed the crowd to 'Teguz', and once again struggled to earn a by-line. The competition was much more intense, not only on the battlegrounds but also among the press corps. You had to work hard to get a scoop, and no one was sharing leads. Rumour and hearsay had everyone frantic, some reporters spreading false stories designed to lead their colleagues astray while they pursued the real scoop.

It was in Honduras that my main flaw as a war correspondent was blatantly exposed: I couldn't handle the tensions of war. The guns and random explosions scared the hell out of me. I dreaded the journeys to the battle zones along the Nicaraguan border, the long rides over precarious roads to interview corpses. The person you spoke to that morning was dead by nightfall; ten seconds later and fifty metres over, it could have been you.

Within weeks of arriving in Teguz, my world became narrowly restricted to the bars, the Maya Hotel – where the major news agencies had set up their offices – and the occasional and thoroughly pointless press conferences held at the US embassy.

I spent many an evening in the O. Henry Bar, a favourite haunt of expats and foreign journalists, the kind of place referred to by a popular mercenary magazine as a 'major networking bar'. Like the bar's namesake, the patrons of the O. Henry indulged in the telling of tall tales, most of which concerned the places they had been and the things they had done as war correspondents or mercenaries or daredevil adventurers. A macho code governed cantina discourse. There were stories about roadblock confrontations with military goons, about long mountain treks, blindfolded, to meet rebel commandos, and about ambushes in which the speaker had been invariably standing right next to someone struck down by stray fire.

During these story-telling sessions, a mirror ball shot blue light around the bar and the sound system blasted out mood music in keeping with the scene. Merengue. Reggae. Hard rock. Disco. Salsa. I remember the Clash and Steely Dan and Talking Heads and Bob Marley and the Rolling Stones, all blurring together (I'm so bored with the USA, psychokiller, throw down the jam till the girls say when and don't worry about a thing). Now and then a mercenary or a Nicaraguan rebel pulled a hooker onto the dance floor and rubbed himself up against her, but as often as not the floor was empty. The clients of the O. Henry didn't come to dance. They came to drink. They came to deal. They came to argue and scoff and boast.

CHAPTER 2

The ghost of O. Henry

IT was in the O. Henry Bar, Tegucigalpa, Honduras, that I first heard about the Río Plátano Biosphere.

One night, after a few drinks, I related my Amazon adventure to a table of tough talkers. It served well enough as a 'bad travel' story – one of the favoured genres of expat discourse. The narrative was weak on macho deeds, but the climactic river plunge won me a few appreciative nods and sneers from the party. One of my listeners was a Brit named Hogan who taught English at the American School.

'If you want wild,' Hogan said, 'take your arse out to the Mosquitia – not a damn thing out there – not even a road, for god's sake.'

'There's a new UNESCO biosphere there,' said a biologist, down in Honduras on a US government grant.

'What the hell is a biosphere?'

'A nature reserve, basically. But the people can stay put, on the theory that natives are an integral part of the ecosystem. This one's out on the Río Plátano in the Mosquitia, one of the first UNESCO-sanctioned biospheres in the world. Supposed to be quite a place, but hard as hell to get to. Like Hogan said, no roads. Nothing.'

'Have you been?'

'No, but I wouldn't mind going.'

An old, almost shredded map of the country was tacked to a wall of the O. Henry. The Fulbright biologist traced his finger

over the split folds until he came to the Río Plátano in the far
north-east, in the seemingly misnamed department of Gracias a
Dios – Thanks to God.

'So how do you get out there?' I asked.

Hogan said he knew some Peace Corps workers in La Ceiba.
They'd gone out to the Mosquitia, to a place called Brus Laguna,
on a weekly flight operated by a local airline called SAHSA.
Supposedly, some missionaries living in the village had put them
up for a few nights.

We located Brus Laguna on the map; it was close to the Río
Plátano.

'It sure would be worth a try,' the Fulbright biologist said.

'I'm game,' Hogan said. 'What about you?'

'Why not?' I said. 'Beats going back down to the border. I'll
take a biosphere over war any time.'

Before the night was out, we had begun to plan our trip. The
biologist would try to get information from the university, while
I'd visit the SAHSA office to see about tickets.

'You do know what the Peace Corps workers say SAHSA
stands for, don't you?' Hogan said. 'Stands for Stay At Home,
Stay Alive.'

'Is that a warning or a challenge?'

'Same bloody thing, don't you think?'

❂

In those days, I was young and carefree in my travelling. I tended
to overlook obvious obstacles and thought nothing of lighting out
for new territory whenever the whim took me. Faced with the
same conditions today – a long, gruelling trip with no facilities of
any kind at the other end – I would probably balk. But at the time
it sounded like the kind of adventure that would earn me standing
with the likes of Mick and the hard-core sorts in the O. Henry. I
guess I longed to be in their league.

Certainly, if I had paused to think about it, I would have questioned the wisdom of the whole enterprise. There was, first of all,

a paucity of information on the Mosquitia. To the people of the capital, it was a distant and forbidding region, more remote and exotic than Miami. Then there was the question of our competence in undertaking such a journey. The biologist, I presumed, had some adventure travel experience, but other than a willingness to take risks, *I* was certainly no intrepid traveller. And then there was Hogan.

I had met Hogan in the O. Henry a few weeks earlier, and we had since gone on some binges together, including a wild weekend up at Lago de Yojoa with the nurse and some of the teachers from the American School. Hogan thought he could get me a job at the school. 'They always need teachers,' he said. 'People come down and last a few months at best before splitting. Honduras is pretty much of a pit, you have to admit. Nobody stays long if they don't have to.' Hogan himself had stayed in the country for four years. He wouldn't say what kept him in Honduras, but it certainly wasn't love of the work he was doing. He considered teaching a bore, especially at a school for 'spoiled rich kids and diplomat brats'. And it certainly wasn't love of Honduras. He disparaged the country every chance he got. 'A tropical sinkhole', he called it, and 'the cesspit of the Americas'. In Hogan's view, every Honduran minister was 'a bloody Yankee whore'.

So why did he stay?

He shrugged. 'The third world itch.'

'What's that?'

'You'll know some day soon enough.'

Well, that was Hogan. He was a cadger, a liar and a drunk. And when he drank, he started spouting off. It was all so much profane nonsense, but it was beautiful nonsense, too. He kept me entertained, but he wasn't likely to be of much help in the hinterlands.

This is a true story about Hogan. One night this guy called Willis comes into the O. Henry. It's the first we've ever heard of him, but everyone else seems to know him. He's a big name in correspondent circles – stories in all the major magazines and newspapers, even some on-camera work for an American network. And he's really full of himself. He's got this Teddy

Roosevelt swagger and a cocky, I-already-knew-that look on his face whenever anyone talks to him. The thing is, everyone wants to talk to him. The other correspondents – normally arrogant and aloof themselves – turn positively obsequious in Willis's presence. He seems to know *everybody* and he's always dropping names, talking about his encounters with Castro and Somoza and Comandante Zero. 'Willis is here, now we'll get some stories,' the correspondents say. 'Now the place is going prime time, you wait and see.'

So Willis holds court all evening, telling his best stories to an enamoured crowd. 'You've got to expose yourself to get the exposé,' he says. 'I've helicoptered into combat zones, been through mortar barrages, dodged machine-gun fire. I know the kind of shit going down here.' He's really *on* this evening, his audience in the palm of his hand, and he's feeling awfully good about himself because he's come down to Honduras to file a major exposé for a well-known men's magazine – the *real* story of Reagan's secret war, told in between doctored photos of nude women in compromising poses. It'll be the definitive report, the one that will cast a shadow over all Central American reporting for some time to come. 'Yeah, but Willis already reported that,' editors will say.

Of course, the moment Hogan sees him, he can't stand him. He wants to bring him down a notch. But Hogan never confronts anyone straight on, so he goes over to this other guy across the bar, a writer for a mercenary magazine down here to report on fighting opportunities with the Contras. A fall-down belligerent lush. Hogan can't stand him, either, but he needs to use him just now. 'You hear what that prick's saying about your boys, the Contras?' Hogan says. 'Says he's going to bring them down, expose your boys for the fascists they are, get Congress to cut off funding, and bollocks up the whole operation.'

'The prick says that? I know that prick. That prick's a real prick.'

'You said it,' Hogan says.

And the next thing you know, the mercenary hack is hitching

his pants up and waddling over, pushing his way through Willis's lackeys, and without a word he throws a punch which Willis parries with his bottle of beer. And then the two of them are hopping around the bar in a bear hug, falling over tables and banging into walls. Willis, who's got a pretty good set of muscles on him, breaks free and sends one good punch into the mercenary's gut, knocking the wind out of him. But before Willis can strut back to the bar and begin transforming the episode into legend, the hack has his gun out and is waving it around. The thing is, the gun has a hair trigger, and before you know it, before he himself knows it, the harebrain's blasted a couple of rounds into the ceiling. Of course, that scares the hell out of everyone, no one more so than soldier boy, who collapses backwards and drops the gun, while Hogan and Willis and the rest of us stampede the exit, leaving it to the Honduran national guard to deal with the mess.

This was the sort of adventure Hogan specialised in. A jungle expedition was another matter altogether.

❂

I tried to track down some information on the biosphere, but no one seemed to know anything about it. Given everything else that was happening in Honduras, with rebels and mercenaries and CIA agents everywhere, the news of a biosphere was easily lost.

First I went to the Instituto Geográfico Nacional, where supposedly the best maps were sold. An elderly man with a pince-nez and a neatly trimmed moustache presided over the nearly bare office. He remained at his desk reading a newspaper, undisturbed by my entry. On one wall hung a large plastic topographical map depicting the country's mountains as bumps of moulded plastic. Something – roaches perhaps – had eaten holes into it so that the entire southern section of the country appeared to be riddled with sinkholes. Another wall displayed an old tourist poster of the Maya ruins of Copán. The paper had yellowed, and one corner had curled over to reveal the original colour of the wall's badly faded paint. The Maya god depicted on the poster appeared to be grimacing in agony.

I interrupted the clerk's scrutiny of the newspaper to ask if there were maps of the Mosquitia. At first he was annoyed at the interruption, then surprised.

'The Mosquitia?' he said.

'Yes. Gracias a Dios Department.'

'We have maps of Honduras. Gracias a Dios is part of Honduras.'

'I need a map that shows the Mosquitia in detail.'

'There are no details in the Mosquitia. This is the best map available: 1:100,000.'

He pulled a map from a desk drawer and unscrolled it on the counter for me. 'It shows all the roads. There is Gracias a Dios,' he said, sweeping his hand dismissively over a nameless green arrowhead fragmented by thin lines indicating rivers.

'There are no roads in the Mosquitia,' I said.

He looked up at me over his glasses, and flashed a sarcastic smile.

To buy the map, I had to take an invoice (which the clerk typed out, rather laboriously, in triplicate) all the way across town to the *palacio* in the centre of the capital, where all accounts were to be settled. A guard directed me to the line for *Pagos* – Payments – but when, after twenty minutes in line, I finally reached the window and presented the invoice, the *Pagos* clerk informed me, as though it were a personal insult that I had brought this invoice to his window, that I needed to go to Window 21. A few turns in the labyrinthine halls brought me at last to Window 21 and another line. After fifteen minutes, just before I could reach it, Window 21 closed: lunchtime for bureaucrats. Those of us in line, fearful of losing our places, moved to a nearby bench and fell into conversation.

'I'm planning a trip to the Mosquitia,' I told my partners in waiting.

They stared at me in mute incomprehension, as though I had said, 'I'm off to Vladivostok.' Then a short, chubby man broke into laughter.

'The Mosquitia!' he said. 'Don't bother. I know – I'm a shoe salesman and I've been out to Puerto Lempira. Hell cannot be any worse. And the people!'

'Did you sell any shoes?' someone asked.

'Sure, they lined up to buy them. But listen to this – they put the shoes on top of their heads and walked home barefoot, the fools!'

Before the clerk returned to validate our purchases from the government, the shoe salesman had everyone laughing – laughing at the primitive people of the Mosquitia and at the crazy gringo who wanted to go there.

When I returned with the receipt to pick up my map, I asked the clerk at the Geography Institute if he knew anything about the new biosphere. He frowned and had me repeat the word several times until he was content that my Spanish was so poor he would never understand me.

'The Río Plátano Biosphere,' I said. 'In the Mosquitia.'

He shook his head in exasperation, tired of having to make the same point again and again to someone so stupid. '*No hay nada en la Mosquitia,*' he said. 'There isn't anything in the Mosquitia.'

❁

That night, I spread the map out on my bed in the grim hostel where I was staying. Not that there was anything to study. The emptiness of the map east of the sierra that cut the country in two was remarkable, with only a handful of settlements indicated and most of the rivers lacking names. A vast, unknown region awaited our exploration. A journey to the Mosquitia was a journey to the furthest edge of the earth. That was all the motivation I needed.

Our plans, such as they were, fell into place. We bought our airline tickets at SAHSA's main office in the capital. It was not the sort of operation to inspire confidence – a dingy little kiosk where the clerk hand-wrote our tickets with a pen that kept running out of ink. Hogan, meanwhile, had succeeded in finding an American missionary in Tegucigalpa who, though not of the same church, knew the Mosquitia missionaries and supplied us with their names. He also offered to radio news of our visit to the coast in order to give the missionaries some notice of our arrival. Beyond that, we had no idea what would happen after we landed in Brus Laguna.

But even these sketchy plans began to fall apart. Two days before our departure, the biologist came down with amoebic dysentery. He would need weeks to recover, and even then a journey into an area where sanitation was dubious would be out of the question. It was a severe blow to our expedition – the biologist was the only one of us with any kind of experience in tropical hinterlands (my Amazon credentials notwithstanding), and we had been counting on him as a guide.

Hogan and I talked it over in the O. Henry. He was somewhat chary about undertaking such an ambitious trek without experienced leadership, but by that point I was completely taken with the idea of travelling into remote wilderness. I suggested that we at least fly out to Brus Laguna and visit the missionaries. We were sure to find a local guide, and the missionaries would no doubt have some suggestions. After a few rum and Cokes, Hogan relented. 'Yeah, why the hell not? I'm game for anything.'

CHAPTER 3

Blinded by the light

B EFORE dawn, we waited in a dismal bus terminal for the *expreso* to La Ceiba. Hogan, still bleary-eyed from another protracted evening in the cantinas, went on a groggy search for coffee in the warren of stalls and kiosks – mostly shuttered at this hour – that made a market of the bus station. The waiting area for the La Ceibeña line was near an entrance to the terminal. Black diesel clouds wafted in from the buses idling outside and hung over the waiting passengers. A heap of garbage nearby added to the aroma, a seething decomposition of rinds, husks, peels, pulp and larvae. On the streets surrounding the terminal, fires burned in dustbins and dark ragmen moved in and out of shadows, feeding the fires with trash scraped from the cobblestoned street. Bundled up against the metal-grated storefronts, the homeless of Tegucigalpa lay asleep in cardboard boxes and beneath plastic sheets.

At last the driver appeared and coaxed the Bluebird's reluctant motor to life. We careened over the capital's flame-lit streets and through the industrialised outskirts. Hogan, having found only lukewarm Nescafé, fell asleep, his head bobbing as the bus lurched from pothole to pothole. The highway north out of Tegucigalpa connected the capital to the country's main economic centre, San Pedro Sula, and had been fully paved for only a few years. Even so, the macadam was already deteriorating, and for hours the bus rattled over ridged asphalt. The road ascended faults and descended into rift valleys. In the higher altitudes, it

47

wound through pine forests and pastured hillsides, passing isolated adobe houses and lime kilns. At lower elevations, a riot of
Jurassic fronds slapped at the bus and huge roots pushed up
through the pavement. Sugarcane mills gave off a sickly sweet
smoke that penetrated the bus. Traffic came to a standstill at river
crossings because only one vehicle at a time could negotiate the
narrow bridges. Rows of food stands were set up at these crossings, the vendors selling snacks to stalled travellers.

Hogan and I left the bus at one such stop to buy coffee and
bread. We had reached the lowlands – hot, insect-loud, tetchy.
After a few hours of sitting in vinyl seats, our clothing had turned
damp and sticky. 'To hell with coffee,' Hogan said. 'I'm going
for beer.'

He came back with a plastic bag filled with jaundiced fluid, the
bag pinched off at the top and a straw stuck in it. 'She wouldn't
let me take the bottle,' Hogan explained, sucking on the straw.

'How is it?'

'Warm. Bloody warm.'

'Welcome to the tropics.'

The driver honked us back on board. 'The houses here are full
of frights,' he said as we came up the steps. Or something to that
effect – I always had trouble following the slurred speech of
Honduran men. 'You have to sing to buy your ticket,' he said and
cackled. *Hijo de puta.* That I understood: Son of a whore.

❁

In the afternoon we had a hot hour's wait in steamy San Pedro.

'Hell of a ride,' Hogan said.

'You slept the whole way.'

'Bad dreams, you know. Fire pits. Insect plagues. Shit, I'm still
shaking. I need a drink.'

After a greasy sidewalk lunch, we reboarded the bus and
pressed on through the coastal lowlands, mile after sweltering
mile of banana plantations giving way to an occasional glimpse of
the sea and the villages where the banana workers lived. The dri-

ver kept the stereo on at full volume. Over and over, a distorted Rod Stewart asked if we thought he was sexy.

'Hey, turn that shit off,' Hogan called.

'*Hijo de puta,*' the driver said, grinding the gears with impressive fury.

With exasperating frequency, the bus stopped in the middle of the banana groves, picking up passengers, dropping them off – every one of them hauling huge burlap bundles, which cluttered the aisle and spilled over the seats. Live animals – goats, chickens, pigs – were lifted onto the roof and lowered down. The bus coughed and sputtered and then rebelled against the driver's ranting. Two tyres blew out along the way, and near the end the brakes entirely failed, leaving us to limp along in first gear, the driver first importuning and then cursing the BVM, who continued to gaze dolorously from the purple and gold banner above the windshield.

When the bus finally reached La Ceiba, the sun had already set, and carousers jigged in the sulphur light of streetlamps as we walked the streets of the noisy town. We stopped at five hotels, each seedier than the last, before Hogan found one he deemed cheap enough.

The next afternoon, we called on Hogan's Peace Corps friends. Bruce and Chris were sitting in lawn chairs at the rear of the Peace Corps cottage. Bare-chested and barefoot, they were spending the afternoon 'soaking up rays and rolling joints,' as Bruce put it. They were planning a party for that evening, and Springsteen was growling from the stereo about being blinded by the light. Chris lit up and passed a joint around. 'Never too early to start,' he said.

'Bloody well right,' Hogan said. 'Perfect timing.'

For an hour we sat in the hot sun while Hogan and the PC boys recalled past escapades. They remembered with particular hilarity a wild night in Teguz that ended up in a police cell – 'A filthy pisspot,' Hogan said – before the Peace Corps director for Honduras arrived to straighten things out.

While the boys spread tanning oil on themselves, I moved into the shade. Springsteen was still singing, his rust-belt angst sounding somewhat surreal with a tropical backdrop. I lay back and watched the coconut palms wave in a listless breeze.

A local boy rode into the yard on a rusted bicycle. He had live crabs for sale. Bruce bought an entire burlap sack of the creatures, spilling them onto the dirt. We watched them crawl all over each other in confusion, befuddled by the hot, dry soil and bright sunlight. Chris picked up a stick and poked at the moiling crustaceans, and when one crawled free from the circle he flicked it back into the fray. Fifteen minutes, thirty minutes passed, and Bruce, Chris and Hogan were still laughing over the crabs.

'Hey, Chris,' Bruce said. 'You know how to cook these things?'

'Boil them. Live.'

'Boil 'em live? That's wild. Too fucking wild.'

Then we were driving to a *supermercado* to get beer for the party, riding in what Bruce and Chris referred to as the PC Jeep. Bruce drove and I rode shotgun; Chris and Hogan stood in the back, holding onto a roll bar. Bruce aimed for the potholes just to rattle Chris and Hogan, while I clutched the seat, my head spinning.

'I'll knock you bastards off yet!' Bruce shouted.

Then the *supermercado*. Beer, chips, bread, rum. A butcher with a machete whacked chunks off a cow carcass and wrapped them in newspaper. Chris invited the checkout girl to the party and gave the address to a girl in the candy aisle.

The Jeep bounded through the streets. Bruce shouted in blunt Spanish to a group of teens on a street corner. 'Why don't you just get a bloody bullhorn?' Hogan yelled. 'Invite the whole frigging town.'

We were grilling meat, while the crabs turned bright pink in a boiling pot. The sun had gone down, and there was a fire in the yard and a fire in my head. When some mini-skirted girls arrived, Hogan howled. Chris passed around a tray full of joints, as Hogan was having a hard time getting the bong going. Soon a knot of people were dancing and smoking.

I tried to talk to Chris about the Mosquitia, but he didn't sound too impressed. 'It's pretty boring out there,' he shouted above the music. 'But it's cool if you're into, like, total deprivation. And howler monkeys. The howler monkeys are cool. We saw a guy kill a snake, a big fucking snake. Poisonous.'

Then I was talking to a girl. She didn't like La Ceiba, she said; Honduras was boring and dirty and poor. She wanted to go to Miami. Miami was the most beautiful city, she'd seen it on television. She didn't like Honduran men, they were mean and crude. American men were nice. She wanted to marry an American and live in Miami. She looked up at me and smiled, her olive brown eyes as wide and deep as a jungle river. Her name was Veronica.

Chris came up to join us. I saw the glowing dial on his watch: four a.m. The joints had disappeared and the beer had long run out. Most of the people had vanished. 'Let's go to the beach,' Chris said, grabbing Veronica's arm. '*Vamos a la playa.*' We climbed onto the Jeep, ten of us barely on board when Bruce ground the clutch and we lurched into the dark, empty streets of La Ceiba.

Near the port, we turned onto the sailor's street, where the bars were still open and music blared. Sailors stumbled around, responding to our calls with obscene gestures. Asphalt gave way to sand, and tyres spun as the Jeep ploughed through sea-wrack and beached jetsam. Bruce brought us to a halt and we tumbled from the Jeep into the sand. A pile of driftwood became a bonfire, and a strong wind blew over us, hot, even in the darkness. Someone played a guitar and the Hondurans with us sang a folk song about roses, a night of roses. The dawn seemed to rise from the sand; there was no sunrise, just a dull grey light.

'Sing something in English,' said Chris. The guitarist strummed a few chords and I finally recognised the words through his thick accent. 'Imagine,' he sang, 'Imagine all the people living for today.' I closed my eyes and lay back in the sand to listen.

✪

On the eve of our flight to the Mosquitia, Hogan and I stopped in a cantina for a last night out before submitting to the austerity of life among the missionaries. An American sailor we met in the cantina told us we were mad for even thinking of a sojourn in the Mosquitia.

'You'll wither and die out there,' he said. 'There's nothing but swamp and malaria. Besides, the rainy season's coming on, and you're likely to get stranded out in that hell-hole.'

He suggested we go instead to the Bay Islands, just offshore from La Ceiba, where we could snorkel and chase black women and drink rum. 'You won't last a week out in the Mosquitia,' he said. 'It's worse than being at sea. No beer. No women. Trust me, leave the frigging mosquitoes to the God-boys.'

By that point, Hogan was already losing interest in the Mosquitia. It sounded too dreary to him, too deprived. He preferred the idea of the Bay Islands. 'So which sounds better?' Hogan demanded. 'A couple of weeks on a beautiful island getting drunk and laid, or a couple of weeks in a steaming, stinking jungle picking ticks out of your arse.'

'I guess it's obvious,' I said.

'Bloody well right.'

I returned to the hotel, leaving Hogan in the bar with the sailors and their molls. The next morning he was sprawled across the bed, still in his clothes. We only had an hour before the flight to Brus Laguna. 'Fuck off,' he growled when I shook him.

I didn't care. I was too curious not to go through with it now. Sometimes it's that way when you're travelling. You just need to go through with it, push on ahead, even when the signs are bad. I left Hogan and flagged a taxi for the airport.

CHAPTER 4

Brus Laguna

THE aeroplane, an ancient DC-3 that had seen service in World War II, followed the coastline, trailing its shadow in the avocado sea like bait on a fishing line. Near the shore, trawlers bobbed in the white waves. Further out, an occasional freighter specked the horizon beneath incipient thunderheads. The settlement of Trujillo appeared and vanished, followed by mile after monotonous mile of empty coastline, the white strip of beach demarcating the boundary between two vast green zones – the sea and the jungle. From Trujillo onwards, there was hardly a hint of human habitation.

❂

The people of the Mosquitia, a region that includes the eastern third of Honduras and the Caribbean coast of Nicaragua, are called the Miskito Indians. They are not, in fact, 'pure' Indians but a 'mongrel breed', as one early traveller called them, mixing indigenous blood with that of Europeans (especially the English) and blacks who escaped from slavery in the West Indies and ended up in the backwaters of the Spanish Main.

For centuries, the Spanish neglected the region, this negligence allowing British buccaneers to use the mangrove shores, lagoons, cays and rivers of the Mosquitia as hideouts and as a base for their raids on Spanish treasure ships. Captain Edward Mansfield, Sir Henry Morgan and the notorious Blackbeard roamed the coast, looking for laden vessels. One particularly brutal pirate named Brewer lent his name, now corrupted to 'Brus', to the lagoon and village where I was headed. British rulers covertly supported the buccaneers in an attempt to undermine Spain's colonial pretensions. England, of course, had pretensions of its own; by the late seventeenth century, the British had established numerous trading posts and towns in the Mosquitia, where they conducted a lucrative trade in logwood, mahogany and pine – the first assault on the rainforest. By the middle of the eighteenth century, the population of the British town of Black River (near present-day Palacios) had passed three thousand.

To legitimise their colonial claims the British chose and crowned a 'King of the Mosquitos', thereby establishing a spurious protectorate as a direct challenge to Spanish hegemony. For the next century, the two European powers engaged in desultory battles, until a treaty was signed by which the British agreed to abandon their colonial designs in exchange for extended logging rights.

But the Spanish and their descendants, preferring the cooler mountainous interior, never succeeded in colonising the coast. After Honduras received independence from Spain in 1821, the new government found no reason to pay attention to such a remote, desolate region. Consequently, British and American traders dominated the economy of the Mosquitia, while their governments jockeyed for control of the territory. As the century progressed, the Mosquitia, particularly on the Nicaraguan side of the border, experienced boom and bust cycles as warring traders exploited the region's timber, rubber, bananas and pitch. But the booms were never significant enough to sustain development, especially in eastern Honduras. By the turn of the twentieth century, the Mosquitia had become a forgotten land, languishing in a long and profound torpor.

Forgotten, that is, by everyone except the Moravian missionaries, who made the Mosquitia their great evangelical cause. They came north from their Nicaraguan missions in the late nineteenth century, bringing the gospel to a region that the Catholics had timidly ventured into and then abandoned. A small, zealous church with limited resources, the Moravians chose the Mosquitia largely because no one else seemed interested. God had called them to go where no one else would venture, and dutifully they went.

❂

After a couple of hours in the air, we abruptly banked toward the coast, crossed over a narrow spit of land and then a glinting sheet of shallow water: the erstwhile lagoon of the pirate Brewer, now Laguna de Brus. My first glimpse of the village was, appropriately, through a passing rain cloud. We came in low through the shower, and I saw the huts, the wide grassy paths, the silver roof of the church. In fifteen seconds, we passed over the entire village and listed toward a wobbly landing on a wide muddy savannah. I don't know why, but up to the moment of splashdown, I expected a tarmac. A laughable notion in hindsight: the nearest pavement was hundreds of kilometres behind me.

I was the only passenger destined for Brus Laguna; the other ten or so on board were headed further south for Puerto Lempira, the Mosquitia's biggest settlement. The co-pilot came down the aisle to the rear of the plane and kicked open the stubborn door for me. I jumped down into a gentle rain, the remnants of the storm that had passed over the village, and wherever I stepped, my shoes sucked down into the thick mud. I took my pack over to a small shelter – four poles and a tin roof – and watched as the DC-3 slipped and slid and struggled into the air, leaving me alone and sweating in the humid air.

I set out across the saturated land, following a footpath that somehow managed to skirt the large puddles and pools of muck left behind by the rainstorm. In the three or four places where the path met with an unavoidable depression, half-mired wooden planks provided a reasonably clean passage. The path took me across a vast savannah that presented an aspect considerably different from my expectations. I had thought that in the Mosquitia I would find dense rainforest; I had fancied myself hacking through vines and fronds and spider webs to reach a concealed village. Instead, I

55

found this wide-open savannah and a panorama that extended for miles and miles too incredible to comprehend in a first encounter. Great silver and grey thunderheads moved like man-o'-wars across the sky, dragging their tentacles of rain. Inside the larger cloud masses, lightning lit up the roiling vapour and broadcast deep rumbling threats, the drumming of an angry timpanist.

Islands of trees interrupted the savannah, stunted palms mostly, but here or there stood an isolated giant – a ceiba or pine. Up ahead, clusters of conifer and fruit trees – and the tell-tale wisps of cooking-fire haze lingering around the tree tops – indicated the presence of a village. I passed some bean fields, a small enclosed papaya plantation of perhaps thirty trees, and finally the first of the outlying huts. A few head of cattle, ribs much in evidence, stood knee-deep in puddles, their dewlaps, udders and hocks mottled with dried mud. A handful of children came tumbling out of a hut, spotted me, then turned and scampered back inside. A man wielding a machete against a tree stump stopped to watch me. I waved as I passed, and he brought up his hand as if to respond, but couldn't complete the gesture. Instead, he traced his thumb along the blade of his machete.

The path led past a small graveyard, a collection of mounds and wooden markers, and brought me to a large grassy commons surrounded by several wooden buildings raised on stilts. The largest of these structures was the turquoise church, its zinc roof red-streaked with rust, its squat steeple slightly askew. Next to the church, in the same compound, stood a large white house with blue trim, which I took to be the mission house, my destination.

The names of the missionaries were written on a card in my pocket: Pastor Mark and Jeannie Reed. I entered the compound through a wooden gate in the barbed-wire fence and passed under a stand of tall pines, the needles dripping water from the recent storm. A flight of steps on the side of the house took me up to a screen door.

Jeannie Reed answered my knock. She was in her late thirties, short and spinsterish, with a narrow, bony face, rag-coloured, shoulder-length hair and thick glasses. There was something earnest about her: you could tell she was a humourless person, the kind who never understood jokes or sarcasm. Like most missionaries I had met, her clothing was conservative and dowdy.

'Well, goodness me,' she said. 'A visitor. Oh, you must be with the Peace Corps crew.'

'Not exactly,' I said. I introduced myself and explained my purpose. 'The mission in the capital was supposed to have radioed word.'

'Land sakes,' Jeannie said. 'It's the first I heard about it. The pastor – my husband – didn't tell me a thing. He's off in Lempira just now putting a new roof on the church there, and won't be back until next week. As to a – what was it – a biosphere? Goodness, I can't rightly say I've heard of any such thing. What on earth is it?'

It was an awkward moment. The plane was long gone, and there wouldn't be another for a week. Brus Laguna had no hotels, no restaurants. I was stranded and at a loss.

'Well,' Jeannie said. 'It's unexpected. But maybe we can arrange lodging for you. It won't do for you to stay here, what with Mark gone and all. The village is plumb full of gossips, believe you me. Let's go visit Otho Wood and see if he can provide a place.'

Twilight had fallen, and we crossed the commons following a footpath which, like the others I had taken that day, managed to dodge the muddy depressions where rainwater had pooled. Jeannie pointed out the classroom and its adjacent dormitory where students from outlying villages stayed during the school year. The frail glow of candlelight flickered in the windows. I heard a guitar and someone singing a hymn; the tune was familiar, but the words were Miskito. I could hardly concentrate, however, because I was under attack, besieged by a buzzing, whirring, whining horde. I waved, slapped and shook my clothes in a clumsy and frantic dance.

'Now you know why it's called the Mosquito Coast,' Jeannie said.

✺

Otho Wood was an elder in the church and a prominent citizen of Brus. 'You are welcome to stay in my home,' he said with great formality, offering me a limp hand and bowing his head slightly. Despite his small, wiry frame, Otho had an aristocratic air, an air that was somehow enhanced by his gestures of humility.

Otho's house stood fifty metres from the commons down a grass avenue. Vegetation enveloped the property: luxuriant umbrella trees fronted the avenue; a prolific mango tree towered over the yard; red flowering shrubs hid the porch. Very few of the houses in Brus were as fine. Most were simple, one-room bamboo huts with thatched roofs; the better ones were constructed from wooden planks, raised on posts and maybe roofed with zinc. But Otho Wood's bungalow, three or four times the size of the humbler abodes, seemed palatial in comparison – especially at night, when kerosene lamps gave the house what in Brus passed for a glow. Painted in bright turquoise and ochre, zinc roof glinting, it amply represented Mr Wood's prominence in the village.

What exactly that prominence was based on, I never discovered. Otho had gone to a school in San Pedro Sula and married a Spanish-speaking woman. He owned cows and a horse, and had some sort of government commission. For decades the Wood family had worked closely with the missionaries. All this seemed sufficient to endow him with status and wealth that no one else in the village possessed. For example, in the compound behind his house, among the orange, papaya and cacao trees, Mr Wood had such luxuries as an outhouse, a shack for bathing and a large metal container fitted with a spigot at its base that collected runoff from the roof for drinking water.

The family included Otho and his wife – I guessed they were in their mid-thirties – and their two boys, Sammy (aged eleven) and Lester (eight). On that first evening in Brus, the boys were doing schoolwork at the dinner table by the light of a kerosene lamp. Mrs Wood – Otho introduced her only as *mi señora* – brought me some coffee and coconut bread as I sat with the boys and answered their many questions: Where was I from? Did I like football? Could I ride a bicycle? Had I ever been to New York? Meanwhile, Otho and his wife sat in the living room and listened to a short-wave radio broadcast: a gospel hour in English that originated from Las Vegas.

Amongst themselves, the Wood family spoke Spanish – a somewhat unusual trait on the coast, where most people spoke Miskito and had only a rudimentary knowledge of Spanish. The Woods spoke Miskito, too, of course, but Otho preferred to use Spanish because it was the language of his wife and 'more cultured'. Most cultured of all, in his mind, was English. In fact, his hospitality toward me was motivated in part by the hope that my presence would facilitate the boys' learning of English. If the boys learned English well enough, the missionaries had told Otho, they could attend a Moravian school in the States and perhaps one day become pastors, the most prestigious occupation one could have in the Mosquitia. In return for room and board, I was to tutor the boys and speak with them in English as much as possible.

Later that evening, I had the chance to speak to Otho. I joined him in the living room, where the Woods' collection of furniture, like the clutter in the yard, suggested their wealth. Some of the furniture had belonged to Mrs Wood's family, and formed, I gathered, part of her dowry. Other pieces had been discarded by the missionaries of years past. I sat on a vintage vinyl couch, while Otho occupied a tattered upholstered rocker. A poorly executed painting of boats in a harbour hung on the wall in a gaudy gilt frame. There were also a director's chair with a torn back, a stained coffee table and a footstool losing its stuffing.

Not surprisingly, Otho knew nothing about the biosphere; but it was not difficult to reach the Río Plátano, he said. After crossing the lagoon to the sandbar, one would only have to walk along the shore a few kilometres to reach the Plátano's mouth. There were some scattered settlements along the way – very small, not even big enough to be named – but beyond them, nothing. Maybe it was possible to hire a boat to go upriver, maybe not. As for a guide, there were some men in the village who might be willing if the pay was good. But the rainy season was imminent, and a long river trip was inadvisable. Otho told me all this in his deliberate, gentle voice. At first I thought he was somewhat effeminate or precious, but later I came to find his manner priest-like.

'Tomorrow we will look for a guide,' he said, carefully pronouncing each word. 'But now, day is done.'

CHAPTER 5

Going native

ON that first night with the Woods, I began the arduous task of learning to adapt to the village routine. Back in Tegucigalpa, I had kept late hours, staying in the cantinas to three and four in the morning; in Brus Laguna, I discovered that bedtime was eight o'clock. At the conclusion of the Las Vegas gospel show, the kerosene lamp was extinguished and everyone retired to their cots. I lay awake for hours, unable to sleep.

Sleep, in fact, proved difficult to come by throughout my stay on the coast. It didn't help that a symphony of sounds erupted whenever I dozed off. I heard scratching, creaking, scraping, rattling, popping, buzzing, whirring, clicking, croaking, snapping and more – all coming from the floor beneath me and the walls around me, or from just beyond the bungalow's gapped planks.

The cot was short and narrow. Wedged between the two bars that poorly supported the sagging canvas bed, I found that any position I assumed was intolerable. Not even months of bad mattresses in cheap hotels and hostels had prepared me for discomfort of this sort. No matter how I arranged myself, part of my body rubbed against the mosquito netting that cocooned the cot, so that at any moment either my knees, my feet or my head were exposed to skilled parasites who had no trouble needling me through the netting. Rain rattled on the zinc roof. I would later find this a pleasing sound, but during that first long night it drove me to distraction.

When I did manage to fall asleep, the insufferable heat gave way to chills induced by the malaria pills I was taking. All night long, and almost every night for the two months that followed, I alternated between the extremes of profuse sweating and profound chills. Malaria itself, I came to think, could hardly be much worse than the side effects from taking the pills.

❋

Morning in Brus Laguna began well before dawn with the roosters' shrill call, and soon the rest of the Woods' menagerie joined the chorus: the pig, leashed to a post, snorted and rooted around the outhouse; the chickens bickered over yesterday's seeds; the guinea hen and the turkey complained from the top of the water bin; while the dogs – craven, skeletal curs with sunken ribs and bulging eyes – yelped and yowled.

The cacophony reached its crescendo when Lester came out to throw some feed around the compound. As soon as the boy appeared on the back steps, the animals yammered at his feet until he started flinging handfuls of grain around the muddy yard.

Sammy had the task of drawing water from a pump at the back of the property. He filled several buckets and left them inside a backyard structure that I called the shower shack, in which we bathed ourselves by dipping a coconut shell into Sammy's buckets and pouring water over our bodies. The system worked well enough, but it had one major flaw: mosquitoes loved the damp, enclosed space of the shower shack, and of course found it convenient to be presented each morning with a completely exposed body. For the mosquitoes, the shower shack was a banquet hall.

Sometime after breakfast (coffee, beans and eggs), a clanking bell called the children to school. For the first couple of days, I walked with Sammy and Lester to the mission school where Jeannie was the English teacher. I sat in the back of the room while she delivered the lesson, an endless recitation of the alphabet followed by skits of simple conversations. Because their teacher came from the American South, the Miskito students all affected a drawl, especially exaggerated on the vowels. 'Good morning, class,' Jeannie would say to begin the day. 'Good morning, teachuh,' they responded. 'Hower y'all today?' 'Ah'm fine, tank you. And you?' 'Ah'm fine, too.'

After the English lesson, when the class moved on to other subjects, I sometimes sat with Jeannie on the school's veranda and helped her grade tests or prepare materials. For Jeannie, materials preparation involved cutting out pictures from the pile of magazines that her sister in the States collected for her, donations from the women of her home congregation. The magazines were her link to home, the only news she got apart from the shortwave. She had to force herself to ration her reading to two articles a day, one in the morning and one in the evening, so that she always had something new to read. When she had finished with a magazine it joined the resource pile, which we culled for pictures that Jeannie thought would make 'good visuals' for vocabulary development.

While the children murmured their lessons and women crossed the commons carrying water pails, Jeannie and I leafed through *Good Housekeeping* or *Woman's Day*, pausing at pictures of whiter, brighter laundry and revolutionary waterproof makeup and no-bake brownies. It seemed to me that Jeannie was more interested in pretty pictures than in useful vocabulary. 'Oh, here's a nice one,' she would say, snipping the photo of a lemon meringue pie or a swimming pool from an advertisement.

❂

When Jeannie's husband returned from Puerto Lempira, I visited him at the mission house. Pastor Mark Reed, I learned right away, was a big sports fan. He tuned in to American Armed Forces radio and listened to American football on Sundays after church and basketball during the evenings. Coming from North Carolina, Pastor Reed loved college basketball and listened intently for the results. He all but worshipped the University of North Carolina's basketball coach, and his favourite topic of conversation was how Coach Smith and the 'Tar Heels' were doing that season.

'I don't think they've got the depth they had in years past,' he would say in discussing a Tar Heel triumph, 'but Coach Smith gets the most out of his boys. He'll find a way to win.'

Around the village, the pastor stood out even at a distance. He was most noticeable when jogging, his white bulk bounding through the village or across the savannah. In shorts and sweat-soaked T-shirt, his blond hair plastered to his head, the missionary splashed up mud as he slogged through puddles, waving at the villagers who paused to watch, hands covering their mouths to keep from giggling.

Pastor Reed was himself as large as a basketball centre: tall and bulky, he towered over the Miskitos, who were clearly in awe of him at close quarters. Even though he was a good-natured man, with a pleasant manner and disarming grin, his parishioners seemed to shrink from him when he stood over them in the church house, preaching in his thick, mannered Miskito.

At that first meeting, Pastor Reed turned down the radio and studied my map with me. He remembered hearing something about a new nature reserve, but that had been a few years ago and as nothing more had come of it, he had put it out of his mind. He pointed out places he had been, mostly along the coast from Laguna de Brus to Laguna Ibans and the nearest village to the west, Palacios, on the Río Negro. In between were a few small settlements that he had visited and ministered to.

'Now the interior is another matter,' the pastor said. 'Up the Plátano, it's rugged going and almost uninhabited. There's one village, Marias, but it's your Pech tribe there – different language, more primitive than your Miskitos. I don't go there.'

As evening set in, the pastor went down to a shed behind the mission house to start up the diesel generator that supplied electricity to the house and the church, the only two buildings in Brus that were wired. The generator allowed the missionaries to run appliances – oven, refrigerator, washing machine – at least for a few hours each evening.

While the pastor and I studied the map, Jeannie busied herself with domestic chores, ironing clothes and running the vacuum cleaner over the rug and floorboards. I soon discovered that Jeannie was in fact fanatical about cleanliness, hating the thought of dirt and mould. Bottles and bottles of cleaning products and insecticides lined a shelf in her kitchen, and the house smelled of the aerosol disinfectant she sprayed everywhere. She was so particular about housekeeping that she refused to hire a maid; a local woman just wouldn't do the chores right. 'They just sort of stir the dirt around.'

But despite Jeannie's array of disinfectants and insecticides, mould grew on the shower curtain and around the kitchen sink, while ants investigated the counter tops and termites colonised damp boards and tunnelled them into sawdust. Jeannie had a strong aversion to Brus Laguna's many pests. In her mind, they were nearly the equivalent of Biblical plagues. 'Lord have mercy, but Brus is just full up of bugs, every kind you can think of. Have you seen those horrible huge beetles that tunnel in the garden? Big as a mouse. The mosquitoes are awful, of course. But it's the no-see-ums I can't stand most. Look at these red bumps all over my ankles – the itching never stops. You know, when we go back home for fund-raising, it's these bumps more than anything else that gets the attention of the church folk – because you know these bites last for months, believe you me. I'll be with the ladies auxiliary at a tea, showing pictures of the school, the students, the church, but when I show them how we're just bitten to death down here, why, you should see the horror in their eyes. They surely become most gracious givers when they see what the Lord's servants suffer in his name!

'But you know who is truly a servant of the Lord? Old Doc Brady over in the Ahuas clinic. Why, the man is practically a saint. Thirty years of doctoring out here. They tried to get him to retire, but he keeps coming back. Says he's got the place in his blood. Imagine, all those years without decent food, putting up with the dirt and bugs. And the loneliness! Why, it's nearly twenty years since the poor man's wife passed on. The Lord is working through him something powerful. It's been just over three years for us, and that's trial enough.'

Tapping the map, the pastor showed me the location of Ahuas, where the Moravians had a medical clinic, some twenty-five kilometres south of Brus on the Río Patuca. The Missionary Air Force had a pilot stationed there, and between them the doctor and the pilot knew the interior better than any gringo. 'You might want to consider paying them a visit,' the pastor said.

CHAPTER 6

Searching for a biosphere

A FTER thinking it over, the pastor decided to accompany me to the Río Plátano. We planned a Monday departure, following the Sabbath, but meanwhile, I had several days to kill in Brus. For an outsider, there was really very little to do in the village. My main activity was walking up and down the four or five broad grassy avenues that formed Brus Laguna's centre. The village lacked obvious signs of modernity: no cars, no wires (other than the few electrical wires connecting the mission house and church to the generator), no television antennas and no glass windows. The missionaries used screens, while all other windows in the village were covered by boards that were propped open in good weather and pulled shut in storms.

But as I became more familiar with my surroundings, I began to notice the inexplicable presence of certain artefacts from the developed world: concrete slabs that had been poured for no discernible purpose, scores of rusting steel drums, spent cylinders of pressurised gas, piles of iron rods, odd lengths of rubber hose and plastic pipe, and even old tyres that had somehow migrated to a region that lacked motorised vehicles. But the most remarkable of these foreign artefacts was the barbed wire: a few thousand metres of the stuff crisscrossed the local landscape. It demarcated virtually every compound, yard and plantation in and around the village, dividing it into a weird geometry. I wondered how it had come to Brus in the first place. Pastor Reed didn't know. Nor could Otho Wood recall exactly. At first he remembered it as a missionary import from some years back, but then he changed his mind and said the government had left it behind after abruptly abandoning some ill-conceived development project. Whatever the story, it had required significant effort on somebody's part to get that much wire out to the Mosquitia.

If no storms appeared on the horizon, I'd continue my walk and leave the village, taking one of the footpaths out to the satellite settlements of Twitanta, Kuswapaika, Haraslaya or Husopan, where the dwellings – called *palapas* – were crude and conditions primitive in comparison with the relative comforts of Brus. The footpath out to Kuswapaika followed the shore of the lagoon, and sometimes I saw shrimp boats out in the middle of the water. Closer to shore, the older boys paddled canoes, while children splashed in water the colour of guava pulp.

The red-dirt path ran along a ridge of high ground, a solid causeway through depressions that turned to swamp and muck after rain. Several log and plank bridges spanned the culverts, but sometimes the planks were missing, forcing one to tightrope walk along the log. I passed a few *palapas*, some half-built and apparently abandoned. Sometimes a woman or child would peer through the doorway, keeping a wary eye on me.

Numerous trails branched off from the lagoon and plunged through brambles that caught at me as I passed. No matter which path I chose, I eventually came up against a body of water – a river, creek, rivulet or swamp, an arm of the lagoon, a finger of river delta. I knew from flying over the region that much of it was waterlogged, but in walking outside the village I came to comprehend the extent of this inundated terrain and to appreciate the beauty of the swamplands.

Mangroves and palms cluttered the banks and extended into the muck left by the receding waters of the dry season or the neap tide. Bamboo groves rose fifteen metres or more into the air, and the crimson and white flowers of epiphytes wrapped around long lianas. In the buttresses of the water-bound trees, fish passed the hours in little root-formed rooms, while grey crabs scuttled along the shore. Snakes swam in the black river water and slithered along hardwood limbs. Marks in the sand and mud revealed the passage of large creatures that I rarely saw: a wide trough indicated the passage of a caiman; the little prints of iguanas followed winding trails; some dog-like tracks signalled the presence of racoons or coatimundis. The largest prints – rare to find – were those of the jaguar, the most elusive of the rainforest mammals.

❂

One day while walking beside the lagoon, I found an old man standing in my path. Small and dark, he wore a pith helmet, a yellow shirt and a pair of stained, threadbare jeans tucked into rubber boots. He smiled at my approach and said, in English, 'Mister, I waiting you.' With that he beckoned me to follow him toward a modest bungalow surrounded by a prolific garden.

This man proved to be Old Jim Goff. I had often heard his name mentioned in the village, for he was regarded as a town father and an authority on the flora and fauna of the Mosquitia. Otho told me that once, years before, Old Jim Goff had walked the coastline all the way to La Ceiba and back – some 650 kilometres of difficult hiking. The old man was either the son or grandson (even he wasn't sure which) of the first Goff, a Frenchman who came to the lagoon in the late nineteenth century and joined with Mr Wiley Wood of Texas to found the village of Brus. The European strain had long since been absorbed into the native bloodlines, but the names Wood and Goff were found all over the region.

Old Jim Goff brought two glasses of lemonade and invited me to sit on his porch. His English was passable – he had learned it from one of the missionaries years before – but limited to phrases like 'God bless!' and 'Jesus good man!', which he blurted out at intervals. We worked out a pidgin of our own using English, Spanish and the few Miskito phrases I had picked up.

A visit with Old Jim Goff could be quite entertaining. On several occasions over the next few days, I sat on his porch while he showed me some of the many objects in his possession. He would suddenly think of something and say, 'Wait please!', disappearing into his house – which looked like some extraordinary curiosity shop – to emerge with something for me to examine. Many of his precious objects were ordinary trinkets from the 'civilised' world: place mats with pictures of ducks in flight over a snowbound lake; a ceramic toad; and, of all things, a pliable Gumby toy.

But Old Jim Goff also showed me leaves and flowers and pieces of bark, describing how 'in old time' the Miskitos used plants to treat ailments. Nobody in Brus knew as much about the flora and fauna of the region, and yet he himself didn't regard the information as valuable. 'In old time' meant that the natural remedies were no longer used, for everyone, including Old Jim Goff, relied on the medicines imported by missionaries. He liked to show me the empty pill boxes the missionary doctor had given him – everything from antacids to antibiotics. He took especial delight in having me read the names of the different medicines, repeating after me as though I were giving him a language lesson. 'Tums,' we would say. 'Tetracycline.' To the Miskitos, the very words had potency, and I'd heard that they loved them so much that they had given the names to their children. Supposedly, somewhere in the Mosquitia lived people with the names Penicillin and Aspirin and Insulin.

Now over eighty years old, Jim Goff was one of the few villagers who could remember the time before the missionaries had arrived in the region. He was a repository of his culture's knowledge and wisdom, one of the few left who knew the old lifeways, but even he depreciated the value of that knowledge and put his trust in the foreigners' science. The knowledge of 'old time' would die with him.

❃

Old Jim took an interest in my journey to the Río Plátano and volunteered to accompany the pastor and me. I was a little sceptical. Even if he had once walked to La Ceiba, the man was now very old, small and shrivelled. I thought that the trek would prove too much for him, but the pastor laughed. 'Don't worry, that old fellow can walk us both into the ground. He does it all the time to visit relatives.'

On the prescribed day, the three of us took the small motorised canoe that belonged to the mission and set out at dawn across the greyish green lagoon. The clouds were light and few, the lagoon water glassy and smooth: perfect travel weather.

About a kilometre from shore, we circled the boat around the tail of an aeroplane which jutted out of the water. Old Jim told me its odd story. On a flight from El Salvador to the US, the plane had apparently developed engine trouble and plunged into Laguna de Brus. A salvage operation was hastily organised, and the villagers recovered the body of the pilot and his cargo: counterfeit blue jeans. The smuggler was buried on the shore, and the cargo distributed among the villagers. Old Jim Goff still sported his baggy pair, stains from the sea water still evident on the denim.

Leaving the plane wreckage behind, we continued on to a small island at the western end of the lagoon, where, according to the pastor, some old cannons lay partially buried in the sand. The island was once the refuge of Bloody Brewer, the pirate for whom Brus was named. The British later established a fort there, and sometime in the eighteenth century a skirmish between the British and the Spanish had taken place in the waters nearby.

It took us about an hour to cross the lagoon – I guessed it to be something like fifteen kilometres – and it was a great feeling to be gliding over the smooth water, sea spray in my face, the bright tropical sun bearing down. There was nowhere I'd rather have been, nothing I'd rather have been doing – one of those quintessential travel moments, when everything has worked out for you, and you feel you are at long last pushing the limits.

And it was good, too, on the little island, walking around with the place all to ourselves. Old Jim dug the sand away to show me two cannons and a remnant of wall left over from the lagoon's pirate past. The cay rose from the water in two mounds, and the snouts of caimans poked out from the muddy shoals. Probably no more than a handful of outsiders had set foot on the island in the last hundred years, and I thought it unlikely that more than just a few visitors would arrive in the next hundred to come. It was truly a place that had been left off the map, uncharted, fixed in its solitude.

The island might have been stuck in time, but we were not. The sun was approaching its zenith and we had to push on toward the true coast, the Caribbean Sea, a few kilometres to the north, where a long, narrow sandbar separated sea from lagoon. The midday breezes gave the water a light chop, just enough to bounce the boat and make steering a little more difficult than at dawn.

We landed just shy of the *barra*, a gap between the mainland and the sandbar that allowed a choppy passage from lagoon to sea. A short walk on a sand trail brought us through some palms to the beach and a wide vista of the sea. We sat down in the shade of the palms and drank in the scene. The waves rushed toward the shore in a series of breakers. A flock of pelicans in file skimmed the surface of the sea. In either direction, the beach was completely devoid of life, the empty littoral matched by an unbroken horizon with no ships in sight.

Once we started our hike, however, it didn't take long to find evidence that ships did occasionally pass nearby. We came upon scattered pieces of trash washed up on the sand: a plastic cola bottle; a chunk of Styrofoam; an orange life jacket; a piece of cellophane turning in the surf. It was all rather strange flotsam to find among the sand dollars and crab shells and dried starfish and turtle tracks of the Mosquito Coast. None of this debris escaped Old Jim's eyes. To him, it was all treasure. He picked up whatever glass, plastic and metal objects he could find and secreted them in a satchel slung over his shoulder. The biggest find that day was the pink torso of a plastic doll. Old Jim washed it carefully in the surf, then added it to his eccentric collection.

It was a five-kilometre walk from Laguna de Brus to the mouth of the Río Plátano, and for two hours we trudged along the shoreline, pausing occasionally in the shade of palms to drink some water and admire the ridge of breakers crashing toward us. It was a monotonous walk – sand, surf, sandflies, broiling sun. Moreover, the fifteen-kilogram pack I was carrying added discomfort to the drudgery, which nearly became a torment as time and distance slowly passed. My calves were searing from the labour of sand walking, and my shoulders chafed under the weight of the pack. The blinding glare of the hot sun on the white sand stabbed my eyes as my skin reddened and burned.

But for all the agony, and maybe in part because of it, that tedious walk made for a nearly perfect afternoon. On many occasions since that day I have longed to be making that trek once again, for there came a point when pain yielded to satisfaction as I lost myself in the moment.

We each kept to our own pace, each plodding along as best he could in the soft sand. The trick was to keep to the meandering strip of firm wet sand left by the wash, but to do so without soaking your boots – wet boots would mean blisters and excruciating pain. The pastor, with his greater girth, soon fell behind. Every so often, I turned to see him huffing along, his face bright red with strain and sunburn. I fared a little better, but could not keep up with Old Jim. The spry old man fairly scooted ahead of us, his bare feet slapping the surf, eyes scouting sea and shore for treasure as he went. From afar, I watched his slight frame dart back and forth – into the waves, up to the tree line – as he spotted some piece of flotsam and hurried to retrieve it. When he got too far ahead, he paused in the shade to show me his discoveries while we waited for the sweat-soaked pastor to catch up.

❂

We reached the tiny settlement at the mouth of the Río Plátano late in the afternoon. A cluster of *palapas* stood upstream from the sea, and we headed directly for the largest one, a stilted structure near the river that Old Jim called the *depósito*. Old Jim's cousin worked there, and while my companions went in to speak to him, I sat on the steps and contemplated the river.

The abstract line on the map I had studied back in Tegucigalpa was now before me. It took a few moments for the realisation to sink in: here it was, the object of my quest, the Río Plátano. I should have felt exhilarated, but in fact I felt vaguely disappointed; I had no idea why, exhaustion perhaps. Or perhaps the biosphere had become in my mind something so fantastic, a place so sublime that the reality was bound to seem anticlimactic: a collection of ramshackle huts; a turgid, muddled river; a muddied bank on which a pig rooted and squealed; a cloying hothouse stink. Was this really the 'pristine rainforest' UNESCO had designated for protection?

I joined the others inside the *palapa*, where the fate of my journey upriver was under discussion. The building was some kind of store or depot, a musty place filled with large sacks of rice and beans. Huge stems of green plantains lay on the floor. In the corner I saw a stack of something that looked like army helmets, and when my eyes adjusted to the dim light, I saw that they were turtle carapaces.

Old Jim's cousin looked just like him – small, dark and wiry. A perfect double. When we were introduced, the cousin stared up at me, wide-eyed, as if to say, So this is the crazy gringo.

'What's the verdict?' I asked.

'He says it's not a good idea,' the pastor told me. 'Maybe not even possible. The river's already high, and more rain is on the way. But they don't have any working motors available anyway.'

Old Jim said something in Miskito and the pastor translated. 'He says there are many things in the river. Branches. Logs. It's dangerous.'

I couldn't admit it, but in a way I was glad to be relieved of the obligation of going upriver. I had reached the Río Plátano, I had tried. At that moment, it seemed enough.

With the plans for a river trip scotched, we set about preparing a place to pass the night. Since the stilted *depósito* was the highest, driest structure around, the pastor and I were given the honour of spending the night on the floorboards among the beans, rice and plantains. We rigged up the mosquito netting with some twine looped around a beam. It looked like feeble protection, but it would have to do. 'I don't care about mosquitoes so much,' the pastor said. 'It's the roaches I want to keep out.'

When we finished arranging our quarters, we sat out on the steps to await the return of Old Jim, who had gone to his cousin's hut where he would spend the night. The sun had almost set and an evening breeze picked up. The smell of rot lifted, and new, redolent fragrances drifted from unseen night-bloomers. In the last light of day and with the air freshened, the Río Plátano seemed every bit the sublime place I had imagined. The obsidian river whispered past. Frogs croaked. Birds cawed. Crickets chirruped. Fireflies filled the purple air.

Even the mosquitoes, besieging us in hordes, added a certain perverse charm to the scene. After all, you reminded yourself, it wouldn't be the Mosquito Coast without them; the place's isolation depended upon the *sine qua non* of their iniquitous presence. The pastor and I slapped and waved in a futile attempt to fend off their needling. The best we could do was don long-sleeved shirts and jeans and accept the annoyance with stoic disregard, accept it as the sting inevitably associated with the sublime in nature.

With nightfall, the locals came to call on us. No one lived permanently along this stretch of the Plátano, the area serving as a temporary fishing and hunting camp and transit zone. Sometimes men came from the interior, dropping off crops and fruit at the *depósito* and taking back staples and other supplies. Cargo boats arrived by sea to exchange rice for plantains, beans and fruit. Miskitos sold hawksbill turtle shells to the boats, a prized commodity that eventually made its way to Japan as *bekko* – ornamentation for furniture.

Three men visited us. Short, dark, smiling, gregarious, they shook our hands and asked the pastor for a prayer. The pastor muttered a few words as he touched their bowed heads, and we stood for a few moments in silence. The quarter-moon had climbed above the treeline and gilded the edges of some clouds – the billowy, innocuous kind, not the thunderheads that habitually beset the region. It was then that I realised we'd been lucky to avoid thunderstorms during our afternoon walk.

It turned out that the men wanted more than prayer from us: they wanted to do some business as well. One of them reached into a sack and pulled out something long and shiny for our scrutiny. The pastor switched on his electric torch and played the beam over the object. It was a snake skin.

'A fer-de-lance,' the pastor said. 'Deadly. Around here they call it a *masagua*.'

'*Masagua*,' the men nodded. I looked closely at the splayed skin in the electric light. It was maybe two metres long, an olive-grey colour crossed by dark bands.

'They want to sell it to us,' the pastor said.

Even after we rejected the offer, the men remained before us, holding out the skin as though the temptation to possess it would soon overwhelm us and lead us to change our minds. After a long silence, the men asked if we wanted to see the *tigrillo*.

We followed them into the darkness, along a path that took us along the river toward a collection of *palapas*. The pastor's beam revealed mandala-like spider webs and a trail of leaf-cutter ants in the gleaming mud. One of the men stooped and caught something – a tiny yellow frog. He showed it to me, pinching it between his fingers, its bulging eyes fighting the light that shone down on it. I nodded and then the man flicked it toward the river, where it plopped and vanished.

Behind one of the *palapas*, we came upon a makeshift cage made of wooden slats and odd pieces of barbed wire. '*Tigrillo*,' the men announced. The pastor lit up the animal, an ocelot. It lay curled in a corner, like a large house cat, breathing heavily. We pressed closer. It tensed and tried to stand, and then I saw that its leg was broken. The injury had allowed its capture, and now, frightened and in pain, the wretched creature trembled and hissed at us.

'What will happen to it?' I asked.

The pastor spoke with the men.

'They say they will kill it for you if you want the skin.'

'They seem pretty convinced we want animal skins,' I said.

The pastor shrugged. 'They make some money that way. It's

one of the few commodities they can sell to the outside world. Animal skins. Turtle shells.'

'It's a shame.'

The pastor shrugged again. 'Somebody, somewhere's buying.'

Just then Old Jim turned up to lead us through the trees to the beach, where about a dozen men of the Río Plátano had a fire going and a pot simmering atop the flames. We sat down on the trunk of a fallen coconut palm and were given plastic bowls steaming with turtle soup. For the second time in a month I found myself sitting by a fire on the Caribbean shore. But the two experiences seemed separated by much more than a few weeks and a few hundred kilometres.

I looked up at a sky sequined with stars and listened to the singsong voices of the Miskito men blend with the sounds of the rushing waves and the crackling fire. Most of these men lived upriver in small villages and settlements. For a few weeks at a time, they came to the coast to fish and hunt turtles. One of the men spoke Spanish, and I asked him about turtling. He told me how they caught the turtles in nets, hauled them aboard their boats and clubbed them – not an easy task given that the turtles weighed over fifty kilos. Sometimes they'd catch a nesting female coming ashore at night to lay her eggs. The eggs were very good to eat, the man told me. They'd find maybe a hundred eggs buried in the sand beneath the bushes. But nowadays it was difficult, for few turtles returned to this part of the coast. The hunting was better to the south, on the islands off the coast of Nicaragua. The men hunted two kinds of turtle: green turtle (which we were having for dinner) and hawksbill, very valuable because it had a beautiful shell. The man's father had caught many, many hawksbills in these waters, maybe ten thousand he said, but now there were very few. They stayed away and didn't come to nest any more, he said sadly; this year the catch was very small.

Old Jim came over to ask me if I had liked the turtle soup. 'Very good,' I lied. In truth, I couldn't bring myself to taste it, and had spilled my bowl onto the sand behind me. I was, in fact, very hungry after the long walk. In the course of a year's travel, I had eaten guinea pig, piranha, stork and iguana – but I balked at eating turtle. In college, I had read the naturalist Archie Carr's book *So Excellent a Fishe*, in which he described the brutal procedure for extracting calipee – the essential ingredient of turtle soup. Calipee was cut from the bones of the bottom shell, often while the turtle was still alive. Once the calipee cartilage was retrieved, the turtles were abandoned, left for scavengers. I didn't know if that had been the case with this turtle – probably not – but the recollection of Carr's account had quelled my appetite.

'Yes,' I told Old Jim, 'very good soup.'

'Amen,' Old Jim said. He then presented me with the turtle's green and yellow carapace, a good-sized one at about a metre long, and squatted in the sand next to me in the dying firelight to point out the shell's qualities. 'Look,' he said, tracing a finger over the smooth, marbled scutes. 'Good, good shell,' he said, rapping his knuckles on it.

At some point in the evening, clouds had moved in to blot out the stars. Out over the sea, the massing cumulonimbus trembled with heat lightning, evanescent flashes touching the beach, the sea and the circle of men with a ghostly blue light. Thunder began to rumble, and the temperature dropped suddenly as the wind picked up. We hurried back along the trail toward the *depósito*, and I heard the first drops of rain splattering in the foliage above us. The pastor held the flashlight as he jogged ahead of us, the beam jumping over the path, the ferns, the thick snake-like trunks of the trees, the river. We passed the *palapas* to the sharp crack of lightning – the jungle suddenly seared white with electricity – and there was a deep rattling explosion as we passed the cage where the ocelot was dragging itself painfully in a nervous circle, droplets of rain glinting on the strands of barbed wire.

We reached the *depósito* just as the torrent was unleashed, and for the better part of an hour the heavy downpour battered the tin roof and thunder shook the timbers. I was exhausted but couldn't sleep. I lay on the floor under the mosquito netting, trying to find the least painful position. A damp, noisome smell rose from beneath the floor, and I imagined the river in flood rising to carry us out to sea. I was especially glad, just then, to be relieved of the obligation of travelling upstream to visit the biosphere.

The storm finally passed, and frogs emerged to serenade the night. I finally dozed off, but a scraping sound woke me. It stopped when I stirred and reached for the pastor's flashlight. I played the beam over the room and saw the turtle shell Old Jim had given me rocking back and forth: a rat was inside it, gnawing at the residue that lined it.

❀

We were woken early in the morning by Old Jim. It was still dark, but the old man said we had to hurry: he was worried about the weather. Dawn came abruptly as we walked along the beach, retracing the previous day's march. Daylight revealed a grey, sultry sky, the sun a sallow circle lurking behind the murky mass of stratus that stretched low and thick from horizon to horizon. The air was heavy and difficult to breathe. The sea's salt smell predominated, caustic in the nostrils and throat. Old Jim walked quickly, no longer pausing to pick up flotsam. Drenched in sweat, the pastor and I struggled to keep up, drinking water on the move, kicking our way through sand and surf.

'What's he worried about?' I asked the pastor.

'Change in the weather. Rainy season's about due.'

'I thought we were already in the rainy season.'

'Well, yes, technically from May on it's the rainy season. But September's the peak. We get some real bad weather then. Days and days of rain. Hurricanes.'

'You think this is the start of it?'

'Who knows? It's not like there's any warning. Four years ago, we got hit pretty hard by Gilbert. Roofs blew off. Floods. People drowned. Never knew it was coming till it hit. Government doesn't take enough interest in the Mosquitia to issue warnings. If Old Jim Goff is worried, that's enough for me.'

It was late morning when we reached the *barra* again and

recovered the boat. Normally we would have a few hours before the afternoon winds whipped up the lagoon waters and made the crossing precarious. But on this day the wind was already up, and we were in for a rough trip. Old Jim took over the helm and gave us a wild ride over the whitecaps. Several times I thought we were on the verge of capsizing, but thanks to Old Jim's skill the trip wasn't added to my list of boating accidents. When we finally arrived at the rickety jetty and scampered onto the yellow mud-bank, the pastor let out a howl of relief: 'Oooeee, praise the Lord!'

'Amen,' Old Jim said; I echoed the sentiment.

CHAPTER 7

Walkabout

FOR the rest of that day and the next and the next, the grey skies and sultry air hovered over Brus. Now and then the wind picked up and blew hard; thunder grumbled, a few drops splattered the earth, but the storm never came. Finally, on the third night, a squall blew through; the rain cascaded down for an hour or so, but in the morning the sky was blue, the air fresh and filled with thousands of newly hatched insects.

With a Río Plátano trip no longer a possibility, the pastor and Otho Wood tried to devise a substitute excursion for me up the Río Patuca to Ahuas, where the Moravian missionary Dr Brady operated a clinic.

Eventually, they arranged for me to ride upriver with Rolando, one of the local men who delivered cargo to the mission. A shipment of diesel and several bags of cement were squeezed into his six-metre-long mahogany dugout, which was outfitted with a motor.

We left the landing early in the morning, Rolando, his son and I. The heavy load dropped the *tuk tuk* low into the mustard-coloured water (*tuk tuk* being the name the Miskitos of Brus gave their canoes, imitating the sound the engine made as it struggled against the current). A caiman rested on the embankment, ignoring and ignored by the women slapping clothes on boards in the water. A short way upriver, we passed the large, rusted hulk of a dredge, its chain and buckets snagged in the mangroves – a monument to the failure of some long-forgotten government project.

Somewhere around noon, about halfway through the ten-hour trip, the river opened up into a broad lagoon, thick with water lilies. For five hours we had seen only an occasional hut and maybe three people, but on the lagoon a number of fishing boats and canoes came into view. We kept close to the reed-thick shoals and soon drew alongside a small jetty, where we tied up and climbed ashore to stretch. A tiny settlement, seven *palapas* in all, sat between the lagoon and the savannah, beneath the imposing blue dome of the sky. Rolando was hoping we would find some food, but instead we stumbled across something unexpected: a wake.

An old woman took us to see the corpse. The body of a young man lay on a reed mat spread on the dirt floor of a dim hut. The brown skin had gone yellow, but otherwise he still appeared lithe and virile. The muscles were tensed, and his hands balled into fists as though ready for a fight. Women were anointing the body with soaked grasses, to keep the flies away. A breeze rustled the palm thatch and a pungent smell – a mixture of mould, smoke and herbs – turned the interior of the hut into a dead zone of heat and sickly sweet odours. Feeling faint, I stepped outside. Rolando soon followed.

It was a traditional funeral, he said, not much practised any longer, since the missionaries came. Tomorrow they would beat a drum and place the body in a *tuk tuk*. They would build a hut over the canoe and burn it. He pointed to a turtle spear rammed into the ground; it was symbolic of something, but he couldn't explain what. When I questioned him about it, he shrugged. 'I am a Christian,' he said.

We left the village and continued to follow the river's meandering course. As the afternoon wore on, the experience of river travel palled. At each slow, exaggerated river loop, we seemed to double back and repeat the previous segment of the journey. At least it all looked the same – a muddy embankment, an indolent caiman, a wading stork startled into flight by our sudden appearance, a stand of hardwood speckled with iguanas, an abandoned hut – the same recurring images with each tedious mile. The only change in the scene occurred on the horizon, where thunderheads were massing for their march inland.

Six, then seven, then eight contorted hours cramped in the canoe left me feeling decrepit. I was wedged into a spot among the fuel containers and sacks of cement mix. Some diesel had leaked from its containers and formed rainbow swirls in the bilge-water.

The storm broke before we reached Ahuas. For half an hour, a hard rain pelted the river and flooded the *tuk tuk* as lightning cracked over us. We seemed on the verge of capsizing or splitting in two, but Rolando, impervious, kept course, and we ploughed ahead through the tempest. His son pulled a plastic sheet over the sacks of cement, though it hardly mattered with the bottom of the boat filling rapidly. Drenched and paralysed, I could only think to myself, This is stupid, this is really stupid. I was certain that the next bolt would hit us, but I could see that we had nowhere to go, no shelter to find anywhere on the river or the exposed savannah. We had no choice but to endure the pummelling.

The worst of the storm finally passed, and we rode the rest of the way through its drizzling aftermath. At a place called Paptalaya, Rolando steered our waterlogged craft toward the dock – little more than a few rotten posts sunk in the shallows.

Drenched clothes clinging to our skin, hair plastered to our scalps, we set about unloading the cargo and carrying it up the bank. Some children and dogs gathered to watch us. The sacks of cement were thoroughly soaked, heavy to haul, and probably useless. The intended project, whatever it was, would have to wait for another day, another delivery.

❂

We left the cargo next to the river, where it would await the carters sent by the mission to transport it by ox and cart to Ahuas. Rolando and his son went to spend the night with a relative before returning to Brus the next morning with several passengers. I passed through Paptalaya's small collection of huts and walked the three soggy kilometres from the landing to Ahuas, where I was to stay with Dr Brady.

I arrived at the clinic in the middle of supper and was invited to join in the meal, a simple affair of iguana, beans and yucca. Seated at the table with Doctor Brady were a young nursing student, who was visiting for a few months as a volunteer, and a tall young man called Jeff, the missionary pilot stationed at Ahuas. Most of the information I had gleaned about the doctor came from Jeannie. He had spent decades in the Mosquitia. On several occasions he had retired, only to chafe in his exile from Honduras and subsequently return to the one meaningful task of his life, doctoring in the wilderness. He was now in his late sixties, and it was apparent that he would stay in Ahuas until he died. There was nothing for him in the States. He had family there, but he no longer needed their presence; he was content to hear their disembodied voices over his ham radio. He found the American lifestyle intolerable – too busy, too bright, too loud – even in the small Washington town where he had been born and raised.

The doctor rarely spoke; his mind always seemed to be elsewhere. When asked a question, he answered with an uncomprehending stare until, a second or two later, he caught up with the conversation and mumbled a laconic response. Over the years, he had become uncomfortable with English, and at times I thought he must be mentally translating the English phrases into Miskito so that he could understand what was said. Only when the maid appeared and spoke to him did he become alert and somewhat quicker-witted.

The pilot was more talkative, especially if the conversation concerned anything related to mechanics and engineering. Head bent down to his plate, he scooped the beans into his mouth in great rapid spoonfuls to the accompaniment of appreciative grunts. Between servings, he said whatever came into his head. 'Word is they want to install lights at the Teguz field. But you ask me it'll never happen because number one they can't afford the right kind of bulbs, never mind nothing's even wired for it. Besides, no pilot in his right mind would land there at night. Runway's like a minefield and those mountains are too close, not to mention always covered with smoke. Might as well try to land on the dark side of the moon. You betcha, Josefina, I sure will have some more iguana. We got us a good one here.' He turned toward me. 'Sometimes, you see, your iguanas can be a little – uh – funny tasting. But this one here is one fine tasting lizard. That's right, Josefina, lay some on me.'

Jill, the nursing volunteer, didn't say a word at dinner. Thinking she might have an interesting perspective on the mission and its clinic, I hoped for an opportunity to speak to her. When she left the table and went out onto the porch, I followed.

She stood at the railing and stared up through the long unkempt branches of a flowering shrub at a full moon that was startlingly white and fine, like a china plate. The flowers, damp with dew, released a cloying scent; breathing in that fragrance was like eating a rich and heavy dessert. Somewhere in the night, the generator choked to a halt and left us in a sweet, dark silence.

At first I thought Jill was exceptionally shy. She kept her back to me and hesitated before tersely answering my questions. I persisted, and got nowhere. Finally, I recognised in her demeanour and in her tone something with which I was already quite familiar: Jill was like many of the gringos I had met up with, especially the young ones who fancied themselves travellers, not tourists. She was protective of what she regarded as her territory and was annoyed that another gringo had invaded it.

I saw this attitude all the time as I travelled the gringo trail. Whenever I encountered another expat traveller – maybe in a cantina, maybe on a mountain bus, maybe on a remote stretch of beach, or maybe just in passing on a city street – the initial reaction was always the same: lowered eyes, a refusal to acknowledge my presence, or perhaps a glance of haughty and cold disdain. And the reason for the hostility was simple: in their eyes, I had no right to be there; I detracted from the authenticity of the experience. It was a territorial dispute of sorts. Jill exemplified the attitude: a couple of months in the country, and she thought she had

exclusive rights to the place. She loathed me for daring to tres-
pass. I left her alone.

The house was now dark except for the pale flickering of a
kerosene lamp. Back inside, I felt my way to the couch where I
was to sleep. The light came from the doctor's office, just down
the hall. I could hear him in there, tuning the ham radio. I lay
down and listened to the weird whoops and whines of the radio
frequency and to the doctor's slow, tired voice repeating his call
numbers every few seconds, casting them into the void, like seeds
carried on prevailing winds to distant reaches. Over and over he
repeated his identification, finally raising an answer. An
American voice, made peculiar by the sound waves, reached us
from Florida. A brief conversation followed. The doctor gave the
Florida radio operator a phone number in the States and asked
him to call it collect. It was a familiar procedure on ham radio –
Florida would connect the phone to his radio and in this way the
doctor could from the middle of nowhere speak to someone
stateside. Next, I heard a female voice, the telephone operator,
followed by a familiar repetitious buzzing. 'I'm sorry sir, that
number is busy,' a voice said. Then another: 'Sorry. No go,
Honduras. Busy. Over.'

❋

The next morning I visited the clinic, a concrete block structure
that smelled of antiseptic and chemicals. It was just after sunrise,
but the tiny waiting room was already crowded with seven people, and more waited outside. Most cases could be handled by the
nurse, a Miskito man trained in the capital and in the States. He
took temperatures and blood pressure and distributed medicine
from the 'pharmacy', a room stacked with boxes donated by
American congregations. Aspirin, diarrhoea medicine and topical
antibiotics sufficed in most instances. The doctor handled the
more serious cases – amoebic dysentery, dengue fever, hepatitis,
malaria and typhoid fever.

On this particular day, the doctor was concerned with two

cases – a boy with typhoid and a man who had injured his hand while fishing. The boy had spent the night in the clinic, in one of the antiseptic rooms reserved for critical cases. The problem was that the boy had been ill for several days, maybe a week, before the parents brought him in. The clinic's supply of amoxycillin had run low, and without enough for a full treatment, the doctor was worried that a partial course of the antibiotic would not be sufficient to knock out the infection. If the boy relapsed, the doctor would be unable to check the disease from spreading. He pointed to pink spots on the boy's chest, a tell-tale symptom of typhoid, patted the boy's fevered head, and spoke to him softly in Miskito.

The night before, the doctor had looked old and incompetent, with his unkempt white hair, slow mannerisms and apparent inattentiveness. But once in his clinic, with his white coat and his doctor's equipment, he became alert and lively. When he spoke in Miskito to the patients, his voice turned animated and warm – very different from his senile English. He paid attention to the smallest details, even giving lengthy instructions to the cleaning woman mopping the hallway with bleach. It was readily apparent that doctoring was his life, that it kept him alive, and that he would keep at it until the day of his death.

It was also apparent that the doctor wasn't interested in talking to me – or rather, didn't have the time to talk about something as remote to the tasks at hand as the interior of the Río Plátano. He had been there; he'd doctored there, and he knew the people, but right now he had more pressing concerns. He paused long enough to brush off my questions about travel to the interior with a stern, piercing glare and a gruff response. 'Only the man who travels with God goes there,' he said. 'He's the only guide who can take you.'

Not especially eager to witness the amputation of the fisherman's hand, I walked over to the airstrip, where Jeff was tinkering with his single-engine Cessna.

'This old gal's like a wife,' he said. 'She sure requires a lot of attention.' He laughed at his joke, then gazed with admiration at the plane. His real spouse lived in the capital; she had found life on the coast too primitive and preferred to stay where she had a maid and groceries and a telephone. On the coast, the aeroplane was Jeff's companion.

'Well, she's a good one,' Jeff said. 'This little lady has logged a lot of miles.'

I asked him about his work, or, as he called it, his mission. Basically, he said, it was his job to support missionary operations in the Mosquitia. That could mean anything from flying in supplies – he had hauled medicine, food, building materials, even animals in his time – and taking the doctor out to remote villages, or sometimes bringing critical cases in to the clinic. He had flown in thunderstorms and landed in mud pits. He had flown to places where no aeroplane had ever been. He really loved that – dropping in from the sky like a creature from outer space, bringing the aeroplane, and with it the modern world, right down smack in the middle of some primitive village. He liked to see the faces of the people as they gathered around the stilled plane, curiosity and wonder in their eyes. He let them touch the plane, and joined in when they all laughed nervously; it was especially amusing when an older person touched the tail or prop ever so lightly and made some comment in the native tongue that got everyone giggling.

I asked him what it was like in the Río Plátano region. That deep in the interior, he said, you found tribes like the Tawahka who were living in another century. These were places where the people still ran and hid in fear when the aeroplane landed amongst them. To tell the truth, he was a bit scared himself sometimes, but he hadn't been roasted and eaten by cannibals yet, praise God! When he brought the missionary or the doctor into those places, even the Bible the Moravians had translated into Miskito was no good. They had to use picture books of Bible stories. It was like show and tell – show them the pictures and tell them the story of Jesus, with the help of a translator, of course. And everywhere they went, the people loved to hear those stories – how Jesus came to heal the sick and even raise the dead. They had converted whole villages at a time, praise the Lord. It was truly the work of the Holy Spirit.

'Speaking of the Holy Spirit,' he said, 'you know what they call us in some of the villages? Ghosts. That's right. They call us ghosts because of our white skin and also on account of we're always talking about praying to the Holy Spirit, see, so they think we talk to the spirits. Must be ghosts ourselves. Goes back to the early days on the coast when the traders came to cut down the trees. They had all these goods, you know, saws, axes and such. The natives decided that the white people were sorcerers who got these things from deep pits in the ground that were like entrances to the spirit world. Gifts from the spirits, that sort of thing. The first missionaries straightened them out, but even today, in some places way back there, you find some people who think we've got magical powers. We tell them we're not ghosts, that it's just God working through us. We tell them to touch us as proof. You should see it – they jump back like they were touching fire. But they still call us ghosts, so I guess that's what we are – ghosts on the coast.'

Was it possible to fly into the interior now?

'Possible? Sure, it's possible. But not advisable. This time of year you could get stranded for a week, ten days. Believe me, a week in a wet Tawahka village would do in anyone. Come back in March or April, that's the driest time, and we'll take you out to Never-Never Land.'

❉

I left Ahuas the next morning. My plan was to take the footpath back to Brus, about a twenty-five-kilometre hike. I was a little worried about the rainy-season showers, and the possibility of getting caught out on the savannah in a violent electrical storm. Jeff offered to fly me, but I declined: I had my mind set on a walk-about.

For the first three kilometres, I retraced my steps to the Paptalaya landing and the Patuca River. Like a dead soul at the River Styx, I gave some coins to an old man to row me across the river. And then I was on my own, following a well-worn yet seemingly unused trail across the wide savannah. Mile after lonely mile, I marched on under the broiling sun, resorting frequently to the bottle of drinking water the doctor had given me. Near the river, I passed small bean fields (enclosed, as usual, in barbed wire), plantations of fruit trees and an occasional ox. The few farmers I saw looked up from their work to watch the ghost, the unexpected apparition, drift past and vanish into the savannah. Further out, I met nobody for hours.

The terrain wallowed in rainy-season mud. Hordes of flies and bees skimmed the mudflats and investigated the intruder. Now and then the path skirted pine stands, where I saw deer grazing. Occasionally, I came upon poles placed for no apparent reason out in the wilds. Some were erect, some stood at an angle, but each was topped by a turkey vulture that took – I imagined – an amused interest in my unlikely passage. I began to wonder if it might be the same vulture on each pole, flying ahead of me and waiting, checking to see if I had wilted yet.

If my reading of my map was correct, somewhere along this stretch of the trail I would skirt the boundaries of the biosphere. I looked to the north-west, where what I took to be a distant line of trees undulated and shimmered in the strange light. That was the biosphere, I decided. An uncertain line on the far horizon, wavering, indistinct, a mirage of a jungle wall, and for me out of reach.

The sky, meanwhile, had turned metallic. A thin layer of clouds stretched from horizon to horizon but brought no relief. If anything, the heat seemed to intensify. The mud and muck seethed, hissed, popped, as if the hot conditions were working a transformation upon it. At first I was glad there was no sign of the usual thunderstorms, but then I began to think that this sky, so peculiar, seemed ominous in an entirely different way. Overhead, a lambent nimbus indicated the sun, a luminous pool surrounded by a great sulphur-coloured aureole, and far to the north I spotted just a hint of a very strange greenish tint. As the afternoon wore on, this tint intensified into a luminescent jade band unlike anything I had seen before, and I knew for certain that something dire was in the offing.

I tried to quicken my pace, but with no way to mark the kilometres as I crossed the redundant landscape, I began to worry that I had taken the wrong path and had veered off course. I focused on the green horizon and let it draw me forward, assuming that it marked the sea. I expected at any moment to see the smoke of Brus in the distance, but the kilometres passed and I came upon nothing but the same palm-dotted expanse of savannah, now turned still and soundless. The noise of frogs and insects had vanished, and there was no breeze at all. The air was dead, as if in a vacuum; I hadn't seen anyone for hours. It was with enormous relief that at long last I spotted the little shelter of Brus's airstrip and, further off, the trees and the haze of Brus itself. I was even glad to hear the distant grumbling of the mission's generator.

Just outside the village, I came to the graveyard, a place I had often visited during my walks around Brus. Now, suffused with the queer green light of the imminent storm, the place presented a strange and alien aspect. I paused at the gate and studied the graves, which were indicated by mounds of earth. A few were marked with leaning wooden crosses, the wood weathered and splintering, and even the newer crosses were only partially whitewashed, as though the painter had lost interest and abandoned his task. Only a few graves were marked with names, and those that were bore strange symbols, such as a downward-pointing arrow with dots on either side. One cross read simply, 'I am Presentación Granwell P'. But for the most part the graves were unmarked. A number of poles had been placed around the tract, but these did not seem related to the mounds. I counted five concrete tombs in the cemetery, three of which had been painted white at some point, but even these more auspicious tombs lacked identification. Though I had been past the cemetery several times, I had never noticed that it lacked the usual signs of Christian influence. Despite one hundred years of missionary involvement on the coast, the few Christian symbols in evidence were strangely mutated.

But when I entered the commons, I found the church lit against the gloom and heard the voices of prayer and psalm competing with the generator. Through the windows, I could see that the church was quite crowded; in fact I seemed to be the only person left outside. I wondered what was going on, but didn't want to enter the church – I might never get out if I did. Every Sunday for what seemed like weeks I had attended the marathon services – hour after hour of singing, praying, sermonising, all of it in Miskito – while cramped, shoulder to shoulder with the other men (the men occupied the left-side pews, the kerchiefed women the right). On those interminable Sundays the church must have been the hottest place on earth, the sun bearing down on the zinc roof, the air inside turned stifling. Many people passed out, but the sermons continued. It was infernal.

Instead of entering the church, I went over to the mission house and collapsed into a hammock, exhausted by my walkabout. I lay there listening to the counterpointed sounds of the service and the storm – first the singsong Miskito voice, punctuated by the amens of the congregation, then the mighty voice-of-God thunder grumbling in response. Flashes of lightning lit up the commons and left a brief skeletal image of the surrounding buildings in my mind.

Finally, the villagers emerged from the church in clamorous groups, just as the first few heavy drops of rain splattered onto the already muddy commons. I could tell right away that this rain was different. It was not the warm, voluptuous, unguent downpour that accompanied the usual thunderstorms. There was something colder and crueller about it. This rain stung: sharp, intense pricks at first, then harsher lashings, like stings from a barbed whip. The fury of the pent-up storm was unleashed, and people scurried off into the darkness. There were shouts – no hosannas now, just laments and complaints.

CHAPTER 8

Rainy season

FOR days on end, the rain did not stop. It fell in torrents, drumming so loudly on the tin roof of Mr Wood's house that we couldn't hear the radio gospel show. Ponds formed all over the village; rivulets replaced pathways, depressions filled with water and marooned patches of higher ground into islands. I couldn't go anywhere. For hours I sat by the back door and watched the deluge. Mr Wood's menagerie took refuge under the house, silenced for once in sheer awe of the storm. Waterlogged branches sagged to the ground, and torrent-stripped petals lay splattered in the soggy compound. Trips to the outhouse became mad, futile dashes across the slick brown mud.

Rain, rain, rain. It went on and on. Six, seven, eight days of it, a plague visited upon the land that in turn brought plagues into the household: we found scorpions and tarantulas and rodents in every room – in corners, on beams, on shelves. With doors and windows shut, everything sweated and a humid reek invaded the house. A slick film developed on surfaces, a prolific mildew spewing spores into the clammy air. My sinuses clogged, my eyes watered and I sneezed constantly. I had to remind myself that I was in the finest native house in the village, up on stilts above the flood. I could only wonder what it was like in the ground-level huts, where the thatch dripped and earthen floors were transformed into mud pits.

I found an old deck of cards in my backpack and taught the boys a few card games. Brought up under the conservative strictures of the church, the Woods disapproved of card-playing, and seemed to think that merely touching a deck could instantly tempt some-one to gamble. But I promised we would play only simple games in English, for the boys' sake, and in the end Mr and Mrs Wood found it very funny and endearing when the boys yelled, 'Go, fish!'

I had had very little contact with Mrs Wood to this point. She was somewhat reclusive, and always seemed to stay in her room whenever I was in the house. I didn't even know her name; like the maids, I referred to her as *la señora*. She was a small woman, with fine features and beautiful long jet hair that made her look younger than her thirty-five years. As Mr Wood's wife, she was a prominent person in the village, but because she had grown up in San Pedro Sula, the big city, and because she was not Miskito, she never adapted entirely to life and society in Brus. I never heard her complain, but she always seemed somewhat melan-choly. Doting on her beloved boys was her only pleasure, and the only time I ever saw her laugh was during those games of Go Fish. I had the feeling she was something of a tragic figure, a Tennessee Williams' character removed to the Mosquitia.

Several days into the storm, I splashed my way over to the mis-sion house. Jeannie and Pastor Mark were playing Monopoly for what, as Jeannie said, 'must be the tenth time in three days.' Mark tuned in the short-wave to Armed Forces Radio and we listened to a football game being played in San Francisco, a place that seemed light years away from the isolation of Brus. There were more people in that faraway stadium than in all of the Mosquitia, and if it were transplanted to Brus, the stadium itself would dwarf the village. More food was being consumed in the stadium that night than the villagers would eat in a year. While the ritual drama played out, the football fans were happily creating enough trash to bury Brus a foot under. None of the villagers had ever eaten a hot dog or sipped from a Styrofoam cup; probably no one in the stadium had ever butchered an iguana for dinner or heard a sen-tence spoken in Miskito. The silent waters of the lagoon named for a bloody pirate sparkled with the reflection of stars and the glimmer of phosphorescent fish; the busy bay named for a gentle saint sparkled with the reflection of illuminated bridges and super-tankers. The radio announcer had no idea that his words drifted through the darkness to a place he had never heard of, in a country he couldn't find on a map. It was strange – and wonderful – to contemplate the contradictions occurring simultaneously across the planet.

❂

Lying in my cot at night, listening to the rain drumming down on Otho Wood's roof, I pondered my departure from Brus. I couldn't leave until the rain stopped long enough for the land to dry out, SAHSA having cancelled flights to the coast two weeks in a row. I was exasperated by the rain, fed up with feeling trapped. I yearned to get out of the Mosquitia and back to the city, back to the cantinas and movie theatres and *fútbol* matches.

After eight days of downpour there came a Sunday of intermittent showers, and at last the storm began to break up. The first patches of blue sky appeared on Monday, along with brief interludes of sunshine, but at night more rain fell and the land seemed no less sodden. I doubted that a DC-3 could make a landing on the mucky savannah, but I prepared for a Saturday departure anyway.

The village slowly returned to its routine. The animals emerged from beneath the houses to resume their foraging. The men visited their bean fields to salvage flooded crops. Fishermen launched onto the becalmed lagoon waters. The schoolbell resumed its clanking, calling the children back to their English-language lessons with Jeannie. And Pastor Mark took up jogging again. As I walked around the village shooting my last rolls of film, I saw him in his shorts and jogging shoes, splashing through the puddles, looming in the mist like a great white whale.

I wasn't fond of using my camera, in part because it seemed so intrusive. During my time in Brus, I had taken very few pictures, most of them quickly and furtively. To use up my last rolls, I went around the commons, quickly taking pictures of each building:

95

the church, the mission house, the school buildings. But I wasn't quick enough. By the time I had made a circuit of the commons, the students in the mission school had spied me and, their curiosity piqued, they bolted from Jeannie's lesson. A group of ten or so gathered around me to examine the camera and look through the viewfinder. Then one of the girls asked me to take her picture, and within seconds they were all clamouring to get their own taken.

Curiously, excited as they were, not one student smiled for the camera. Despite my prompting, they stared at the camera and adopted a look of solemnity – dignified, yet so different from their ordinary warmth and grace. To embellish the portraits, they shared a watch, the only one amongst them, each wearing it in turn, then handing it ceremoniously to the next person.

Word of the photo session got around. The rest of that day and the next, as I walked around the village, people came over to me and asked me to photograph them. They all had ideas about the arrangement of the composition, treasured possessions proving a popular motif. One man insisted on holding a prized rooster in his photo; another wanted to wear my sunglasses. I had to wait while a woman scrubbed clean a blue metal pot that she thought would enhance her portrait. Rodliana, the Woods' maid, spread a blue blanket on the damp ground, picked some flowers from the shrubs, then kneeled on the blanket, spine erect, smock smoothed, hair tucked behind her ears. Like all the others, Rodliana giggled and smiled both before and after the picture, but at the precise moment the shutter clicked, her face turned grave, the embarrassed smile vanished and solemn eyes stared into the camera.

❁

Saturday arrived at last, the day the SAHSA plane was scheduled to visit Brus and the Mosquitia. For three days the sun had shone in between brief showers, but the savannah was still soggy and I didn't believe a DC-3 could land and take off in such a quagmire.

My goodbyes, therefore, were unceremonious. I tossed my things into my pack, thanked the Woods, and stopped at the mission house to wish Jeannie and Mark well.

I really didn't think that this was it, my final farewell to the villagers and the people who had hosted me. I told everyone I was going out to the airstrip to see if the plane would make it in, fully expecting to be back in the village within a couple of hours to begin another week of waiting.

As I walked out on the miry savannah, I was more and more convinced that the plane would not attempt the landing. I figured it would take at least another week, maybe two, for the earth to drain dry.

I waited at the airstrip for an hour, and was on the verge of giving up when I spotted a figure coming out from the village, slowly advancing toward the shelter. Soon I recognised the diminutive frame, the pith helmet, and instantly I felt chagrined, for I had not made the trip out along the lagoon to say goodbye to Old Mr Goff. And now here he was, all of eighty years old, walking seven maybe eight kilometres to see me off. But if he intended any reproach, I couldn't detect it. He smiled broadly as he approached me, an irresistible boyish smile on an old man's face. We clasped hands, and he held mine in both of his.

'You go home,' he said.

I shook my head. 'No plane.'

Old Mr Goff said, 'Yes, plane is come. You go home.'

I scanned the skies, the brooding clouds. It looked hopeless.

But Old Mr Goff was adamant. 'Yes, plane is come.'

Then he took something from the pocket of his stained counterfeit jeans and handed it to me. It was a wooden cross inlaid with pieces of tortoise shell. Old Mr Goff cut short my embarrassed thanks and pointed into the distance. 'Now is come.'

I looked in the direction he pointed and saw nothing; listened, and heard nothing. A minute passed, with Old Mr Goff smiling and staring into the distance, beatific as if he saw the Angel of the Lord approaching. Then he reached up, put his hand on my head, and recited a prayer in Miskito. When he finished, I heard the distinctive drone of the aeroplane and detected the speck moving against the clouds.

As it drew closer, however, I saw that it was not the SAHSA plane but Jeff's Cessna flying low under the rain-heavy clouds. He circled twice, apparently looking for the firmest section of the airstrip for his landing, and brought her down onto the muddy savannah. The plane skidded and slipped and tailspun to a stop, mud splattering the wings and windows. Jeff killed the engines, popped open the door, and shouted to us, 'Praise the Lord! That was a tricky one!'

'Jesus good man!' Old Mr Goff chirped.

'Sure didn't expect to find anyone out here,' Jeff said. 'You all get enough rain up this way? I almost decided not to bring her down, but then I saw you all out here.'

I explained I was waiting for the SAHSA plane. Jeff laughed. 'Those boys ain't gonna fly in this mess. I'm the only one in the whole country crazy enough to try it. That's 'cause I'm flying on a wing and a prayer, praise God.'

We helped Jeff unload the cargo destined for the mission house – a case of fruit cocktail tins, several boxes of disinfectant spray, five cases of Coca-Cola and a box filled with bottles of aspirin. Later, some boys from the mission school would ride their bicycles out to fetch the cargo. For now, we stacked it all under the shelter; it seemed like a meagre delivery, not worth the reckless touchdown that the weather conditions necessitated. But that was Jeff: he just grinned and winked. That's what he was here for, to fly in the worst of it. 'Got God for a co-pilot,' he said.

Jeff was headed for La Ceiba to retrieve a supply of desperately needed penicillin for the clinic, and he offered to take me along with him. He scanned the savannah and decided there was enough firm earth along one side of the landing strip for him to attempt the take-off.

'Got her up outta worse in Ahuas,' he said.

Maybe Jeff didn't sweat it, but I did. After saying a heartfelt goodbye to Old Mr Goff, we sputtered and spurted and finally found traction enough to build up speed and get off the ground. I clutched the cross Old Mr Goff had given me. The plane bucked in the wind as we banked over Brus and headed for the coastline. I was so nervous, I didn't even pause to think that I was seeing the village for the last time.

❂

But several hours later, alone in La Ceiba, I did think about it. Stupefied by the noise and lights and carnival crush of its incipient urban blight, I rued my return to the developed world's orbit. Walking down the main drag, I spotted the PC Jeep careening through the traffic, Chris's blond hair waving in the wind, Hogan seated next to him, smoking a cigar. I turned down a side street to avoid them and headed the other way.

The rigours of life in the Mosquitia had become wearisome to me during the week-long rain, but now that I was back on the frontier of civilisation, I knew I would have a hard time readjusting, and I regretted having given up. But there was no going back now; I would have to press on toward whatever obscure destiny awaited me.

I did, however, have one last obligation to the people of Brus. Before leaving La Ceiba, I took my film to a studio and had it developed. The portraits of the villagers came out better than I expected; in fact, they were the best photos I'd ever taken. I visited Jeff at the airport, and he promised to take them to Pastor Reed, who would see that the portraits were distributed.

I often think about those photos. I imagine that they decorate the walls and shelves of huts all over Brus, their colours fading in the tropical humidity, corners curling. Because of them, I am still present in Brus. I am nowhere to be seen in the pictures themselves; nevertheless, I am there, an imperceptible image captured in the pupil of each staring subject. And I am there, too, just beyond the frame, a ghost presence, the unseen eye that gazed, that still gazes, and that will go on gazing until time and the elements have erased from village memory the fading images I once recorded.

Costa Rica, 1996

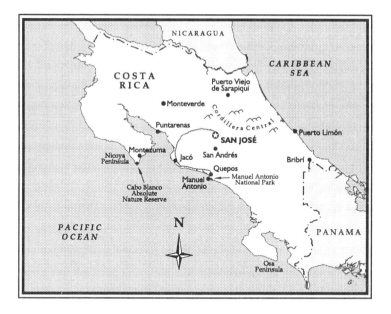

Interlude

A FTER my sojourn in the Mosquitia, I gave up journalism. I was tired of chasing corpses and tired of rejection. When an alternative presented itself – teaching English at a secretarial school in San Pedro Sula – I took the offer and left behind the seedy demimonde of the war correspondents in Tegucigalpa. Later, through connections, I landed an even better position teaching at the national university of Guatemala. I thus relocated to Guatemala City.

Those were dark days in that sad country, a time of mayhem and worse, when the dead were dumped on the road in the night and foreign journalists vanished in the highlands. There were curfews, tanks in the streets, American helicopters hovering over the massacre of mountain hamlets. More than 100,000 people died or disappeared in a thirty-year-long crescendo of violence. Volcanoes spewed ash and fire, the earth trembled and shook, and the ravines filled with mutilated bodies. On the long blacked-out nights I lay in my room listening to the Uzi bursts that rattled the adobe boneyards in the outskirt slums.

I stuck it out for two years, and then couldn't take it any more. I had no choice but to return to the States and take up university teaching there. For nearly a decade, I read the news coming out of Central America – the escalation of the Contra war and its implosion in scandal, the fall of the Sandinistas, the end of war in Salvador, the ensuing economic crises brought on by the spread of fundamental neoliberalism. And, in the wake of the peace process, the growth of ecotourism, a development I found especially interesting, if somewhat odd, given the region's vicissitudes.

I noticed an increasing number of advertisements for ecotours appearing in the back of travel magazines. At first, most of the ads were for Brazilian Amazonia, and then a few for Peruvian excursions began to appear, including the now-thriving operations around Iquitos. By the early 1990s, however, more and more space was dedicated to Costa Rica, the emerging star of ecotourism.

I was surprised and intrigued by this development. In the mid-1970s, when I was there as an exchange student, Costa Rica was a little-visited way station on the gringo trail, meriting only seven pages in the popular alternative guidebook to Latin America that I carried. A mere twenty years later, Costa Rica had become the second most popular Latin American destination, and entire books were devoted to travel information on the tiny country. The statistics coming out of the place were impressive: between 1990 and 1995, the number of international visitors grew from 435,000 to 790,000 a year, while earnings from tourism more than doubled.

❂

Costa Rica's sudden popularity is easy to understand. Few countries match it for natural beauty and variety. Despite its tiny size (just over 50,000 square kilometres), Costa Rica's stunning diversity of habitats harbours a wealth of fauna, including over 200 species of mammals, 850 species of birds (ten per cent of the world's known species) and 150 species of amphibians. Some 1400 different kinds of trees have been identified. In all, five per cent of the life forms on earth live in an area that covers only .03 per cent of the planet's land surface, and more than 1000 of these species are found nowhere else.

Furthermore, no other country in the developing world has attempted to preserve its biodiversity to the extent that Costa Rica has. Around twenty-seven per cent of the land area is under some type of protection – in twenty national parks and eighteen natural reserves. Guidebooks call Costa Rica an environmental paradise and a global model for 'sustainable development'. In just a few decades, the country has gone from having one of the highest deforestation rates in the world – well over half of the forested area was destroyed between 1940 and 1990 – to a country with zero deforestation in 1997, at least according to official statistics. In the process, Costa Rica has transformed itself into eco-tourism's wonderland, the place where green dreams come true.

Interested in seeing this transformation for myself, I looked for an opportunity to revisit Costa Rica. My chance came when an academic organisation I belonged to sponsored a Latin American Studies conference in the capital, San José, and my university agreed to pay my way.

CHAPTER 9

Ecotourism's wonderland

COMING upon Costa Rica from six thousand metres, you see the place as a kind of epiphany, God's great green dream suddenly and unexpectedly revealed. For twenty minutes, the jet glides in gradual descent through a sea squall – beads of rain on the portals, a grey shroud pulled across the sky. Then in an instant the shroud slides free, and there below, much closer than expected, the emerald earth erupts in verdure, a turmoil of cloud forests and rift valleys and dark green ravines interrupted here and there by the jutting cones of stark volcanic peaks. Maybe this manifestation is not unlike what Milton's Lucifer saw when, hovering over Eden, he beheld 'in narrow room Nature's whole wealth, yea more: A Heav'n on Earth'.

And, indeed, my aeroplane was full of North American passengers anticipating adventures in Eden. They were headed to Costa Rica to hike, bike, surf, fish, sail, canoe, kayak, raft, hang-glide, gaze, gawk and photograph. This is going to be great, they told one another. A week in paradise. Their expectations were reinforced by the numerous ads and stories in the airline's magazine. I counted five uses of the word 'paradise' to describe some aspect of Costa Rica: an island, a resort, a national park, a bed-and-breakfast, a river excursion.

The elderly woman sitting next to me had a somewhat different agenda. Agnes was on her way to Monteverde, in north-west

Costa Rica, to visit the Quaker community there. She hoped to do some volunteer work with a school located in a forest reserve where children learned about ecological issues. A former college professor, she had become active in social causes since her retirement. For the first two hours of the flight she had shared brochures and newsletters with me, telling me about the programmes and organisations she supported. Her favourite new issue was conservation in Costa Rica.

Costa Rica was a battleground, she said, because it was a progressive country with much popular support for conservation, yet the destruction of its forests continued apace. If conservation was going to succeed anywhere in the developing world, Costa Rica was the place. If not here . . . she shook her head and fell silent.

When we dropped out of the clouds and the country was there beneath us, startlingly verdant, she stared out the window. I assumed that, like me, she was in awe. But I was wrong. She was focused not on any manifestation of God's grandeur, but on the evidence of human transgressions.

'Look down there,' she said. 'You see?'

I looked out the portal: a river valley, hills chequered with farmland and pasture. It looked idyllic.

I nodded. 'It's beautiful.'

'Oh, but don't you see it,' she said, disappointed. 'Look again. The road along the river? The cleared areas? That's logging. Illegal logging. Look at the water: brown. Soil erosion silting the water, that's what that is. You see? Costa Rica has the laws, but they're not enforced. And do you know what those trees are turned into? Popsicle sticks. Imagine.'

I agreed, it was sad; but from our vantage the destruction didn't seem rampant. As we approached the capital, we flew over vast tracts of unbroken rainforest. 'That's probably the Braulio Carrillo park,' the Quaker woman told me. 'The parks and reserves aren't the problem in Costa Rica. It's what's going on *around* the reserves – that's the problem.'

❄

When we came out of the immigration area, we were besieged by tour operators waving cards with the names of hotels, resorts, agencies, cruise ships, lodges and expedition outfitters. Agnes spotted the representative of her organisation and we said good-bye.

I was met by Warner, a university student and conference go-fer who had come to the airport to transport participants to the hotel. Along with three others who had just arrived, I climbed into a minibus for the ride into the city.

Right away, it was evident that Costa Rica was undergoing rapid modernisation, most of it related to the tourist industry. Warner, who spoke English and seemed to like practising it, gave us the lowdown. He pointed out several new hotels, most of them foreign outfits, and the site of a new amusement park under construction. The roads, however, had not been modernised. The main highway into San José was a rutted, deteriorating macadam that made the trip into the city an amusement park ride in itself. I was a bit surprised, because Costa Rica was certainly the wealthiest of Central American countries – yet its roads were the worst. Wouldn't tourism have brought in enough money to pay for road repairs?

'The thing is,' Warner explained, 'much money is dedicated to extend the roads to where tourists want to go. Maybe later the roads we citizens use are for fixing.'

I was sharing a seat with a middle-aged man who introduced himself as Pedro Cocinero – 'That's Peter Cook in gringo,' he informed me – a Spanish teacher from Tennessee who from the moment we'd boarded the bus had kept up a jovial badinage in a twangy combination of tourist Spanish and down-home American. 'Hey, amigo,' he said, 'you presentin' a paper at this conference or are ya here for the *cerveza* and *señoritas*? *Vengo para las señoritas* myself. Well, glory be, lookee there, they got a Pizza Hut down here. *Qué bonito!* Like I was saying, I'm here for the ladies. Lookee here.'

'Pedro Cocinero' showed me a thick book, a photo album with hundreds of pictures in it, pictures of women. It was a catalogue, he explained, of women who wanted to meet and marry gringos. Beside attending the conference, he planned to attend some get-acquainted parties where he could meet some of these women. Pedro told me his story in brief: 'Just turned fifty, newly divorced for the third time and basically tired of American women. *No más gringas* for me. But take a look at these *señoritas bonitas*. Look here, look at this one, number 294 – ain't she a doll!'

He flipped through page after page of stunning women, most of them half his age and, given his crusty looks and off-beat clothing, way out of his league. But Pedro wasn't deterred by these discrepancies.

'You see, there's a lot of American men pretty much fed up with all that women's lib stuff. I like my ladies more traditional – you know, the home type who'll love and cherish her husband and won't feel oppressed by a little housekeeping and cooking. For their part, these gals are tired of the macho thing the men down here got going. The drinking and fooling around. They want American husbands, clean, sober, someone to respect 'em and treat 'em right, like proper ladies. Gringos are more sensitive, and that's what they're looking for.'

'You don't think it has anything to do with the money American men have?'

'Oh, no doubt. But what's wrong with that? I'll earn the bread and she'll bake it. That's the way it's supposed to be.'

But if Pedro wanted to come across as the sensitive type, he'd have to learn some tact first. In the course of the bus ride he managed to malign everyone else on board. The two American women in the seat behind us stopped their perusal of the conference schedule to listen in. They snorted, gasped and gnashed their teeth during Pedro's speech – but Pedro didn't notice. Nor did he seem aware that Warner, the driver, fell into the category of Costa Rican males he'd just denigrated.

For his part, Warner pretended not to hear. When we reached the city centre, he pointed out the central plaza, the cathedral and the theatre. When we arrived at the hotel, he helped us with our luggage, refusing offers of tips, and let us know that he'd be working at the conference's registration desk if we needed anything. He was deferential, polite, pleased just to be of help – national characteristics of the 'Ticos', as Costa Ricans call themselves. I well remembered their irrepressible friendliness from my stay in the mid-70s. They answered questions with alacrity and were only too willing to provide information, even if it was the wrong information. Thank them and they came right back with the Tican motto: *Con mucho gusto* – with pleasure.

❉

After checking into the hotel and registering for the conference, I went out for a late-afternoon walk around the city I'd once lived in and hadn't seen for fifteen years. The grid of east–west avenues and north–south streets was familiar to me. The big landmarks – plaza, national theatre, cathedral, train station – looked the same. But in many ways San José had changed markedly. The small provincial capital that I once knew no longer existed. The city was now smart, urbane, congested and Americanised. A seventeen-storey Holiday Inn towered over Morazán Park. American fast-food restaurants had taken over the city centre. English was everywhere – on signs, on products, on the radio in restaurants and on the televisions in department-store display windows. Numerous bars and cantinas catered to foreigners – the Key Largo, the Blue Marlin, Risas – all of them glittery places loud with slot machines and American pop music and satellite television on numerous screens. The centre of San José had become a generic tourist zone.

But San José was still a lovely city – the nicest of the Central American capitals – enveloped by abrupt hills and gentle volcanic slopes, giant trees shading the parks where lovers were locked together on kissing benches and Central America's most literate shoeshine boys read newspapers and magazines, even novels. Flowering shrubs enfolded walls, fences and gates in their boughs, spreading dashes of red, yellow, purple and white against concrete and iron and razor wire. The smell of roasting coffee permeated the centre at certain times of the day. Even with the fast-food joints

111

that occupied every other storefront, the promenade of Avenida One gave Ticos and tourists alike a fine place for strolling or window shopping. Fruit sellers rang bells on their carts and called out special offers; beggars blew trumpets, banged tambourines, waved bubble wands and recited poetry; the sound of children singing out their school lessons wafted from second-storey classrooms.

At one point during my walk, I turned a corner and started down a street that was immediately familiar to me. After I went a block or so, I realised where I was. Somewhere on this street, on this same block, there was a cantina I used to frequent, a place called Arturo's; it was the favourite hang-out of budget travellers, drifters, hippies – the sort of directionless traveller that Costa Rica attracted in the days before ecotourism and adventure tourism and speciality travel. In fact, back then low-budget drifters were likely to be the only travellers besides businessmen who found themselves in Costa Rica – and even they tended to be on their way to somewhere else, Costa Rica being just a brief interlude in between more exciting places like Guatemala or Colombia.

I had spent a lot of time in Arturo's, after classes at the university, drinking long into the night and listening to travellers' tales and drifters' idle chatter. It had been in Arturo's, on those evenings, that my wanderlust had been born. It had been in Arturo's that I'd first dreamed of travelling up and down the Americas for no real purpose other than to go, go and keep on going. It had been in Arturo's that I had learned and accepted what I took to be the proper travel philosophy: that an unplanned journey was best, that the journey itself was more important than the destination, that you discovered more en route than you did on arrival. It had been in Arturo's, over bottles of Imperial beer, amid a cast of characters I once would have shied away from, that I had signed on for the ride.

But now I couldn't find Arturo's. Back and forth I went, certain I was on the right street. No Arturo's. The people I asked had no idea. The place was long gone.

❂

It was soon clear that ecotourism was the hottest game going in San José. Virtually every downtown store and hotel window had a poster or board, in English, announcing ecotour specials on surfing, rafting, diving, fishing, boating, mountain biking, horse-back riding, trekking, even hot-air ballooning over the rainforest canopy. Sidewalk touts handed out leaflets to passing tourists. The lampposts were stickered with offers: 'Tortuguero, $79! Raft the Reventazón, $99!' The whole capital seemed consumed with a kind of eco-craze. The prefix was used everywhere – there were eco-lodges, eco-resorts, eco-buses and an Eco-Rent-a-Car. The airline I'd travelled on billed itself as the Eco-Airline.

At the conference registration desk, I asked Warner if he could suggest a good ecotour. He pointed out that in fact the conference had arranged some optional tours for its participants. One was to Tortuguero to see the turtles, but Warner didn't recommend it because it wasn't nesting season. He thought maybe I'd like the 'Jungle River Cruise', which the programme described as 'a cruise through the tropical rainforest on a comfortable modern jungle river boat. Buffet lunch included.' It sounded a bit suspect, but I figured why not, I was only going to be in the country for a little while and I might as well take advantage. I signed up for the trip, scheduled for two days time.

❂

In the meantime, the conference opened with a reception dinner. The US ambassador delivered the keynote address. He talked about development in Costa Rica and how the country was poised to enter a period of sustained economic development. The ambassador noted that historically Costa Rica had remained undeveloped and untapped because the Spanish had found nei-ther gold in the region nor an Indian population to enslave as labour for the hacienda system. Now, however, Costa Rica found itself in better shape than most other Latin American countries, with a larger middle class and a more educated population. These attributes, along with the country's extraordinary physical beauty and wonderful climate, made it attractive for investors. Costa Rica was 'an acknowledged paradise', the ambassador said, and that fact had prompted a number of companies to relocate and establish their headquarters in the country. A recent example was Intel, the computer giant, which had chosen Costa Rica as the base for its Latin American operations. Progress was not without costs, however, the ambassador warned. Industry required infrastructure, and Costa Rica would have to deliver: from its first day of operation, Intel would use one-fourth of the country's electrical output. It was clear, therefore, that Costa Rica would need to develop its capacity to generate electricity.

At this point, I expected the ambassador to make what to me was the obvious point: to increase electrical output, Costa Rica would have to dam rivers – and indeed several projects were under way on wild rivers – which would necessarily alter the environment and mar the picture-perfect qualities that had attracted companies like Intel in the first place. But the ambassador refrained from articulating this dilemma, and he issued no warning about destroying that which had made the country attractive. No doubt the ambassador was aware that the local press would cover his every word, and that tomorrow a detailed summary of his speech would appear in the newspapers. Not wishing to offend his hosts, the ambassador opted for prudence and left the inevitable conclusion implicit. Or did the ambassador even perceive the dilemma? His speech gave no hints, and I was left wondering.

❁

On the day of the Jungle River Cruise, I joined the others who had signed up for it – including Pedro Cocinero – in the hotel lobby. A huge Mercedes Benz tour coach arrived with our guide, Johnny, a jovial and energetic man who, while evidently a good student of English, had mastered the lessons on tag questions a little too enthusiastically.

'OK, everybody, we got a big day, don't we? So we have to get started, don't we?' he said over the microphone as we boarded the bus. 'We gonna have some fun, aren't we?'

My own hopes for having fun were severely diminished when Pedro Cocinero took the seat next to me.

'I'm looking forward to this, *sí señor*,' Pedro told me. 'We don't got so many jungle rivers in Tennessee, no siree.'

The bus took us through the city, and out into the surrounding valley. The road climbed past cattle pasture, coffee farms and large tarp-covered plantations where exotic flowers were grown for export. All the while, the guide prattled into the microphone, and his amplified voice, exploding on the p's, directed our attention from one side of the bus to the other.

'You see how the coffee plants need shade, don't they? So the farmer, he plants the shade trees first, and it's maybe five years before he gets his first crop. That's really amazing, isn't it?'

'OK, everybody, look here to the left, we see the farm for the flowers under the big plastic. That's a lot of flowers, aren't they?'

'OK, somebody ask me about the roads. Our roads are pretty bad, aren't they? But you know, the new president he's really doing something. He holds a news conference, you know, to say to Costa Rican people there used to be 10,000 potholes in Costa Rica. Now only 5000. So he's doing pretty good job. Then we find out the potholes they got so big, the 10,000 little holes now make the 5000 big holes. Pretty good joke, isn't it?'

In between the guide's comments, I foolishly asked Pedro Cocinero how his dating sessions were going.

'Not so good,' he told me. 'Only been to one. The ladies are fine and all – you wouldn't believe how pretty they are. But the whole thing's not too well organised. I went to the get-acquainted party. It was supposed to go from seven to ten, but we didn't get started until nine. That's too late for me. I have to be asleep by eleven so as to get my eight hours.'

'Why's that?'

'Insomnia. I got to take these pills to fall asleep. If I don't fall asleep right quick and get my eight hours I'm messed up all the next day. Today's a good day, I slept real good last night. I took

115

a double dose just so I could be ready for this trip. Had to put in earplugs, though. There's a lotta traffic noise in this town. But I got my eight hours and I'm rarin' to go.'

'Good for you,' I said. I could see why Pedro Cocinero was twice-divorced. I felt sorry for whichever Costa Rican girl he selected as his new partner, but at least she'd have the advantage of not speaking English. It would be an unbearable torment to have to hear this tedious recounting of the previous night's sleep, day in and day out.

We arrived at our first stop. According to the itinerary, we were about to have 'a delicious buffet lunch at one of the most beautiful jungle lodges in Costa Rica'. The lodge proved to be one of those places that had proliferated since the coming of eco-tourism – run by foreigners for foreigners who wanted to penetrate the rainforest, to find themselves 'surrounded by jungles and colourful gardens', without having to give up the comforts of their first-world lives. From the look of them in the slick brochures available in my hotel's lobby, Costa Rica's lodges recalled those I had seen in the Peruvian Amazon: air-conditioned transportation, *haute cuisine*, wine lists, the promise of nature-viewing from a balcony, an escape to paradise complete with twenty-four-hour bar, all-you-can-eat buffets and 'pleasant walks along prepared rainforest trails'. In Costa Rica, as in the Amazon, the selling point was nature, but the majority of the lodges took pains to assure clients that they served up nature without com-promising on first-world comforts.

Luncheon over, we followed the guide along a gravel trail to a stream for an opportunity to photograph some frogs. Frogs were one of the main emblems of Costa Rican ecotourism. They appeared in promotional brochures, on T-shirts, postcards and gift mugs. But, as in the rest of the world, Costa Rica's amphibians were disappearing. The golden toad was gone. The harlequin frog had disappeared. The prospects for other frogs and toads were not good, even in the new, ecologically aware Costa Rica.

Photographing rare and vanishing species is one of the biggest thrills for ecotourists, and much of ecotourism's popularity is due to the popular desire to see forests, animals and tribal cultures before they disappear for good. Johnny, our guide, knew this, and when he captured a small green frog, he had a little trick in store.

'OK, everybody, get your cameras ready. Focus on this spot over here with the nice ferns.'

He held his cupped hands up to his mouth and said, 'Very sorry, Mr Frog.' Then he shook his hands hard. When the frog had had enough, Johnny placed him on the spot with the nice ferns as a backdrop. 'OK, everybody, now you take nice pictures.'

The semicircled tourists leaned forward, cameras clicking, video cameras whirring. 'Wild frog. Costa Rica,' one cameraman said into the microphone as he shot a few seconds of film. Meanwhile, the dazed frog sat inert at our feet, as apathetic as any zoo animal. Its translucent lime green skin glistened as the cameras flashed, its limbs so thin you could see through the skin to the bones, as though the frog were made from jelly.

'Well, glory be,' said Pedro Cocinero, 'I never seen such a critter before. So tiny and green.'

Finally, the frog regained its bearings and hopped first one way, then another – the ecotourists backing up as though it might attack – before finally finding the ferns and disappearing from view.

We reboarded the bus to travel to a landing on the Sarapiquí River, where the itinerary called for 'a cruise through the tropical rainforest' on a 'comfortable modern jungle river boat'. From the embankment ten metres above river, we looked down at the dock and a row of the 'modern jungle river boats': fibreglass longboats fitted with plastic seats and a canopy. Four of them, loaded with tourists like us, already plied the river, their engines coughing clouds of blue smoke. Our group descended the embankment and climbed aboard one of the boats.

Over the loudspeaker, Johnny introduced Captain Pedro. The captain, he said, had lived all his life in the region and knew the jungle river 'like his back or his hand'. He would show us many interesting things, many animals. Captain Pedro, wearing a white captain's hat, turned and grinned at us. He had maybe five teeth.

The boat drifted in the current while Captain Pedro fooled with the starter. The engine growled once, twice, then came on full force and a wave of exhaust passed over the passengers. 'OK, here we go!' shouted Johnny. 'Look for animals everybody!'

It didn't take long. Just ahead, up on the embankment, we made our first sighting: a cow tied to a tree. Down in the river, three young humans splashed water on one another. The tourists aimed their cameras at the children, who obliged by standing up and revealing their glistening brown and very naked bodies.

Then, all of a sudden, Captain Pedro pointed up at a tree. 'Look everybody,' our guide said over the loudspeaker. 'Captain Pedro sees something. What is it, Captain Pedro? An iguana, everybody! Two, three . . . *five* iguanas!'

The boat rocked as the tour group shifted weight, everyone leaning out to see, grabbing for their cameras. The tourists frantically fiddled with fancy video equipment and cameras – screwing in lenses, popping in cassettes, unzipping leather camera bags. The humans below were in a panic, but above them the lizards lolled, sunning themselves, blending in with the leaves and fading from sight. About half the group saw them and tried to point them out to the more near-sighted members.

'Right there, see? Follow the branch out to the cluster of leaves. See him?'

The flurry of excitement over the iguanas proved unnecessary, for soon they were everywhere in the trees above us as we chugged past. For twenty minutes, in fact, they were the only wild animals we saw, and Johnny's amplified call of 'Iguanas!' prompted little enthusiasm.

The section of the Sarapiquí River we were seeing could hardly be called wild. Up above, on the steep banks, shacks and bungalows stood in clearings. There were corrals and fences and gardens, pigs and cows and horses. For a good part of the river trip, we passed through a banana plantation – row after row of monoculture. Blue bags covered the fruit, protecting it from insects. Discarded bags were everywhere, turning like jellyfish in the river current, snagged in overhanging branches, stuck in the muddy banks.

Just when it looked as though we would have to be content with iguanas and the odd heron, Captain Pedro came through. Or rather his comrade captains came through, and Pedro was sharp enough to get in on the action. What Pedro had seen, some 150 metres downriver, were the manoeuvres of his comrades as they converged near the riverbank. A growing cloud of exhaust indicated that at least one boat was trying to hold steady against the current – the sure sign of an animal sighting.

Immediately, we were roaring at full throttle to join the flotilla and catch a glimpse of whatever had deigned to show itself. With our arrival, four boats bearing some one hundred tourists idled in the current, bows pointed to the bank, while the guides' distorted voices broadcast facts about the creature – a modest-sized caiman.

It rested on the riverbank, perfectly motionless in confronting the human gaze and the commotion of clicking cameras. The caiman bore it all with such reptilian aplomb that a few tourists wondered aloud if it were still alive. Even though we were within ten metres of the caiman, we didn't have a good view. The breeze carried the engines' bluish exhaust over the passengers and the riverbank, enveloping the caiman in a gasoline cloud. The tourists murmured complaints – first that they couldn't get clear pictures, then that they couldn't breathe.

Eventually, Captain Pedro backed us away from the shore, and the current swung the boat out of the exhaust cloud. We continued downriver in search of more exotic fauna. Whenever Pedro thought he saw something, he threw the engine into reverse, holding the boat steady whilst the vapours once again rose against us. Pedro was seeing phantoms, however; no other animals materialised, and after an hour on the river, the tourists no longer cared. The fumes were too much, and the complaints were getting louder.

But just as we started back upriver, we scored big. A terrible roar shook the air and startled everyone, including Pedro, whose captain's hat came tumbling from his head when he jumped in his seat.

Another roar, and the guide made the sighting up in the trees ahead: a family of howler monkeys. Our boat churned straight for them, the other tour boats close behind. There was a bustle in the boats – monkeys are the golden fleece of ecotourism, the prize animal everyone hopes to sight and photograph. Even Johnny seemed fairly surprised that we had actually encountered a family of them. 'Ohmygod, look everybody,' he said, 'one, two, three, four howler monkeys!'

The monkeys seemed less pleased. They peered down through the leaves at the posse of boats circled beneath them. The male let loose with a tremendous, throaty roar, then broke off some twigs and threw them toward the boats. Undeterred, the boats manoeuvred to give the tourists a better shot at the monkeys. Johnny used his loudspeaker to coax them with kissing sounds into plainer view, but the howlers stayed coyly behind their branches until they had seen quite enough of the humans and headed for denser canopy.

On the bus ride back to San José, Pedro Cocinero got an early jump on his eight hours, and I was left alone to think about the jungle river cruise. 'Nature', as experienced on this tour – and I presumed it was typical of what was being offered by many of the so-called nature tours in Costa Rica – had been kept at a distance, safe, tame, packaged for viewing. We'd looked at it from platforms, from paved paths, from boat decks. It had stayed alien and removed from us. By the time we came to the Braulio Carrillo National Park, the nature experience had been reduced to absurdity. We gazed at the Carrillo – an expanse of territory as wild and unknown as any place in Costa Rica – from the air-conditioned bus as we sped along the new four-lane motorway that had recently been gouged across the national park to facilitate motor traffic from the capital to the Atlantic coast. The guide entertained us with stories about the feral region we were passing through – stories of adventurers disappearing, of animal attacks, of a terrain so rugged it had never been mapped. But all we saw was dense vegetation clinging to the cloud-forest slopes. Most of the tour participants had fallen asleep; the rest of us had to wipe mist off the windows to see – the air conditioning was so strong that it clouded the panes as we passed through the cool, rain-soaked mountains.

Warner greeted me when I got back to the hotel. 'How was the tour?' he asked politely.

I didn't want to offend him, so I lied. 'It was very nice,' I said.

❁

The day after the jungle river cruise it was back to the conference sessions, but for a few hours in the afternoon, I sat on the patio outside the Gran Hotel watching the sidewalk traffic and reading the newspapers. Several had articles concerning environmental issues, some conservationists disagreeing with the government's claim of zero deforestation and asserting that logging continued unabated, while the opposition party accused the government of continuing to do nothing about toxic agricultural runoff in the country's rivers. Meanwhile, three separate stories recounted the deaths of ecotourists in outdoor accidents: one had been attacked by an alligator, another had slipped off a cliff, and a third had dropped from the ropes hoisting her up a tree at an eco-camp.

While I sat on the plaza, the big tour coaches pulled up to let out scores of sunburned tourists, some laughing, some complaining about the mountain roads they'd just travelled on. Two American ladies at the table next to me discussed the face-lifts they'd come for – where the incisions would be, how little the operation would cost compared to cosmetic surgery in the States. One of the women, uncertain where she was, kept referring to 'Porta Rica'.

'I just love the colours of this Porta Rican money,' she said. 'But I wish it was simpler to figure out what everything costs.'

I, too, was wishing things were simpler to figure out. Ever since I had returned from the jungle river cruise, I'd been thinking about the whole ecotourism enterprise, and especially about the travesty in which I had just participated. It was a low point for me; I seemed to have come such a long way – in the wrong direction – since I had left the Mosquitia. I felt by turns sheepish, disappointed and annoyed that in growing older I'd become so much like the sort of tourist I had once despised – safe, plodding, predictable.

I was also wondering just how representative the jungle river cruise was of ecotourism in Costa Rica. As the buses unloaded their passengers, I looked for signs that the other tours weren't as spurious as the one I had taken. I was not encouraged. Given all the cameras, the luggage sets and the expensive gear that the tourists carried, one thing was clear: ecotourism was primarily for well-heeled holiday-makers more interested in sport than ecology. Sure they wanted Costa Rica's natural beauty preserved, but they wanted it preserved as a playground to which only they – those with the money – had access. Such were my cynical thoughts as I watched the tourists prepare for a night of drinking and gambling at the gringo bars and casinos.

Among the people strolling on the plaza that afternoon was Agnes, the Quaker woman I had met on the aeroplane. Her sweatshirt extolled the 'Creative Learning Center'. I remembered she shared the organisation's newsletter with me during the flight. I waved, and she came over to greet me.

'So tell me about your travels,' I said. 'I take it from your shirt that you got to the school all right?'

'Oh, indeed,' she replied. 'It was a most wonderful time. This children's rainforest project is really something. The curriculum integrates ecology into every class, and they have a fund so that schoolchildren from around the world can contribute to preserving the forest. Oh, it's so beautiful. You should go to see what they're doing up there. It will lift your spirits.'

Agnes told me she planned to return to Monteverde after taking a little tour of the country. She wanted to visit Puerto Limón and travel south along the Caribbean coast to the Panama border and the reserves of the Bribri Indians. This, I knew from my reading, was some of the most difficult territory to access in Costa Rica.

'What company are you going with?' I asked.

'Oh, I'm just going on my own,' she said. 'No tour groups for me. I learned years ago it's better to give it a go on your own. I've studied up on the route. It won't be easy, but I like it better that way. Say, maybe you'd want to come along?'

'Well, I don't know. The conference . . .'

'I understand. I'm just rattling on. Many years ago my husband and I used to travel together. Just like a couple of tramps we were. Well, I guess I'm just an old lady daydreaming. I'd love to travel with a smart young man again. My Maurice and I had such a grand time.'

'Travelling must have been quite different back then.'

'Oh my, yes. It wasn't so easy to get around as now. We even rode on *burros* across the Venezuelan sierra. Can you imagine?'

Agnes and I ended up ordering some afternoon coffee and pastries in the Gran Hotel's cafe. She told me more about her travels with her late husband. South America, Africa, Asia, Europe: they had gone around the world on a shoestring, the greatest time of her life. As we talked, the slot machines in the hotel lobby bonged and chimed as the tourists played machines with names like Jungle Juice and Hurricane. Beggars approached us – playing maracas, waving bubbles from a soapy wand, blowing on a flute. Agnes placed a ten *colón* coin in the palms of each as they passed. She had a purse for the purpose – her 'almspurse', she called it.

By the time Agnes and I parted, I was sorry to have had too little time to travel down to Bribri town with her. I couldn't have imagined a better travelling companion.

If nothing else, Agnes had both shamed and inspired me. I felt ashamed because at seventy-five she showed more energy, insight and vigour than I did at half her age. At the same time, I was inspired by her adventuresome spirit to try again, to forgo the spurious tours and revive my taste for independent travel. By the time I reached the hotel, I'd decided to skip the last days of the conference in favour of taking an improvised journey somewhere.

At the conference desk, the ever-present Warner helped me out once again. I tried to explain to him that in the end the jungle river cruise had been disappointing because every aspect of it had been staged. I wanted a more spontaneous experience, I told him, an off-the-cuff adventure. He seemed to understand: 'Yes,' he agreed. 'Tours have many restrictions. Why don't you just choose a national park and go? There are buses. That is what we Ticos do.'

'Well, then, where would you go if you had three days?'

'For me,' he responded, 'my favourite park is Manuel Antonio. I like best the ocean.'

CHAPTER 10

Queasy in Quepos

EARLY in the morning, before dawn, I walked down Avenida Central to the bus terminal – a maze-like marketplace that had taken over the former Coca-Cola bottling plant. I found the dimly lit Quepos–Manuel Antonio ticket kiosk in a row of shuttered market stalls. The woman behind the barred window pecked a manual typewriter, searching out the letters to fill in my ticket. A pack of dogs raced through the terminal, and an old, muttering man, his head bound in gauze, flailed a twig broom at scattered wrappers and rinds, stirring a putrid dust into the dank air. For the first time since I had arrived in San José, I felt like I was back in the Central America I had known all those years ago. I felt a little surge of excitement.

Subsequently, I was a little disappointed, but not surprised, to find that at least half the travellers on the bus with me were foreign tourists. And sure enough I ended up sitting next to one of them, a very nervous, round-faced, balding American named Douglas. It was a six-hour ride over a difficult road full of twists and switchbacks. In places the road was adequate, but many sections were rough, nearly washed out. The descent was abrupt – from San José's 1150 metres to sea level in under a hundred kilometres – but the travel itself was slow-going.

The whole time, Douglas's legs were twitching and he fidgeted with everything – his backpack, his camera, a package of candies. 'Oh man,' he said, agitated, 'I can't believe there's no smoking on the bus.' The only time he calmed down was when we stopped for a break at a roadside diner and he got a cigarette in his mouth.

Back on board, Douglas talked about real estate, about how cheap it was to buy land in Costa Rica. 'You can get two thousand hectares of rainforest for a few thousand bucks,' he informed me, 'but you got to get around the kickback mortgages.' He'd come to 'Cawster Rickuh' to take some tours – like whitewater rafting on the Reventazón River – and to check out some land deals, 'get a feel for what's going down real estate wise.'

I asked him about the rafting. 'Fantastic,' he said. 'The best. But you better go soon. They're building that super-dam on it. River's going to be gone in a couple years.' When I suggested that this was a shame, Douglas shrugged. 'It'll increase land values,' he said. 'Improve the electricity, which has got to happen for development purposes, you know. Besides they got plenty of rivers here.'

Douglas prattled away, non-stop, all the way to the coast, his twitching becoming more severe with each kilometre. During his longer monologues, I looked out the window. The mountain-valley coffee farms had given way to mango orchards and African palm plantations on the coastal plain. Along the coast, the road worsened, and the bus was forced to weave wildly to avoid potholes. Bridges were nothing more than iron bars laid over rattling girders, barely wide enough for one vehicle.

The road drew within sight of the ocean, where billboards announced the opening of model homes in development tracts along the coast. Signs, in English, were posted on every lot of land. Douglas was ecstatic. 'Oh, man, look at that! What did I tell you? It's a buyer's market. Should be some great deals down here.'

We rumbled past Jacó, a funky SoCal surfer colony. The road climbed cliffs high above the beach, allowing views of inlets and humpback islands. Finally we turned into Puerto Quepos, a former banana company town, and followed a rough road over a hill to the entrance of Manuel Antonio National Park.

'This is going to be great,' Douglas declared. 'I'm into this sort of thing. Nature. Birds.' He rubbed himself down with a perfumed insect repellent. I wished him good luck.

The bus dropped us off at the end of the road, where open-air restaurants and souvenir stands lined the beach. To enter the park, I had to wade through an estuary and pay an entrance fee at the guard gate. At five dollars, the fee was a third of what it had been a few years ago when, to discourage visitors, the government had raised entrance fees. So many people were coming to Manuel Antonio that the park was suffering serious degradation. Fearing a loss of revenue if fewer people showed up, local businessmen had complained about the fee hike, and the fees had subsequently been reduced. The park, however, was still overcrowded, and officials were considering the possibility of closing it on certain days of the week.

Trails within the park led to three different beaches and up to a cliff top called Cathedral Point. On the trail to the first beach a sign advised visitors against feeding the monkeys. The animals had turned aggressive and attacked people because of such feedings. The beggar monkeys were everywhere, swinging on the spindly branches of the trees that lined the beach, running through the sandy thickets behind them. Two young Japanese women, cameras at the ready, tentatively approached one small monkey, its head cocked in curiosity. Further down the trail, another group of tourists, barefoot and in bathing suits, advanced on a monkey sitting in the shade beneath a bush. The monkey had found a candy bar wrapper and was licking the brightly coloured paper clean. One man, cigarette in mouth, belly hanging over the band of his tiny swimsuit, crept in a semicircle around the bush, aiming at the monkey with his video camera.

I bypassed the first beach, and decided to climb up Cathedral Point to get a view of the offshore islands. The trail was quiet and almost empty; the majority of visitors came to Manuel Antonio for the beaches. Not interested in tanning, I took the trail to a lookout point, where a middle-aged British couple loaded down with an array of equipment, charts and books were studying a laminated card with drawings that depicted 'Costa Rica Typical

Birds'. Seeing me, the woman gesticulated excitedly, simultaneously shushing me and calling me over. 'Look, look, down there in the bush,' she whispered. 'Oh, he's gorgeous!' She handed me her binoculars and pointed down into the thicket that clung to the cliff side.

I stared through the eyepiece and picked up first a blur of blue and white – the sea below us – then a tumble of green before I focused in on the bush and spotted the bird. It had a black body and a long, sharp, slightly hooked bill. Its chest was puffed up into a bright red pouch, a mating device. I nodded my appreciation and handed the binoculars back to the woman. The man pointed to a drawing of the bird on the laminated card: a Magnificent Frigatebird.

The lookout point was a good place for birdwatching. A number of sea birds glided on the wind currents below us, circling, skimming the water, updrafting to the trees and bushes on the cliff side. Somewhere I had read that about 350 different species of birds were found in the park and environs. I asked the couple if they were having any luck.

'Splendid, just splendid,' the man told me. 'Morning hours seem best. Been at it since near dawn.'

Charles and Lucy, I learned, were birding enthusiasts who had come to Costa Rica from England hoping to see some of the many species that are found nowhere else on earth. Charles was tall, thin and grey; Lucy, short, plump and red-headed. Charles was slow and laconic in speech; Lucy, animated and quick. They seemed like complete opposites except for their shared love of birds.

Charles had a good ear for birds. Even above Lucy's incessant happy chatter, he could detect a whoop, twitter, or po-wheet. Now and again he paused and raised his hand.

'Oh, Charles,' Lucy asked, 'what is it, do you think?'

'Don't know. Sounded trogon-like.'

'Oh! An oropendola, perhaps? I'm dying to see an oropendola: they have the most beautiful tail feathers, and their nests!'

We waited for a repetition of the call, Charles and Lucy scanning the forest with their binoculars. Lucy kept a notebook in which she recorded their sightings. Each entry included the name of the species, the date, the place and a comment: 'Gorgeous!' 'Breathtaking!' 'Ruffled feathers, but very bright colours.' 'Seemed to have a lame wing, poor fellow.'

Leaving the lookout point, we walked together back toward the middle beach, where we came upon an intersecting trail that headed away from the water. Some distance along the trail, we came across two people looking up into the trees. One was a bearded American with a leather satchel strapped across his shoulder; the other was a teenage boy, a Costa Rican.

'Find something?' Charles asked.

'Family of capuchins,' said the American.

We heard rustling above us in the trees and spotted the white-faced monkeys hopping from bough to bough. 'Why, they're darling!' Lucy exclaimed. We chased the monkeys down the trail until they veered too far into the overgrowth. Lucy was disappointed that she couldn't get a clear shot at them with her camera. 'At least we got a look at them,' she consoled herself, stopping to jot in her notebook.

The American, it turned out, was a biologist from a college in Indiana, who'd come here to collect plant samples, leaves mostly, which he gathered in plastic bags and stored in his satchel. He had met the boy near the entrance to the park – one of the touts offering guide service. Many travellers in Latin America tend to shy away from these touts, or openly shun them, considering them nuisances or con artists out to get their money. But wherever I've travelled, I've found them to be knowledgeable and interesting – they've always added to the experience. The same was true here with Carlos; he was young, maybe fifteen, but he'd learned a great deal about the flora and fauna of the park. He brought us one plant specimen after another and explained its medicinal value: a thorn used for brewing a tea that soothed sore throats; a plant whose sap helped diabetics; a leaf used for treating diarrhoea. Carlos told us that his grandmother had taught him all these things. The biologist took careful notes on everything Carlos told him, writing on cards that he slipped into the plastic bag with the sample. Saving the rainforest was imperative, he told us, for any number of reasons, but one of the most important, and least recognised, was the value of these plants for pharmaceutical research. 'You've got an entire living, breathing pharmacy right here,' he said.

❂

Having walked for several kilometres around the park, I left it to look for a place to spend the night. I had hoped to stay nearby, at some cabanas just outside the entrance, but they were all full. It appeared I'd have to try the hotels along the road back into Quepos. While waiting for the local bus, I noticed a billboard at the entrance to the side road that led to the cabanas. 'Tourist Project to be built here', the billboard announced. An artist's conception of Manuel Antonio's future showed a resort imposed on the beachfront, with cars, paved roads, towering hotels and crowds. Soon, it appeared, the area just outside the park would be paved over, the unsophisticated souvenir shacks and seafood restaurants and cabanas replaced by more luxurious facilities. Any pretence of ecotourism would vanish or be watered down, and the Manuel Antonio area would become just another beach resort, like those in Mexico, with sewage seeping into the water and landfills taking over forests. The park itself would become a small, inert tropical garden in the midst of a resort complex.

It appeared that ecotourism in Costa Rica faced a grave threat as developers sought to cash in on the country's new-found appeal as a tourist destination. This is the danger small-scale ecotourism faces in poorer countries. The pressure to develop is enormous; development, so the argument goes, means jobs, foreign exchange and quick profits. Pressure is exerted on the government to expand and improve the infrastructure; investors and developers move in, willing to put up money the government doesn't have. Successful ecotourism, on the other hand, is necessarily small scale and limited; it doesn't provide the kind of jobs and foreign exchange that resorts can. The choice for development, therefore, seems almost inevitable.

And despite its acknowledged concern for environmental protection, Costa Rica was yielding bit by bit to the pressure. Resort complexes were going up on both the Pacific and Caribbean coasts, and developers were planning other projects to accommodate the surge in tourist arrivals. In San José, I had read a newspaper article about a new resort in Guanacaste anchored by a 310-room five-star hotel. The managing director of the $70 million project was calling for more government emphasis on beach tourism to 'supplement' ecotourism. The big question was whether the two types of tourism could coexist.

❂

The Quepos bus arrived, dropped off a load of beach tourists, and picked up those of us waiting to make the return journey. The seven-kilometre road to Quepos climbed up a hill, then wound down into the former port. The entire route was lined with hotels; the driver called out their names as we passed, and tourists got on and off. The holiday-makers looked just as bohemian as the backpack travellers of twenty years ago, the kind I had met at Arturo's cantina – but their backpacks must have been loaded with far more cash and credit cards than those the Arturo's crowd carried. The Manuel Antonio hotels cost fifty, seventy-five, a hundred dollars a night, and the restaurants charged twice the San José price. I noticed that many of my fellow travellers carried video cameras along with their backpacks.

Just before we descended into Quepos, a wave of exhaustion passed over me and my head started to throb; I started to feel dizzy and a little queasy. I couldn't wait to get off the hot, stuffy bus and get some air. It might have been the cold pills I'd been taking; even though I had a water bottle with me in the park, I could have dehydrated myself with all that walking in the heat.

I stumbled away from the bus station into a hot glare, the sunlight sharp and severe against the whitewashed walls. Woozy, I stopped in a store to buy some orange juice and then crossed over to a little park on the waterfront. I leaned against a stone wall in the shade of a mango tree, and drank the juice. I could see the remnants of the banana company dock rusting and rotting in the sun, the shanty-lined estuary glistening, a flock of pelicans flying overhead in formation, and the endless horizon, the gleaming margin as Tennyson called it, stretching forever. Staring at that horizon, I felt lost, dizzy, transfixed by the vast blue glare. I kept staring at it, until the expanse overwhelmed and enveloped me, and I was free-falling into sleep.

When I opened my eyes again, a little boy was standing over me, tapping my head. 'Are you a gringo?' he asked.

'How does it appear?' I said. I tried to focus on the boy, but the light was too bright. I sneezed several times and shuddered.

'To me it appears,' the boy said, 'that the ants are eating your shoes.'

I looked at my feet. It was true. I'd been sleeping near an ant nest, and the advance scouts were exploring my hiking boots and trousers. Even so, I was too lethargic to do anything about it right away. Finally, with the boy looking on in amusement, I managed to stand and stamp my feet until the ants fell free.

The boy wanted to talk. He babbled on and on, but I could only understand every fourth or fifth word because he was missing too many teeth. When I moved back into the shade of the park that fronted the beach, the boy followed. He rode his little bicycle in circles around me when I sat down on a bench. He kept talking – something about school, his mother, and a dead cat.

Nearby, at a concrete picnic table, a dominoes game was in progress. Four men – two old, two young, all wearing big straw hats – slapped the tiles down and cackled over their plays. One old man said something to the boy, then repeated it twice. The boy giggled. At first I thought they were telling him not to bother me. Then I realised they were warning him not to talk to a stranger.

To ease their minds, I farewelled the boy and headed out into the street. The boy followed, making slow loops on his bicycle and mocking my slow pace, before darting off. I stepped over a stream of green scum running along the gutter. A man in a truck shouted at me, telling me to beware of something, but he rumbled past before I could decipher the message. The white-hot sun spun me around again; I had to find a hotel room and get some sleep.

For an hour, I walked around Quepos looking for a place to stay. The hotels were painted in bright colours – pink, coral, aqua, yellow. They seemed friendly, inviting, but every place was full or cost far more than I could afford. The desk clerks looked me over and shook their heads. They wrote unreal figures on slips of paper – $100, $150 in US dollars . . . cash only. I skulked off, an outcast in Quepos.

On the outskirts of town, I came across a decrepit place painted a lurid candy pink. The sign said you could pay by the hour. I knocked on a barred window that read 'Registration', the frame lit with red neon. A yellow eye appeared in a peephole as a garbled voice spoke. 'One hour,' I said. A small trap door at belly level slid open to reveal a black hole. I pulled out a 5000 *colón* note and slipped it through the hole. A hand snatched it away, and a moment later my change appeared, along with a key to room number five. There was a warped plywood door. A bead curtain. A dingy corridor. The overbearing odour of bleach and musk. Number five was a dim room with a fifteen-watt bulb, red and gold Oriental wallpaper, a faucet that dripped. I collapsed on a mattress with a profound sag to it. Didn't matter. I just wanted an hour of sleep.

But of course, the hour wasn't enough. All too soon, someone was knocking on the door and shouting, '*Ya, ya!*'

'All right, already,' I groaned. When I got to the corridor, no one was there.

By this time Quepos was dark. I made my way to the bus station, only to discover that the last bus for San José had left – there wouldn't be another until five the next morning. I'd reached rock bottom.

I tried to keep in mind one of the key lessons I'd learned in my travels: even in the most anguished moments, when you wonder why you bothered to leave home at all, something emerges from the travel experience that you couldn't discover in any other way but by letting go, by crossing the line and exposing yourself to the unknown.

With no plan in mind, I wandered into an open-air restaurant called Dos Locos, where a middle-aged gringo tried to flirt with the waitress. 'See that,' he said, pulling a photo from his wallet. 'That's my sports car.'

'And this is your wife?' the waitress asked.

'My wife? No, that's my sister.'

I ordered a bowl of soup.

At some point, the gringo stumbled off, drunk and alone, and other gringos took his place. They were a jovial lot, drinking beer after beer, teasing the waitresses and talking sportfishing with one another. Like the first man, they were bare-chested, their overly tanned skin an unnatural dun colour.

Suddenly, outside the restaurant, a tour bus pulled to a stop, a big, sleek monstrosity with darkened windows, growling engine and throaty air brakes. The driver hopped down and entered a hardware store. Without hesitating, I crossed the street and mounted the steps into the dark bus. Almost everyone was asleep – a busload of elderly tourists, Germans maybe. The few who were awake didn't say a thing when I passed down the aisle mumbling '*Buenas noches*.' I curled up on the back seat, a stowaway, and fell into a fitful sleep. Even though the air conditioning was too high, the potholes rattled the bus and the driver took the curves too fast, I was more than thankful for the clandestine lift.

I was dead asleep when we reached San José. The coach now empty, the driver stood over me, shaking me. I suddenly realised I was at his mercy. He could demand money from me, threaten to call the authorities – who would surely have shaken me down for all I had. Groggy, worried, I thanked him and hurriedly gathered my things together. '*Con mucho gusto,*' he said, winking at me. 'Hope you feel better.'

CHAPTER 11

Sustainable development

THERE were probably a dozen places in Costa Rica which, like Manuel Antonio, had won popularity among ecotourists and as a consequence had attracted the attention of developers. Cahuita, Puerto Viejo, Tortuguero, Dominical, Drake, Golfito – all were threatened by a sudden surge in development. The once vacant and pristine Nicoya Peninsula, in particular, was poised to become a major resort area. A new airport in Liberia, near the top of the peninsula, was now open to international traffic, allowing tourists to jet in and head directly for the beach without having to go through San José. Five-star hotels were going up along what promoters were calling Costa Rica's Gold Coast. World-renowned golf course architects were busy constructing country clubs.

While in Costa Rica, I had been reading about hotel openings, airport expansions and infrastructure upgrades in the daily newspapers. The Minister of Tourism was quoted frequently on the issue of 'sustainable development'. He promised that ecotourism and environmentally friendly outdoor activities would remain the country's primary attraction. At the same time, the Minister of Public Works was announcing an expansion of the road network along the tourism corridors to allow for an increase in tourist traffic and to provide access to areas of the country that had been difficult to reach.

To me, an outsider, the government seemed uncertain of its course, pulling in opposite directions. I asked Warner if Costa Ricans had a sense of where their country was headed.

'It's like this,' he explained. 'Protection of the environment is important to the country's identity right now. Any government official or candidate knows you can't violate that identity, so they say this and that about keeping Costa Rica green. But the big money is in resorts and these ministers always go for the big money. Remember, they stay in office for only a few years so they're not interested in where the country will be in ten or twenty years. They're too busy getting what they can out of their position. Everyone talks environment, but the real identity of Costa Rica is corruption.'

'So you think the ministers are not sincere when they speak of sustainable development?'

'Of course they are sincere. They sincerely favour development that sustains themselves.'

❄

According to some observers, the model for 'sustainable development' in Costa Rica could be found in the small beach town of Montezuma on the Nicoya Peninsula, where a number of enterprises had attempted to blend tourism with conservation. Like the Manuel Antonio–Quepos area, visitors were attracted to Montezuma by its beautiful beaches and nearby protected area (the Cabo Blanco Absolute Nature Reserve); and indeed a sizeable tourist industry had established a beachhead along the ocean front. But whereas development in Manuel Antonio felt like it had been imposed on the land, in Montezuma it blended in. The emphasis was on keeping things simple and relatively unspoiled – the most popular place to stay didn't have electricity, and some hotel owners had established small private reserves of their own. Established in 1963, Cabo Blanco was Costa Rica's oldest protected area. The rules were stricter than at Manuel Antonio: no swimming was allowed, so beach tourism would be held in check, and the rigorous five-kilometre trail into the reserve effectively limited the number of visitors.

However, just forty-five kilometres from Montezuma (as the

seagull flies) lay Puntarenas, the exemplar of everything that could go wrong in Costa Rica if 'sustainable development' *was* merely a minister's hollow phrase. Puntarenas once boasted an attractive beach, but now the Paseo de los Turistas – crowded with hotels and souvenir shops – fronted befouled waters. Swimming was no longer possible in the contaminated surf, and a nauseating stink hung in the air. This was Costa Rica's worst-case future scenario – development run amok, a once beautiful beach turned into a foul dump.

✿

One morning in San José, I shared the restaurant with a Canadian, a grey-haired man with a bright red, wrinkled face. We met because he was having trouble with his bill. He thought he was being charged for something he hadn't ordered, but his thick, ungrammatical Spanish wasn't up to the task. The confused waitress adjusted the bill several times, but not to the gringo's satisfaction. Finally, I intervened to translate his complaint. The disputed amount was hardly more than a dollar, and in short order the matter was settled.

The Canadian and I then fell into the usual conversation: What's brought you to Costa Rica? What places have you been to? It turned out that he owned a lodge further down the Pacific coast on the Osa Peninsula. 'The only unspoiled place left in the country,' he boasted. 'If it's ecotourism you want, Osa's the place.' He dismissed all other Pacific beach towns with a wave of the hand. 'Ruined,' he said, 'all ruined. Might as well put up a roller coaster in Manuel Antonio. It's nothing but an amusement park now.'

I told him I'd just come from Montezuma and that I'd found it to be better preserved than anywhere else I'd been in Costa Rica. He scoffed at my naiveté.

'Montezuma's a fine place – if you're a drug addict. Nothing but dope dealers over there and they're ruining the place. Used to be nice, I warrant you. Not no more.'

'Not like Osa?'

'No sir. Osa's the last good place here in Costa Rica. Maybe in the whole hemisphere. And we're keeping it that way. You ought to come down and see for yourself. Here, I got a brochure.' He handed me a glossy, fold-out pamphlet with colour photographs of a deserted beach, a spider monkey, a sunset, a tanager – the now familiar signifiers in such brochures. Two pictures showed a pleasant swimming pool set in a tropical garden. I glanced at the text: 'select private lodge', 'last stands of virgin forest', 'far from the bustle of the large resorts', 'resident troops of monkeys', 'soaring canopy', 'fine wines and gourmet cuisine'. I had seen similar phrases in the dozens of brochures available in hotel lobbies.

'You want to see the real thing, you come on down. Call that San José number and we'll arrange everything. Here, I've got something else for you.'

He handed me a photocopy of an adventure magazine article about Osa and said, 'Hope to see you down there. Oh, by the way, what's the Spanish for sunglasses? I need a new pair.'

Later, in my hotel room, I read the article the Canadian had given me. The writer enthused over the pristine peninsula and informed his readers that only in Osa would they get a true 'off-the-beaten-path adventure'. They could forget the rest of Costa Rica, now inundated with 'mainstream tourists searching for packaged adventure travel'. The writer described the lodges and activities available to the adventuresome traveller who wanted to go beyond the tourist zones to discover 'the old Costa Rica, a country of unspoiled rainforest, abundant wildlife, rustic facilities, and bracing physical discomfort'.

The article got me thinking. The writer, complaining about the 'legions of tourists' who had 'overdomesticated' the country, longed for 'the old Costa Rica'. But he failed to recognise that it had been adventure travellers themselves and the adventure magazines they read that had popularised the now-spoiled places, starting the process of degradation. No doubt articles from twenty years back had raved about unspoiled Manuel Antonio. Adventure travellers had then rushed off to see the virgin lands, bringing the contamination they so loathed along with them. Services and facilities had followed, and eventually the less-adventurous tourists they so despised had arrived.

So what did the disgruntled adventure tourists do? They went to the next place down the road, or beyond the road, in search of a new 'authentic' experience. Adventure travellers continually push the frontier further and further into the pristine wilds, but the road inevitably follows them in, bringing the facilities and services and infrastructure they so deplore. So adventure tourism pushes still further ahead, and the pristine places fall like dominoes in its path. Twenty years from now, maybe fewer, the Canadian might well be putting up a roller coaster in Osa.

If, however, Costa Rica could 'develop without destroying' the area, as the Ministry of Tourism's policy statement had it, then the spoilage might be contained. But the pressures were very great to head in the direction that appeared to offer the greatest returns. Most likely, the beach towns would not end up in the degraded condition of Puntarenas; but there were warning signs that should be recognised, with the billboard at the entrance to Manuel Antonio looming as the most literal sign of all.

CHAPTER 12

Mountain fiesta

W HEN Warner asked me about my trip to Manuel Antonio, I talked about the changes that had occurred on the Pacific coast. Twenty years earlier I had camped with some other exchange students on the beach at Jacó. At that time, Jacó had had nothing – no hotel, not even a restaurant. We had bought sausages in town and roasted them over a campfire on the beach. We'd seen no one for two days, spending most of that time skinny-dipping and lying in the sun. Unbeknownst to us, we had been part of the first wave of adventure tourists who would popularise the area, then leave it to the developers and conventional tourists. Now Jacó was jammed with hotels, swimming pools, discotheques and casinos, and the beach was crowded with surfers.

When I spoke about 'the old Costa Rica', Warner said I sounded like his parents, always reminiscing about a more traditional Costa Rica. He thought the boom in tourism was mostly a good thing for the country, and that the quality of life had improved. It was uncertain, however, whether the facts supported his perception. Indeed, some of the statistics were rather gloomy: ten per cent unemployment, seventy per cent of the people living below the poverty line ($100 a month), real salaries falling by ten per cent. For over a decade, the country that had once boasted the best social services in Latin America had faced austerity measures and devaluations and growing foreign debt. These economic pressures made it all the more difficult for the government to resist the developers and promoters who wanted environmental protection laws relaxed.

Warner acknowledged that Costa Ricans themselves had changed since the growth of tourism. 'Many people say that in Costa Rica tourism has cost much. Now we have drugs in San José and more crime. People have more fear. More than anything else, they say tourism has changed us. Before, we Ticos did things for people without thought of reward. But now we are brusque, more businesslike, devoted to money, interested only in what we can get from someone. A few years ago, when the government started to promote tourism, the slogan was *el país de la amistad*, but now it is no longer so much a country of friendship.'

❊

When I called the number in the brochure the Canadian had given me, the price I was quoted stunned me. The other Osa outfits I called gave similar quotes. Ecotourism was clearly the privilege of the well-to-do. With only a few days left in the country, I resigned myself to taking a day-trip or two to the nearby national parks.

But then an alternative turned up. With the casual and easy hospitality for which Costa Ricans are renowned, Warner invited me to accompany him to his mother's town, San Andrés, about thirty kilometres outside the capital. It was a fiesta weekend in the town, and Warner wanted me to see the 'real Costa Rica'. He also wanted me to meet his brother, who was a law student specialising in environmental law.

The trip to San Andrés began early in the afternoon, when Warner's brother Miguel collected us in his small pick-up. We rattled over the narrow, congested streets of the capital, past a movie theatre where people were queuing for the latest Disney movie; past a bare, concrete hospital, where several wheelchair-bound patients had been left lined up along a chain-link fence to watch the traffic; past a gleaming Mormon church; and over a quaking bridge that spanned a trash-strewn ravine.

In the foothills of the sierra, we passed coffee farms and cattle pasture. This, according to Miguel, was the typical landscape of contemporary Costa Rica – agricultural, deforested. Little land outside the national parks remained pristine, he remarked, and whatever was left was being assaulted by the logging companies.

Before long, we turned off the paved road and ascended a narrow dirt track heading into the mountains. It was a slow climb, the road requiring a series of switchbacks to make the ascent. At times we could see back to the Central Valley and the volcanoes Poás, Irazú and Turrialba; at others, the south central sierra came into view, dominated by the 3820-metre peak of Chirripó. Warner pointed out the wheeling flight of hawks and vultures high overhead, riding the thermals in a brilliant blue sky. The landscape changed dramatically – dry scrublands on one side of the sierra, wet forest on the other. Some of the slopes had been clear-cut, leaving eroded escarpments. For several hours, we climbed, descended, and climbed again. When Warner had shown me San Andrés on a map, it had looked like a short trip. But Costa Rica plays bigger than it looks: thirty kilometres can take several gruelling hours to cover.

The road narrowed near the summits, where large boulders had dislodged and tumbled into the road. Miguel swerved, rather too quickly I thought, bringing the truck to the road's unstable brink – there were of course no guard-rails – so that sometimes we were staring hundreds of metres straight down the mountainside. When we had reached the highest point, Miguel stopped the truck so I could appreciate the view. A high-altitude wind shook the truck, and we were level with a hawk that circled over the chasm in front of us. Warner pointed out tiny San Andrés, far below us at the bottom of the chasm. From that height, the adobe village looked like a collection of white stones in a green bowl. A long bone-white ribbon of road twisted and looped its way down the green and brown mountain toward the town. The descent took nearly an hour, and the final kilometre of road was severely rutted. We bounced our way into the dusty plaza to the explosion of firecrackers tossed by a pack of mischievous boys.

Warner's mother lived in a whitewashed adobe house, its walls spider-veined with tremor cracks. The señora hugged each of us as we entered, and the arrival of an unexpected guest seemed to please her immensely. She told me it was a great honour to welcome me into her home. I presented her with a pineapple that I'd bought in the market, a half-dollar purchase that prompted, to my embarrassment, a response well beyond the fruit's value. She called me her distinguished visitor and placed the pineapple in the centre of the table next to our supper, a steaming pot of cow-tongue soup.

The house had no interior walls: the floorspace was divided by several turquoise partitions that were decorated with discoloured photographs and faded diplomas. A dim, bare bulb lit the space where Warner, Miguel and I sat on vintage vinyl chairs while the señora fetched chips and beer. I took the opportunity to ask Miguel about Costa Rica's attempts to protect its environment.

'The law itself is not the big problem in Costa Rica,' he began. 'For us, more important is enforcement. We have good laws. We have good intentions. But that is not enough. For example, it is good to have protected lands, but half of that land is not patrolled or monitored. The reserves around the national parks especially suffer from exploitation. Logging is out of control. Studies show that Costa Rica loses 100,000 hectares of forest every year, which means no forests will exist in the year 2000 except in the national parks.

'One area in which we do need stronger laws is in the disposal of contamination. Agricultural chemicals and pesticides are a major problem in our rivers and coasts.'

I asked him if ecotourism was helping the environmental movement.

'Yes, it helps. But the tourism sector is principally under the control of foreigners. The government is mostly concerned with foreign exchange right now. It is difficult for officials to take a long-term perspective because environmental initiatives conflict with economic development. To me, our best hope is not with tourists but with our own people, with local action and community initiatives. We are trying to encourage neighbourhood associations to take action against contamination.'

As the evening progressed, more and more people arrived – uncles, cousins, nephews. It seemed that the entire extended family had crowded into the house. Whisky and rum were served, and the next few hours blurred past. More people arrived and there were more introductions, more names I couldn't keep straight. We sat down to bowls of soup. Since I was deemed the honoured guest, the biggest chunk of cow tongue went to me. My glass was filled again and again – first beer, then rum, then whisky. The men were telling jokes that made the women titter, cover their mouths and screech. Two men argued about upcoming elections, the dispute becoming increasingly volatile until everybody was involved. 'You see how democratic we are in Costa Rica,' Warner shouted above the din. 'In El Salvador they shoot each other; here, we just shout!'

An attractive young woman asked me about my travels and was horrified when I told her that I had bused through Honduras. 'But the poverty, the violence – such barbarity!' she exclaimed. Another person wanted my opinion on Costa Rica's chances in the World Cup. Then there was a sudden commotion in the corner of the room: flames leaped up from a votive candle that had set fire to a nativity scene. Warner rushed in from the kitchen with a pot of water and doused the flames. The pot, however, had had some rice left in it, and now the white grains were splattered on the singed figures of Mary and Joseph. Baby Jesus lay buried beneath a greyish glob.

The night ended with more shots of whisky and rum and slurred toasts to health, love and money. Eventually, I was led to a cot in a back room. I lay awake for some time, dizzy, the cot spinning.

❂

In the morning, the first concern for Warner's family was a procession to the cemetery to place flowers on the graves of

Warner's grandparents. Rather than intrude on the ceremony, I walked over to the plaza to take a look at the fiesta.

All around the dusty plaza, tents were set up for the selling of foodstuffs – home-made pickles, cotton candy, popcorn, cheese, sweetbread. A row of barbecue grills made from steel drums emitted billows of smoke. A huge generator contributed to an overload of sound that included the chiming and bonging of video-game machines, a boom box at the cassette vendor's tent, two loudspeakers blaring *música romántica* to accompany the preparations for the Miss San Andrés contest and, in the cantina tent, a trio of guitar-players crooning traditional songs. On top of it all, several boys continued to hurl firecrackers into the air; with each bang, they broke into laughter, as though surprised anew by each explosion.

Just beyond the stage where the Miss San Andrés hopefuls were nervously primping, I came across a row of cages containing a menagerie of sorry-looking rainforest animals: an armadillo, a coatimundi, a raccoon, three agoutis curled into a ball. The cages sat in the sun, and the sad creatures had nestled into their dirty straw, avoiding the attention of children who dropped nuts and rocks on them whilst their parents giggled and took photos.

The big event was the procession of the saint, which turned out to be a rather protracted affair. First the palanquin was brought out of the church and set down in the dust. Several old women fussed with a statue a metre high and ghostly white except for its pink lips and coal-black eyes. They placed a ring of yellow flowers around the saint's neck and sprinkled petals at its feet. Then a band of robed men arrived and the palanquin was hoisted onto their shoulders. The saint was marched around the plaza with a crowd of townspeople and dogs in tow, before disappearing down a rutted street. Two trumpeters joined the procession and contributed bursts of melancholy dissonance to the ritual. When the saint had visited and blessed every street in the village, it was returned to the musty nave of the adobe church.

While the selection of Miss San Andrés was being made, Miguel and I had a beer in a makeshift cantina. Imperial Beer streamers decorated the tent and fluttered in the steady, hot wind.

The 'bartender' – who was in fact the church caretaker and sexton – brought us dripping bottles of beer straight from the ice chest. The firecrackers continued to pop, and the same redundant music that had been going all day continued to blare from the speakers. Periodically, the crowd outside whistled and cheered lustily while a teenage girl took a turn around the stage.

Miguel pointed to the massive slopes of the cordillera rising all around us. 'You see how stripped and eroded these mountains are? When I was a boy the forest covered everything.'

'And this is the result of logging?'

'Some logging, especially wherever the newer, better roads are being built. Around here, some of the forest has been stripped for firewood, some has been cut down for coffee farms and for new plantations of export vegetables and flowers. And everywhere in Costa Rica, cattle are a problem. So much of our forests are now pastures for cattle. You cannot imagine what a problem is this animal. The rainforests are disappearing so we can eat hamburgers. Twenty hectares of rainforest for every hamburger. When I was a boy we could see many animals here. Deer, fox, sometimes mountain lion. All are endangered now. Only one animal remains: everywhere, the cow.'

✪

At some point that evening, during the drinking, the dancing and the bingo games on the plaza, Miguel and Warner decided that we should climb a nearby mountain to see the sun rise.

Just after three in the morning, we drove up the mountain to a trailhead that led to a weather station. The cold, thin air felt good once we started hiking. Miguel led the way with a flashlight, the beam bringing into view boulders, ferns, shrubs and – Miguel's principal concern – snake holes. At first our hike was easy, but as we neared the weather station the trail became steeper, and the loose cinder caused us to slip. The night was so clear it felt as if we were climbing into the billion stars that glittered just overhead – a breathtaking experience, and not just because of the high altitude.

The weather station consisted of a chain-link fence surrounding a lone tripod instrument equipped with various data collectors. Miguel shone the beam on a chart box, a rain gauge, a solar panel, a radiation sensor, an anemometer. A cup wheel spun in the wind, which by my reckoning was blowing strong, steady and cold. For thirty minutes we watched the softening of the inky blackness in the east. Then bands of light appeared, growing brighter and wider, as if a luminescent pink dye had been spilled across the horizon. Then, in sync with the rising sun, the shadow line descended the mountainside and the drab world at our feet was transformed into gold.

In every direction, mountains showed themselves, the stark cones of the volcanoes most prominent of all. For fifteen minutes, thirty minutes, an hour, we watched as Costa Rica awoke to the light. When the sun was fully over the horizon and the last dark bands had dissipated, the entire country was spread beneath us, brilliant and golden. Costa Rica is not a large country – we could see almost all of it from our vantage point – and it looked perfectly tranquil, silent, motionless. But at any given moment on any given day, Costa Rica bursts with life, teeming and humming.

I thought of its prolific growth: the cedars, mangroves, mahoganies, laurels, pines, silk cottons, gumbo-limbos, guanacastes, silvertrees, cypresses, alders, orchids, coconuts, mangoes, pineapples, oranges, chayotes, anonas, papayas, zapotes, bananas, corn, beans, sugar, coffee.

I thought of the animal life: the antbirds, tanagers, harpy eagles, parrots, toucans, macaws, hummingbirds, quetzals, flycatchers, cotingas, armadillos, agoutis, Jesus Christ lizards, iguanas, hawksbill turtles, poison dart frogs, basilisk lizards, morpho butterflies, leafcutter ants, peccaries, kinkajous, racoons, skunks, otters, foxes, bats, ocelots, jaguars, tapirs.

I thought of the bustle of human activity: picking coffee beans, cutting bananas, spraying poison, driving cars and trucks and tractors and bulldozers and buses, building dams, logging forests, buying and selling, getting and spending.

Amidst it all, thousands upon thousands of ecotourists would be up and at it – boating, hiking, surfing, fishing, biking, ballooning, climbing, swimming, rafting, kayaking, searching for something missing in themselves, in their lives, and hoping that prolific, profligate Costa Rica could provide it for them.

Here on the mountain, no one had spoken for some time. It seemed that the vision had left us dumbstruck. Finally, Warner leaned over and whispered, 'How is it, Esteban?'

I shook my head in awe. It had taken me ten days of travelling around the country to reach this place, to find, only hours before boarding the plane for the flight back to the cold north, what I had been seeking all along. I was pleased that I had made it here, that once again luck had taken me beyond the confines of simple tourism. And yet, now that I was here, I couldn't help being the tourist. I reached into my pack for the camera.

'It's good,' I told Warner. 'It's very good.' And I peered through the viewfinder to frame my picture.

The Ruta Maya:
Guatemala, 1997

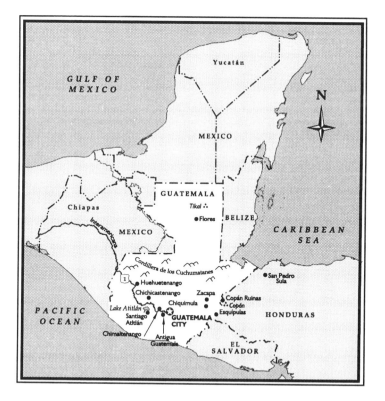

Interlude

A FTER my return to the States, in the depths of a long, bitter winter, I thought often of that morning I had spent atop the mountain in Costa Rica. I had even more time to think about it when I fell ill and went through a long, frightening, painful bout with an unknown virus. For weeks on end, I was drained of energy, unable to move. I lay in bed dazed, drugged and feverish, my world reduced to television viewing and light reading. Nothing made sense. The boundary between dreams and consciousness blurred.

For some strange reason, during that long spell, the Maya haunted my sickness, invading both sleep and consciousness. They appeared everywhere. A television documentary explored 'the mystery of the Maya'. The cover of a weekly news magazine asked, 'Who were the Maya?' A best-selling book purported to reveal the prophecies of the Maya. And geographic journals turned out article after article on the latest discoveries at Copán, Calakmul, Caracol and Bonampak.

The more I came across the subject, the more interested I became. During my years in Central America, I had visited the ancient sites of Copán in Honduras and Tikal in Guatemala without understanding much of what I was seeing. Now, lying in bed sick and disabled, I pinned my hopes for recovery on the Maya: that is, I promised myself that when I recovered I would use my summer vacation – and my savings – to go back to Guatemala and see again, with more informed eyes, the places that were but a hazy memory to me. When I felt up to the task, I called travel agents for information. I pored over guidebooks and maps. The possibility of a journey energised me and helped me return slowly to health.

The trip to Costa Rica had revived my interest in alternative tourism, and so I took particular notice of the publicity attending the creation of the so-called 'Ruta Maya', the Route of the Maya. The concept committed the governments of Mexico, Belize, Guatemala, Honduras and El Salvador to the general philosophy of protecting cultural and environmental sites within their borders. The somewhat vague plans called for the development of ecotourism and cultural tourism in the region, with special emphasis on the contemporary culture, ecology and archaeology of Mayan lands. This development was to take place under the guidance and monitoring of an intergovernmental organisation, currently called El Mundo Maya, or Mayan World.

The great hope was that carefully controlled touristic development would somehow help preserve and protect Mayan culture and the environment of Mesoamerica, while at the same time providing income for the Maya, thereby improving their living conditions. The money that tourism brought in would be used, ideally, to create national parks, protect archaeological sites and promote conservation. People would recognise that they could make more money by preserving the rainforests than by cutting them down. Everything was supposed to mesh beautifully: tourism would bring in money at a local level, inspire the people to preserve their environment, and educate tourists about other cultures and the need for biodiversity. As one promoter put it, the Ruta Maya would 'increase environmentally oriented tourism and sustainable, non-destructive development to provide jobs and money to help pay for preservation'.

I studied maps and plotted a journey that would cover a significant portion of the Ruta Maya. I would start with the ruins of Copán and Tikal, then work my way north, passing through the Guatemalan highlands to Chiapas, Mexico; this part of the trip would take me through the most populous regions of the contemporary Maya. From Chiapas, I would travel up to the Yucatán peninsula, where the ancient ruins of Uxmal and Chichén Itzá play host to the greatest number of tourists on the Ruta Maya.

❂

I had another reason for wanting to visit Guatemala during that summer. At the end of the previous year, 1996, the government and the guerrillas had signed peace accords that had put an end to the longest civil war in Latin America, a civil war that I had witnessed at its worst during my years as a teacher in Guatemala City.

The roots of the troubles could be traced back to 1954, when a CIA-sponsored coup overthrew a progressive, popular government and instituted a long series of increasingly repressive military dictatorships and puppet regimes. By the early 1960s, guerrilla groups were operating in the countryside, and for the next thirty years Guatemala was engulfed in a civil war that attracted world scrutiny for the sheer brutality of the atrocities committed: tens of thousands murdered and 'disappeared'; over 400 highland villages wiped off the map; citizens napalmed by their own Army; the politically suspect kidnapped and tortured by death squads. Backed by the US government, the Guatemalan military carried out a campaign of virtual genocide against the Maya, who were supposedly supporters of the communist guerrillas.

Since I had been in Guatemala during the worst days of the civil war, I found it hard to believe that mere signatures on paper would solve anything. Five hundred years of racial prejudice and inequity could not be easily wiped out, nor fifty years of military totalitarianism for that matter. Only fifteen years before, the Army had engaged in a deliberate campaign to destroy Mayan culture. The oligarchy and the military, largely of European ethnicity, had too much at stake to consider sharing power with the Mayan majority. Many of the members of the wealthy elite I had met despised *los indios*. Such a deep hatred would not soon change, and in going to Guatemala again, I hoped to speak to some old acquaintances to find out what was really going on.

CHAPTER 13

On the road to ruins

SOMETIMES you make bad choices. You go against the prevailing advice and try to do things the hard way, thinking
maybe it's more 'authentic' – whatever that means – or more hon-
est. The truth is you don't know why you make these choices, so
obviously wrong to you even as you make them. You feel
strangely powerless to do otherwise. In the end, you have to write
it all off to bad travelling karma and you push ahead toward whatever obscure fate awaits you.

And so it was for me as I travelled from Guatemala City to
Copán, in Honduras. Ignoring the advice of guidebooks and the
travellers' grapevine – 'join a package tour' – I opted for a staggered journey on local buses: the capital to Chiquimula;
Chiquimula to the border; a switch of buses at the border for the
final leg into Copán.

For the first stage, I chose a bad bus and ended up on an age-
ing rattletrap with neither muffler nor legroom. Its balding tyres
blew out one by one on the hot asphalt roads of Guatemala's
Oriente, an arid desert region of cactus and scrub and heat haze.

Our first delay occurred along a busy stretch of the Atlantic
Highway, stranding us on a steep mountain near ancient obsidian
beds once worked by the Maya. Opposite us, a ghostly wall of
still higher mountains loomed above a dry, dun-coloured gap, the
Motagua Fault, where the isthmus's tectonic plates grind against
one another. Scores of trucks spewing diesel clouds churned up
the grade ever so slowly, coming upon us with their heavy load of

concrete blocks bound for construction sites in the already over-built capital. Brightly festooned buses sped past in the opposite direction, on the road to the shrine of the dark Christ in Esquipulas – horns blaring, holy pilgrims staring out at misfortune's stranded darlings. Every so often a sleek tour bus passed, gliding toward Copán, its load of wiser tourists dozing in air-conditioned comfort; they would reach the ruins by nightfall, while I languished in the desert.

The second blowout stranded us in a more fortunate location. The bang and screech and skidding halt came to pass a mere half-kilometre from a row of roadside stalls and a highway junction: the turn for Guatemala's hot outland towns, Zacapa, Chiquimula, Esquipulas, and the Honduran border. While the makeshift repair job was made, I sucked down a sweet, pulpy fruit drink in the hot sun, and watched the trucks hauling Gallo beer and Coca-Cola and bananas and sealed freight from the Caribbean ports roar past. A Rubios cigarette hoarding announced the fortunate traveller's imminent arrival in Zacapa: a town whose most famous native son was known all over Guatemala as 'the Butcher'. This vicious son of a bitch organised and maintained the Eye for an Eye Death Squad, and as a general in the armed forces took the reign of terror to all corners of the country. In Guatemala's frontier land, folks admired that sort of brutality. They carried guns and knives and were quick to use them. Their quick temper was considered their most endearing trait.

When the third tyre blew, our luck ran as dry as the face of the land we were trying to cross. It came only an hour after the last blowout, at the summit of a spectral ridge separating Zacapa from Chiquimula. The driver and his aide rotated the tyres once more, while the passengers sat on boulders to wait out the repair. The wind blew hot and hard. I jumped a barbed-wire fence and climbed a short distance to a pinnacle, where I glimpsed a landscape that blushed in the pink and rose glow of the setting sun.

'Guatemala doesn't exist. I know. I've been there.' So begins a novel I've never read. Honestly, I don't know what the writer means: I've never travelled in a country so definitely, so defiantly in existence. Guatemala overwhelms the senses. It leaps out at you, knocks you down, takes your breath away. It's a geography textbook brought to life, the entire earth crumpled and compacted into one small, three-dimensional corner. Guatemala most emphatically exists. I know. I've been there.

Nevertheless, I found it an endless frustration when I tried to capture Guatemala in words. The place resisted transcription. Like its national symbol, the quetzal bird, Guatemala wouldn't survive in captivity. The writer could try, but in the verbal cage he built he found only bones and a solitary resplendent feather. Maybe the place doesn't exist, after all.

❂

It was dark when the bus renewed its labours and descended the ridge through twists and turns to the plains below. Just before Chiquimula, the driver halted at a military checkpoint and a soldier waved us off the bus with his rifle. We lined up in the dark for a document check, two sleepy soldiers passing down the lines to glance at the *cédulas* all Guatemalans must carry. My passport gave them pause; they flipped through the pages but then lost interest and handed it back. Further down the line, they selected a victim for harassment: a young man, who was taken to a concrete guardhouse.

'Why did they take him away?' I asked the driver when we reboarded.

'Military service,' the driver replied. 'Guatemala needs more soldiers.'

'Is that true?' To me, that was the last thing the country needed.

'Of course. We already have enough gringos.'

I spent the night in Chiquimula, Guatemala's hottest town, where dry-season temperatures regularly rise above forty degrees Celsius. Even at night, the heat was insufferable, especially inside the shabby *pensión* where I took a room – or, rather, a cubicle.

Needing to stretch my legs after a long day on the bus, I went out for a walk. A thousand blackbirds chirped wildly in the trees and young lovers had taken over the park benches in the plaza. Pungent smells filled the air: grilling meat, blossoming almond trees, rotting fruit. On the side streets, I passed houses open to the night, prodigious families sitting out on porches, listening to the radio.

When I was well outside the town, past the last houses, the dirt track I was following dead-ended in a cattle pasture beneath the outline of dark hills. I stood for a moment, sweaty, feeling the hot draught, breathing in the overbearing stink of cattle. I thought about how often this had happened before – how in Central America I was always following a road that petered out, how again and again the journey seemed bootless, without destination, a journey undertaken for the sole purpose of movement. Wasn't it Horace who said we can change our skies but not ourselves? So be it. I turned back and headed into Chiquimula. I had an early bus to catch.

❈

It was still dark when the microbus blasted its horn and pulled out of the marketplace. '*Jocotán, la frontera,*' the driver's aide shouted, hanging from the passenger door as the bus circled the plaza. The shouting seemed pointless: the bus was already full of passengers and their burlap sacks. Nevertheless, near the highway an old man waved, the bus stopped, and we squeezed together a little more.

About ten kilometres past Chiquimula, the bus left the highway and followed a rough dirt track into the mountain range separating Guatemala from Honduras. Despite the ruts, the bus bounded along, or seemed to, and it wasn't long before the bouncing and jarring and rattling unnerved me. I was squeezed between the window and a woman with a baby at her breast and a toddler on her knee. Their burlap sack squirmed and grunted at my feet. Trying to stretch my legs, I inadvertently poked the sack, and it let out a curdling squeal. The driver said something that got everybody laughing. The only words I understood were 'gringo' and 'pork'.

158

As the morning progressed and the sun rose higher, the interior of the bus turned stifling. The windows were shut tight against the dust; a sour stink strengthened – the baby's drool, the pig's shit, the sweat from us all – and contributed to my growing nausea. I kept thinking of a line from a Beatles song: 'On the way the paper bag was on my knee'. I could have really used that paper bag.

For fifty long, slow kilometres, we rattled past the wattle-and-daub houses of the Chorti-speaking Maya who inhabited the region. The men, dressed all in white, paused in their cornfields to watch the bus's passage. Blue-skirted women hurried along the road, loads of firewood balanced on their heads. Streams coursed over the road, forcing the bus to splash through numerous fords. Valleys of aloe gave way to stands of pine on alpine slopes. Where the trees had been felled, patches of red sandstone stood out like wounds rubbed raw. We came upon two towns, Jocotán and Camotán, both dominated by colonial churches and military garrisons. Guardsmen in dark green uniforms and sunglasses stood sentinel over market-bound Indians laden with mysterious burlap burdens.

The road worsened near the border, but at least the bus emptied out a little. By the time we came to a halt in front of a woebegone shed marked '*Migración – Guatemala*', I was one of the last left on board. Nearly wilted, I headed straight for a kiosk and bought a lukewarm cola. The border crossing was a dusty, ragged place – a handful of kiosks, the derelict Guatemalan post, a chain across the road, a rusted sign reading '*Frontera Guatemala–Honduras*'. The equally derelict Honduran post had a hammock strung up on its porch, where a soldier dozed. Money-changers milled about, every last one of them wearing an oversized business suit, cheap sunglasses and a bogus Rolex.

To one side of the road, an impromptu football game was in progress, the border providing the goal line. While I drank my cola, errant kicks sent the ball out of Guatemala and into Honduras. The borderline itself was a clearly visible swath of dead vegetation burned into the earth with herbicide. The hills above the border crossing were severely deforested and eroded.

The side of one hill had been completely washed away where Honduras had sent its erosion across the boundary.

The cola turned out to be a bad idea. Warm and gassy, it churned in my stomach. Worse, before I could finish it, a sleek tour bus arrived. The guide jumped down, a stack of passports in his hand, and beat me into *migración*.

Suddenly the frontier came alive. The tourists spilled out of the bus to take pictures and change money with the polyester-suited men who punched their calculators and flicked through wads of purple *quetzales* and red *lempiras* and green dollars.

I waited my turn at *migración*, while the tour guide had his charges processed out of Guatemala and into Honduras. By the time I'd paid the appropriate fees (including one for unspecified *servicios extraordinarios*) and had my passport stamped, I'd missed the local bus on the Honduran side. The tour bus churned up dust and left me in its cloud, stranded on the border.

I sat down in the shade to await the next local, but it wasn't long before a plump and jolly man whistled me over and offered me a lift into Copán. He pointed out a small Toyota pick-up. As soon as it was gassed, he explained, we could go. Every vehicle crossing the border had to be 'gassed' with insecticide, supposedly to prevent unwanted plagues from spreading across international boundaries. First the wheels were sprayed and then a toxic cloud was blown into the vehicle's interior. After a minute, the doors were opened and the gas billowed out and rose into the air, leaving behind a foul odour, an oily film on the pick-up's vinyl seats and two unfortunate flies shrivelled on the dashboard. Meanwhile, a million insects buzzed and whirred back and forth across the border.

My driver was a businessman from San Pedro Sula. Every so often he travelled to Guatemala City to buy Mayan handicrafts – several bundles lay in the bed of the pick-up – which he sold in turn to tourist hotels and shops. It was good money, he said, because the handicrafts were very cheap in Guatemala and Honduras had nothing like them to offer tourists.

'There are no Indians in Honduras,' he told me even as we drove past Mayan cornfields. 'We're Spanish here. Look at our women – much more beautiful. Why? We have Spanish features.'

He made me promise him that I would try a Honduran woman while I was in Copán. 'You'll see,' he said. 'The very best women in Central America are the women of my country.'

Later in the evening, I did in fact meet some local girls – three of them, about ten or eleven years old. They were selling carved Mayan masks and little wooden idols.

When I declined to buy, the oldest said, 'Maybe tomorrow?' She had reddish hair and freckles and dirty shins. All three wore plastic sandals. 'Maybe,' I said.

With that hope, for the next hour, they followed me wherever I went in the village, keeping five paces behind and occasionally giggling or singing out, 'Maybe tomorrow?'

The whole time I was in Copán, the girls followed me. If I went to eat, they were waiting for me when I came out of the restaurant, sitting in the gutter of the cobblestoned street. The oldest one, the one with the red hair – a sign of malnutrition? – jumped up whenever I came through the hotel door. 'Maybe tomorrow?' she repeated, extending once again the head of a Mayan god toward me.

Sitting in an ice-cream shop, I looked up to see them paused on the threshold, standing in a pool of light, smiling across at me, cradling their trinkets. For the first time, I truly saw them: they had the faces of innocents; there was an angelic beauty to their awkward bodies and unkempt hair. I waved them over and ordered cones for us all. We sat at a table together, the girls all but falling over with the giggles. I knew they'd be on my heels wherever I went for sure now. I also knew I'd committed myself, whether I wanted one or not, to buying one of the gaudy idols before I left.

❂

The little town of Copán Ruinas was about a kilometre from the Mayan ruins. Although the reason for the town's existence had always been the ruins, for years surprisingly little infrastructure for tourism existed in the place. A couple of mean hotels, a handful of restaurants, a tiny museum, maybe a faltering souvenir shop doing a desultory business. To be sure, there were always foreigners in town – the occasional tour group, a small legion of the more adventurous backpacking travellers and, in the dry season, a cadre of archaeologists, mostly young American graduate students, at work on the site. But despite the foreigners, Copán Ruinas seemed the quintessential Central American boondocks town, with a pleasant little plaza where people sat on benches, ice-cream carts jangled bells and a slow, sad chant issued from the never-ending Mass in progress within the church. The most exciting thing to do in town was to head for the bar favoured by the archaeologists, buy some drinks and talk dirt archaeology.

I discovered that the town was still small, the plaza still pleasant, the streets still cobblestoned and devoid of traffic, but the demeanour of the place had changed. The children following me with their cheap souvenirs were one indication. Then there were the T-shirt and tourist shops on the plaza and the tour buses parked on the streets. Several new hotels, large and luxurious, indicated that a new sort of tourist was frequenting the place. Air conditioning, swimming pools and happy hour were part of the new order.

Ownership patterns were changing, too. Many of the new facilities were operated either by Honduran companies from San Pedro Sula or by foreigners. One Dutch-owned place advertised the availability of European bread, European coffee and European beers, with nightly screenings of American films. Down the street, a vegetarian restaurant had opened up.

In spite of all the changes in town, visiting the ruins was a tranquil, almost mystical, experience. Far fewer tourists came to Copán than Tikal or Palenque or Chichén Itzá. You could still wander around the Great Plaza alone, studying the 1200-year-old stelae dedicated to the powerful but doomed ruler known as 18 Rabbit, here wearing the fantastic costumes of different gods, frozen in a stone dance, surrounded by grotesque caricatures and the weird glyphic lettering that tells, so far as it can be read, the bloody story of 18 Rabbit's decapitation at the hands of an arch rival – a lord named Cauac Sky who came from Copán's colony, tiny Quirigua, to wreak havoc on the great city state and destroy its once omnipotent leader. You could still stand in the shade of a giant guanacaste tree and contemplate the Hieroglyphic Stairway, built in the eighth century by a ruler named Smoke Shell, its thousands of glyph-carved blocks revealing the 600-year history of Copán's ruling lineage. You could still sit on the steps of the ball court – a portal to the underworld, as the Maya conceived it – and imagine the rituals of life and death that played out there under the mute stare of stone macaws.

No matter how many times I've seen it, Copán's stone imagery startles me. Feathered serpents, grinning masks, dancing jaguars with obsidian eyes, fanged mountain monsters, maize gods, crocodile heads decorated with Venus symbols, skulls that represent the maw of the underworld, sun-eyed beasts, magic turtles, water lilies, monkey scribes, and the so-called Vision Serpents, World Trees and Celestial Birds – a weird and sometimes frightening wonderland as conceived by the Maya and interpreted by twentieth-century scholars. *In situ*, the bizarre iconography surrounds you, looms over you, leers at you, confounds you, and strikes you dumb. You wander the site as though in a dream, the strangest dream of your longest night.

❂

On this visit, the stone carving that most impressed me was not one of the masterpieces among the stelae, friezes and altars. It was another piece, unfinished, that I had never seen before. A graduate student working at the site showed it to me.

I met Heather near the Hieroglyphic Stairway, just as she emerged from a metal door at the entrance to an archaeologist's tunnel that burrowed into the stairway's supporting pyramid. A large blonde woman, she had a classic American face, round, ruddy, beaming.

'Sure is hot in there,' she said. 'Gosh, the fresh air feels good.'

163

When I asked her what she'd been doing, she launched into a quasi-technical description of her project. It had something to do with potsherds and cinnabar. She had the habit, common among American students, of ending each phrase with a rising intonation.

'OK, there are these pieces coated with cinnabar? And it's, like, highly toxic? So we have to wear these gloves, right? And, well, it's pretty complicated. I'm probably boring you.'

Heather was one of a dozen or so graduate students at work here; over the years, Copán had undergone more study than any other major Mayan site. It was the first site that John Lloyd Stephens, the father of Mayan archaeology, came to investigate in the 1840s, at a time when the origin of the ruins was a complete mystery. More recently, some of the most exciting discoveries in the Mundo Maya had occurred at Copán. An intact temple had been found inside a pyramid, a rich tomb uncovered, and many of the glyphs on the stelae on the Great Plaza had been deciphered.

I asked Heather what had drawn her to study the Maya. She brushed back her damp hair and sighed. 'Oh, gosh, that's a good question. You know, I think it's the whole mystery thing. Like where did they go and all that? When I was an undergrad I thought it was, like, spooky and a total mystery. Now it turns out we think that here at Copán there was an ecology crisis type of thing.'

'So they didn't really vanish?'

'Not exactly, but actually they did kind of just leave one day, pretty abruptly – like that half-finished altar thing? Have you seen it?'

I hadn't, so Heather offered to lead me over to it. We crossed the alley of the ball court and climbed the spectator steps. The altar was a squat, nondescript affair, easily overlooked amidst the more spectacular monuments. Heather explained that one side of the altar depicted the last king of Copán raising some fan-like object in emulation of the facing figure, presumably his predecessor; on the other side, an inchoate scene of two seated figures struggled to emerge from the stone, but the images were stillborn. It was as if the workman, sensing the imminent collapse, just picked up his tools and fled. The date on the altar, equivalent to 822 AD, was the last ever recorded at Copán.

❂

The collapse of Classic Mayan culture in the ninth century has never been completely explained, nor is the nature of the collapse, especially the seemingly sudden abandonment of the great centres, well understood. Mayanists now believe that certain identifiable factors combined to bring about the breakdown: political, social and economic forces played some part, but above all else, especially in Copán, environmental factors led to the collapse.

Overpopulation was part of the problem. The fertile Copán Valley could no longer support the large population of Copán's heyday, for the valley had been severely deforested. The great building programme that distinguished Copán from its rivals required a huge amount of fuel, its buildings and vast plaza floors being plastered in a shell and limestone mixture that had to be fired in kilns. An incredible amount of plaster was needed for the unending process of plastering and re-plastering the city. In order to fuel the kilns, the Maya of Copán despoiled huge tracts of forest. A great environmental tragedy was inevitable.

The renowned Mayanist Michael Coe has stated that there is no question the collapse was brought on by a catastrophic drought, exacerbated by deforestation and overpopulation. This drought in turn triggered social and political upheavals from which the only escape for the upper class was total abandonment.

Standing with Heather atop the ball court, I could see more recent signs of deforestation in the hills surrounding the ruins. In fact, all along the road into Copán there was evidence of erosion and denuded land, a hint of what the valley had looked like as the crisis had developed. Clearly, the Mayan collapse held a lesson and a warning for our own world. As Mayanist George

165

Stuart has noted, 'the story of Copán is more pertinent to our times than we could ever have imagined – for it illustrates the folly of the misuse of land'.

❂

For the return to Guatemala City, I talked my way onto a tour bus. Actually, I didn't need to talk much; I offered the guide my left-over *lempiras*, and he shrugged, 'Sure, why not?'

The girls were waiting when I left. We walked from my budget hotel to the new luxury resort where the package tourists were boarding their coach. For three days the girls had waited patiently for a sale, and now the time had come. I looked over the choices they offered me, and it was immediately clear that I wouldn't get away with buying just one. I stood before the girls like Paris before Athena, Aphrodite and Hera: an impossible choice. I selected one from each and said goodbye.

On board, the elderly package tourists asked me how much I had paid for the idols.

'Did you hear that, George? That's pretty cheap, and we've got to use up our Honduras money.'

'I guess so,' George responded. 'They won't take this funny money in Guaddymala. Got their own funny money.'

Before the bus departed, half the group descended to buy the girls' masks and statuettes. The three of them grinned and waved, their stock sold out, while my travelling companions photographed them from the windows of the bus.

And with that, we were on the road, bouncing over ruts and splashing through streams for seventy bone-jarring kilometres, the passengers popping pills and groaning. When we reached the paved road, the group burst into applause. I, however, hardly noticed a thing; equipped with functioning shocks and air conditioning and – a rare luxury in Central America – four recently retreaded tyres, this monster tour bus was a roving palace. Once we hit the smooth macadam, I dropped into a sleep that lasted all the way to Guatemala City.

CHAPTER 14

The lost city

YOU can take a bus from Guatemala City to the ancient Mayan city of Tikal – fourteen, sixteen, maybe twenty hours of dull travel across the desert of the Oriente, through the humid banana lands of the Caribbean coast and on into the denuded lowlands of the Petén, the northern third of Guatemala. Once, the Petén was sparsely settled and covered with tropical hardwood forests. If the rainforest were still there, the ride would be more appealing, but the Petén has been opened up to settlers, the trees cut, the land turned over to cattle. I'd made the trip by road before; it was too long and too depressing to repeat.

So I joined all the other tourists and flew to Flores, a jungle town sixty kilometres from Tikal. Riding the bus on the newly paved road from Flores to the site, I saw a good example of what happens when roads are built through the rainforest: the rainforest disappears. Between Flores and the boundary of Tikal National Park, vast tracts of trees had been cleared and burned; scorched stumps stood alone in blackened plots. A smoky haze on the horizon testified to other burnings within reach of the road. It was difficult to divine the purpose of the holocaust: here and there I could see small plantations of corn surrounding a makeshift dwelling, deforested fields given over to cattle, and stacks of timber awaiting retrieval. But mostly I saw a stripped landscape – hectare after denuded hectare destroyed, then left abandoned.

This all changed once we crossed the boundary of Tikal National Park. For the next seventeen kilometres, the road took us through pristine rainforest dominated by evergreen broadleaf trees – sapodilla, ramón, breadnut, cedar and silk-cotton amongst them. The contrast was abrupt and stark: from blighted cattle pastures we passed into the dense, prolific canopy of trees twenty metres high. A few mahogany giants reached up to forty metres, and all the trees were draped with lianas, stranglers, orchids and bromeliads. Hidden in this luxuriant flora would be an abundance of rare fauna: snakes, monkeys, frogs, foxes, ring-tailed coatis, ocelots, oscillated turkeys, pumas, peccaries, tapirs, toucans, macaws, mot mots, oropendolas, harpy eagles. This was the 'unproductive land' that the Guatemalan government and timber companies and cattle ranchers hoped to exploit. The 575 square kilometres of the national park was one of the last untouched sections of the Petén, a remnant of what was once the second largest rainforest in the Americas.

❂

At the heart of the national park lay the ancient city of Tikal, the most famous of the Classic Mayan sites. Ten years had passed since my last visit to the ruins. In those days, I'd travelled simply, unencumbered, needing only a small tent set up under a thatched shelter at the campground. It had been a nice enough place to stay, and cheap, with a grassy lawn where Petén turkeys foraged and the park workers played evening games of football. But now, as a measure of my decline in daring, I booked a room at the Jungle Lodge, a place I previously disparaged. Here I was, forking over my money, signing the registration, taking the key down to Bungalow No 4 – with electricity and private bath, just a few steps from the new swimming pool. Notwithstanding these jungle luxuries, the lack of air conditioning, television and telephone led guidebooks to describe the Jungle Lodge as 'rustic', 'basic', even 'primitive'.

When you visit Tikal, you inevitably collect anecdotes about Humans versus Nature in the rainforest.

One night in the dining room of the Jungle Lodge, for example, a story made its way around the tables. That afternoon, a young European had strayed off the path to pursue and photograph a fox. He'd ended up entangled in a small thorny tree, and been cut up pretty badly. But that hadn't been the worst of it. The branches of the trees were favoured by a type of red ant; when the tourist brushed the tree a small battalion of the ants had fallen upon him. He had been bitten so badly that he'd gone into shock and had to be taken to the hospital in Flores. The guides passed from table to table, imploring their charges not to leave the trails under any circumstances. 'The jungle is very bad to you,' I heard one say.

The next day, in a courtyard of the Central Acropolis, I watched a group of tourists react to the sudden appearance of a coatimundi. The raccoon-like animal, its long ringed tail sticking straight up in the air, was sniffing the ground in the shadow of an ancient wall when the group spotted him. Reaction was swift and well orchestrated: lens caps were unscrewed, film was wound. Amidst excited gasping, the group deployed into a semicircle and pinned the coati near the wall. But the shadow caused a photography problem, so someone threw a cookie, and the coati cautiously crept forward to sniff it. Once they'd drawn him into the sunlight, the group fired off a round of good shots.

The coati, however, was still hungry; it turned to its food source and advanced a few paces with more alacrity than before. The startled tourists scrambled backward; the coati froze and watched their retreat. When the tour guide finished his discourse on the Central Acropolis, the group headed off to Jaguar Paw's palace. Before departing, one of the tourists reached into her handbag for a packet of cookies, still plastic-wrapped, and tossed it toward the coati. When she had gone, the coati came forward, snatched the packet and carried it off into the jungle thicket.

❁

For two days, I heard but did not see the howler monkeys. Their booming barks and groans resounded throughout the rainforest, but the howlers remained distant and out of sight. Late in the afternoon on my second day in Tikal, I heard the howlers close by. The first roar seemed to shake the trees, and it was followed by a dark mysterious howl that stopped me dead on the dirt track. I followed the subsequent roars up a service road that led to a small administration building. The monkeys were in the trees behind the building, ten metres up, a family of five. They were smaller than I had imagined, their bellow belying their size. I stood and watched them rustling the leaves and breaking off pods of fruit.

The cries continued as evening approached and darkness covered the rainforest, drawn-out, plaintive groans bespeaking some unnamed pain. Periodically, all night long, their bellows disturbed the calm of the hotel compound, and they were at last quieted only by a furious pre-dawn downpour that rattled the metal roofs of the bungalow and left the grounds of the Jungle Lodge littered at daybreak with twigs and leaves and fronds.

❂

One evening, I heard a talk by Peter Harrison, an archaeologist who had been working at the site for over thirty years. Afterwards, I asked him if any of the archaeological evidence at Tikal suggested, as at Copán, that environmental degradation figured in the collapse of Classic Mayan civilisation.

Harrison, like most Mayanists, was cautious in his answer. 'There's no conclusive evidence of any single cause of the collapse,' he replied. 'All anyone can say for certain is that it happened.'

Around 900 AD, at the height of the city's cultural achievements, the culture that had produced those achievements fell apart. 'It happened rather quickly, we know that much,' Harrison continued, 'but excavation hasn't revealed many clues other than unfinished construction – an indication that work was abruptly abandoned. There must have been a number of causes to bring on that kind of cataclysm, but more and more we suspect that water management had a lot to do with it. The Petén is a rainforest, but

170

it is susceptible to drought. A long drought, combined with deforestation and declining productivity in the poor soil of the Petén, would have led to a fairly drastic food crisis. Of course, this is all very difficult for archaeology to prove.'

The next day, Harrison invited me to see some examples of water management at Tikal. A tall, trim man, he strode along at a deliberate pace along the causeway, pointing left and right at various mounds, some excavated, the majority still silent under vegetation. Though I was younger than him by some twenty years, I practically had to jog to keep up.

Water was very important to the Maya, Harrison explained. In fact, much of Tikal's architecture was designed to channel water, for the site was located on a major water divide that provided passage from east to west. 'It was a controlling site,' he said. 'Very strategic.' But for all their efforts, there was never an abundance of water – levels in the main reservoir showed that. Much of the tremendous rainfall was lost to evaporation and sinkholes in the limestone. Some of it gathered in lowland holding pools called *bajos*, but in a drought the *bajos* dried up. In an extended drought, the people of Tikal would have literally died of thirst in the middle of the rainforest.

Moreover, in recent times, as the Petén rainforest has been chopped down and burned to create cropland, evidence suggests that deforestation would have hastened the desiccation of the *bajos*. As Tikal's population grew, the ancient Maya must have deforested the Petén in an effort to meet fuel and food demands. To demonstrate what it might have been like, Harrison led me to several hectares of wasteland – a large burned-out reed patch enclosing two small stagnant puddles. He pointed out the house where archaeologists used to live, on the far side of the withered acreage. 'Right here,' he explained, 'was a large pool. It had always been full of water, ever since I first came here in 1959. For a long time a huge crocodile lived in there. I've never seen it like this.'

'So at the time of the collapse, the water supply at Tikal would have dried up like this?'

171

He nodded. 'It would seem so. A catastrophe at hand. Famine, class strife, disease.'

Given our current treatment of the rainforest, I said, it could well be a once and future catastrophe.

Harrison stared in contemplation at the moribund reservoir. 'If so, it could be horrific. At least it was for the Maya. When we excavated the house of the ruler Jaguar Paw, we found evidence of post-collapse occupation. Probably derelict nomads living in the ruins of Tikal, desperate to survive. We found the remains of human bones and skulls in the rooms. There were teeth marks – evidence of gnawing. Cannibalism.'

A hot, dry wind blew over us, and the sun burned our skin red. I looked over the dry reservoir to the visitors' centre, where the tourist crowd, oblivious to omens, was busy buying Coca-Cola and potato chips and T-shirts and faux-jade trinkets.

❁

On my last day in Tikal, I woke before dawn and joined a group of fellow tourists in the lobby of the Jungle Lodge. About twenty of us had signed up for a guided hike into the ruins to climb Temple IV and view the sunrise from the tallest of Tikal's pyramids. I recognised most of the group from communal meals in the restaurant: about half came from a German tour group, another handful were American teachers and the rest were teenagers from a Baptist church in Arizona. A diminutive, machete-bearing man named Jorge was responsible for leading us along the dark jungle paths.

We descended the driveway of the lodge, and turned onto the path that led into the ruins. Like most of the paths at Tikal, this had once been a Mayan road, a causeway of plastered limestone laid through the jungle. The plaster still existed, a hard shell that turned slick when wet and made walking somewhat treacherous, especially on slopes. By the time we reached the Great Plaza, three tourists had slipped and fallen, notwithstanding their state-of-the-art hiking boots.

It was still pitch black when we passed beneath the temples of the Great Plaza – the Temple of the Giant Jaguar and the Temple of the Masks – and made out their imposing dark outlines against the night sky. Already, birds were warbling and chirping, their loud chorus anticipating daylight. The wet air was heavy with the pungent aroma of the ramón trees, a smell reminiscent of cooked beans. We plunged into forest again, marching to the steady knocking of a woodpecker. The causeway took us around Temple III, then along the Bat Palace and past two small mounds – once temples, now stone heaps. In the shadows to our right stood two carved stones, darkness concealing the images depicted on them; one, I knew, a round altar, showed two elaborately dressed men conferring over an altar upon which were laid bones and a skull.

Finally we came to the base of Temple IV, the Temple of the Two-headed Serpent. Unlike the renowned temples on the Great Plaza, the pyramid's stairway was too ruined for climbing, and ladders now led up through the trees and the snake-like roots that entangled the temple's terraces. Jorge scrambled over and around the roots to climb alongside the ladders, stabilising some of the shakier tourists as we made the ascent.

The last ladder brought us to the top platform, above the tree line, where a good-sized crowd had assembled to celebrate the sunrise. A long-haired young man sat cross-legged, playing an out-of-tune guitar, while a group of people circled around him chanted in a language I couldn't identify. Nearby, a man and a woman wearing chic adventure gear had assumed meditative positions; they sucked in deep breaths, then loudly exhaled the malevolent air in their systems. Their breathing exercises continued unabated even when the ramón-pungent smell of Tikal was periodically replaced by clouds of repellent as one or another of the tourists doused themselves with DEET. The whine of the mosquito horde challenged the chanting of the guitar-player's entourage and the Pentecostal murmuring of the Baptist youth group holding hands in prayer. To one side, Jorge and a park guard stood watching it all, sharing a cigarette.

The sudden roar of a howler monkey, eerie in the grey light

before dawn, cut off all the gringo noise. We listened to the slow, disturbed cry coming from the trees somewhere beneath us. We strained to see into the dense vegetation, but the roars were diminishing, moving away from us.

Then, abruptly, day broke without sunrise, the enigmatic horizon grey and misted. Here in the tropics daylight just happened, darkness surrendering all at once to a milky light. The anticlimactic sunrise caught the worshippers off guard. The music, chanting and prayers had ceased; the spirituality we had been seeking was denied us. We stared eastward toward the murky dawn, finally realising that nothing spectacular would happen.

On the walk back to the hotel, I pondered the lessons of Tikal. As one of the more established and more frequently visited sites on the Ruta Maya, it was the model for the government planners and officials who hoped to turn the scheme into a reality. But there was much in the Tikal experience to concern them: the destructive effect of roads, the difficulty of meeting tourist demands for comfort without constructing the environmentally damaging infrastructure that those demands required, controlling the impact made by tourists on protected wildlife. But at least the national park had succeeded in preserving 575 square kilometres of rainforest, and the very existence of these trees demonstrated the success of the preservation efforts. What I'd found here in the park was certainly better than what I'd seen along the road coming from the airport.

We retraced our steps to the Great Plaza and turned down the long causeway leading to the hotel area. An enchanting green light filtered through the dripping canopy, and the loud songs of the birds and tree frogs silenced my thoughts. Just then, a branch above us cracked; we heard the rustle of leaves, some crashing, and suddenly a thud right in our midst. Someone stifled a scream. We turned, startled, then hurriedly scrambled back: a snake had fallen from the branches overhead. Before we could move, the guide dashed forward, waving his machete, and brought down the blade onto the stunned reptile, cutting its body in two.

For several seconds, everyone stood motionless, too stunned to react. Then, slowly, we came back to life – nervous giggles, cautious approaches, exclamations of amazement. The guide was congratulated, photos were taken – each tourist wanted a picture of themselves crouching over the dead snake and another of the guide poking it with the machete. It was, everyone agreed, an incredible occurrence, the highlight of the day. Back at the lodge the snake was the talk of breakfast, and excited descriptions and pantomimes were provided for those unlucky not to have witnessed it. No one mentioned, if anyone even knew, that the snake was a tree boa – quite harmless to humans.

CHAPTER 15

Worlds apart

B ACK in Guatemala City, I visited Rodrigo, a Maya from the highlands of Quiché who for several years had operated a small but successful clothing factory in Guatemala City. I first met him in 1988, when by chance we sat next to each other on a flight from Guatemala to Houston. Rodrigo got his start in business in the mid-1980s, when the civil war in the highlands had been at its most intense. Many other young Quiché his age had joined the guerrillas out of desperation and despair, but Rodrigo had gone instead to the capital, hoping to attend classes at the university. Penniless, he had been forced to take work in a potato chip factory on the outskirts of the capital, and never got the chance to study. He lived in a shanty town, with ten other people from his village crammed together in one shack.

A born businessman, Rodrigo recognised an opportunity and knew how to take advantage of it. Handicrafts from the Quiché region were very popular with tourists, but Rodrigo had noticed that they were hard to come by with the highlands engulfed in conflict. Tourist shops in the Guatemala City market had resorted to selling poor imitations of Quiché clothing made by non-Indians. Rodrigo knew many Quiché women who were unemployed and living in his own section of the shanty town. Under his guidance, the Quiché families pooled their resources and bought some materials. Before long, Rodrigo was selling their products to the shops downtown.

Over the years, Rodrigo had saved money, bought some old

sewing machines and opened a small shirt factory. As his business grew, he'd bought better equipment and eventually moved into a larger space near the university. By the time I first met him, the business was thriving. He had brand-new equipment and ten employees – all young Quiché who worked part of the day and took courses at the university. With his partner, María, he designed clothing that would appeal to young Americans, and he began to travel to the United States to sell his line to US stores. On that first meeting he'd been on his way to Austin, Texas, to close a deal with a store that sold his clothing to college students. Since then, he had achieved some renown as an expert on Mayan weaving, and at the invitation of the Smithsonian Institute had visited Washington D.C. to participate in a 'Traditional Arts' conference.

Now, at his factory (actually a small concrete house with sewing machines set up in the different rooms), Rodrigo greeted me warmly and gave me a quick tour to show off his latest acquisition: computerised weaving machines. He showed me his recent creations, including woollen winter coats which, he told me with pride, were selling very well in New York.

The young students in his employ were polite and softly spoken in the Quiché manner, and eager to talk about their experiences at the university. Just ten years before there hadn't been many Indian students, and those few had not been treated well.

'Now there are changes,' one young man told me. 'First there are changes in our people. Many more of us think of leaving our villages and coming to the capital to study. Some even go to the United States. There are changes in Guatemala, too. I think now more people accept that the Maya are part of this country, part of its present and future, not just the past. For example, the politicians must go to the villages during their campaigns now. They know we vote and they need our vote. We are not ignorant Indians any more.'

'Imagine,' Rodrigo added. 'Once we were not even considered people. Now we are citizens. Once we were abused for speaking our languages. Now look – here are newspapers printed in Quiché and Cakchiquel.'

Why these sudden changes? I asked. After all, the Maya had long been subjected to horrible persecution. Many outside observers used the word genocide to describe the policies of the Guatemalan government and military during the 1970s and 1980s. Was it possible for practitioners of genocide to change so markedly in such a short period of time? What had happened?

'The most important thing,' Rodrigo explained, 'was the Nobel Prize. There was a political awakening. The year 1992 was very important – first for the anti-Columbus marches and demonstrations that brought together native peoples from all over the Americas, and second for the Nobel Prize. After that, the politicians could not ignore us any more.'

Rodrigo was referring to the Nobel Peace Prize awarded to Rigoberta Menchú, the Quiché Mayan woman who had gone from picking coffee and working as a maid to leading solidarity movements. Her tragic and horror-filled story, told when she was twenty-three to an anthropologist, had been translated and read world-wide. In exile in Mexico, she had represented the Maya by alerting the developed world to the Guatemalan government's bloody campaign against her people. Many in her audience had recognised that she shared certain qualities with Martin Luther King, Gandhi and Nelson Mandela.

Meanwhile, in her homeland, she was reviled by the ruling elite; she would be a dead woman if she ever returned. All that changed in 1992 with the announcement of the Peace Prize. The Guatemalan oligarchy was truly stunned that an 'ignorant Indian', a maid, should have won such a prestigious award. But by virtue of that prestige, the elite were forced to recognise her. No longer could she be threatened with death: she had risen above her persecutors.

Rodrigo and his student workers told me that an incredible surge in pride amongst the Maya had followed the award. They wore their indigenous clothing to the university now. They studied the different Mayan languages (twenty-two of them in

Guatemala alone) and wrote in them. They were organising political groups. In short, the Maya had risen up with all the fortitude
of a people who for 500 years had resisted – and survived – the
worst possible oppression. Rigoberta Menchú's Peace Prize had
been the catalyst.

Their optimism impressed me, but I couldn't help being a little sceptical. I had spent too much time among Guatemala's elite,
listening to their racist talk, to believe that this small but powerful minority had changed overnight. The 500-year history of
oppression had continued despite changes of government, peace
accords or even Nobel prizes. Still, it was encouraging that these
young Maya felt optimistic and empowered. That in itself was a
significant change.

Knowing of my interest in Mayan culture, Rodrigo offered to
take me out to the government crafts market near the airport,
where INGUAT – the government tourism ministry – was spon-
soring an exhibition of traditional weaving. The next morning, we
took a bus out to the exhibition. It had been seven years since I'd
last visited Guatemala City, and now, riding through town, I was
completely at a loss. I could hardly recognise anything, the city
had changed so much in those seven years. The one-way streets
headed in the opposite direction from how I remembered; new
flyovers and bridges sent widened boulevards careening off to
city zones that hadn't existed when I lived in the capital; towering glass structures straddled earthquake faults; and shiny,
American fast-food places cluttered the business districts.

Like ghosts, the indigenous Guatemalans, dressed in their traditional clothing, waited in bus queues and hawked fruit at inter-
sections and scampered along sidewalks and across boulevards
hauling huge burdens on their bent backs. Their impoverished
presence on the fringe of things seemed the only constant in a
transformed city.

We passed near the neighbourhood where I used to live. It had
then been an area of fields dotted with Mayan mounds; now the
fields were gone, the mounds buried under the pavement of vast
parking lots. Malls had gone up, huge California-style complexes

stocked with the latest gadgets and styles from the first world, all exorbitantly priced.

Rodrigo pointed to a gleaming glass structure rising several storeys above everything else, its name emblazoned in lights: TIKAL FUTURO.

'What do you think of that?' I asked.

He smiled: 'You have experienced enough in this country to know that Guatemalans love the Maya of the past. Those are the good Maya. The living Maya today are not believed to be so good.'

'The only good Indian is a dead one,' I said. 'That is something we used to say in my country.'

'Well, in Guatemala they still think it. They steal the names and images of our ancestors, but they don't want to have anything to do with the descendants. Except of course for the purpose of tourism.'

The weaving exhibition turned out to be an illustration of Rodrigo's point. In a grassy area outside the government tourist market, women from different highlands villages were demonstrating the use of the belt loom, a 2000-year-old method of weaving that was still a fundamental part of Mayan culture. The loom was portable and could be used almost anywhere. In this case, one end of the loom was fastened to a tree, while the other was attached to a belt that the kneeling weaver passed behind her back. In this kneeling position, the weaver employed eleven different weaving techniques to create the intricate designs for which the Maya are renowned.

We walked around the park, stopping at different stations to learn about the spinning, dyeing and warping of wool. The women, dressed in their finest *traje* – the traditional clothing of their village – were completely absorbed in their work, all but ignoring the crowds passing by, even when a tourist stepped up close for a photograph. Some of their seeming aloofness was due to the presence of young INGUAT representatives who stood in front of each demonstration and explained what was going on to anyone who stopped to observe. The Mayan women were not given the opportunity to speak for themselves; they were the displays in this museum of the Maya, and the INGUAT representatives, dressed in dark blue suits, were the interpreters. No doubt the INGUAT reps were simply being zealous in their interpretive roles, and I was sure they weren't intentionally silencing the Mayan women; but when, for the third time, a blue suit interrupted with an answer to a question addressed to one of the indigenous women, I became annoyed at their facile intrusions.

Finally, we came across a display that INGUAT had left momentarily unguarded. A Mayan woman in a red blouse and blue skirt knelt beside a mat upon which numerous distinctive *huipiles* were arranged. The *huipil*, or over-blouse, is the most important article of women's clothing for the Maya. Months of work go into weaving the intricate designs that make each *huipil* as unique as a snowflake. Certain patterns and motifs are used by all the women in a given village, but each weaver signs her work with her own idiosyncratic touches.

I asked the woman where these *huipiles* came from. She named the villages – San Marcos, San Juan Cotzal, Nebaj, Nahualá, Zunil, Totonicapan. Then I asked her what the symbols represented. She pointed to bees, deer, flowers, vultures, hummingbirds, turkeys, two-headed eagles, monkeys, stars, diamonds. An astonishing repertoire danced across each *huipil*, a dance of symbols that encoded stories of the village, the family and the weaver herself. Each *huipil* recorded a history; for the Maya, textiles have become texts.

The woman politely explained each detail, and called my attention to the beauty of the designs. *'Mire qué bonito el pájaro,'* she said in the lilting Spanish spoken by the Maya. See how pretty is this bird. But our conversation was soon interrupted by the return of the INGUAT representative, who arrived just as the weaver was showing me a *huipil* from her own village. 'That is the *huipil* from Patzicía,' the INGUAT girl chimed in. 'Look at all the decorations. Can you imagine how long it would take to make one of these?'

As we walked back to the bus stop, Rodrigo asked me if I liked the exhibition. To be polite, I said yes, but after a few moments of silence, I added that I hadn't cared for the presence of the INGUAT chaperones.

'Ah,' Rodrigo nodded. 'Exactly. You remember what you asked me about the Ruta Maya? Well, this is the problem, right here. The Maya don't have the control. But yes, the government has it. Yes, INGUAT has it. Yes, foreigners have it. Well, then, tell me – for whose good is it?'

❂

The next day, I had arranged to visit my former landlady and colleague at the university. She had invited me over to meet the ladies of a club she belonged to, today being their monthly meeting. Ingrid lived in Zone 13, near the airport and just off Avenida de las Américas, where several American fast-food restaurants served as upscale hang-outs for the children of the elite. She lived on a quiet street lined with large homes. An armed guard stood on the corner, and Ingrid's house hid behind a high concrete wall trimmed with razor wire. As on every wall in the capital, broken glass had been embedded in the top, the jagged edges designed to thwart thieves. Talking into a speaker on the gate, I identified myself to someone in the house, and shortly afterwards a young Indian teenager wearing the *traje* of her village came out to unlock the gate, her plastic sandals slapping on the asphalt drive. Two strutting Doberman pinschers followed her, and when I passed through the gate they darted up to sniff me, while the girl slapped at them and giggled.

The maid led me through the house. There was a room full of antique furniture and another where a table was laden with pastries and fruit. She took me to a pleasant sun-room, where Ingrid was sitting with three of her fellow club members. Ingrid greeted me flamboyantly, kissing me on the cheek – it seemed we were now old friends – and leading me by the hand into the room for introductions.

There followed the usual exchange of names and pleasantries – all amidst a swirl of silk and rayon, powdered faces, peroxided hair, perfumed cleavages. High heels clacked on marble tiles; jewellery clinked and glittered; a caged parrot added to the clatter. The maid came in with glasses of chilled Chilean wine, served to exclamations of delight. And just when we'd settled into our chairs, four more guests arrived and we went through the whole ritual again.

When all the members of the ladies club were present at last, the meeting was called to order. Under discussion: the club's annual fundraiser for charity. This year, the ladies were planning to donate spectacles to orphaned Indian children. To raise the necessary money, the ladies had decided to hold a fashion show – with their daughters as models – to which they would charge admission.

'Oh, what an emotional night it will be,' a woman who was dressed from head to foot in silk said to me. 'I hope you will be there to see our darlings.'

During the discussion, the Indian maid distributed fruit, cake and coffee. My eyes were drawn to the garden that lay just outside the sun-room. It fairly glowed with brilliant flowers and shrubs: prolific purple and red bougainvillea, shimmering green banana fronds, a three-metre-high poinsettia. A macaw sat in a large white cage gnawing and flinging the fruit the maid had brought it in a silver bowl. A grizzled Indian in a straw hat squatted on the lawn and scythed the grass with a machete. A few blocks beyond the yard's concrete wall, a tall glass office building reflected the thunderheads of an approaching rainy-season storm. I heard the grumbling of thunder.

The walls of the sun-room were hung with paintings of Indian women wearing the *traje* of their villages. The outfits were stunning – vibrant and brilliantly detailed. But the faces of the subjects were missing: in their stead, the artist had substituted dark brown ovals to support the swirling colours of brocaded headdresses.

The woman in silk persisted, trying to exact from me a promise to attend the fashion show. 'You might find a girl you like,' she said salaciously.

In fact, I had already been to a similar fashion show, years ago when I lived in the capital, held at the Guatemalan–American School. On that occasion, the girls had dressed in slinky night-gowns and low-cut dresses and miniskirts and bathing suits to parade before fathers and brothers who'd whistled and stamped and howled with delight. I had no interest in sitting through another spectacle such as that, especially one staged for the benefit of children orphaned in Army massacres.

With the conclusion of the meeting's business came another round of coffee and cake. An elegant woman in a leopard-print jacket asked me what I liked about Guatemala City. I kept my answer simple: the museums, I told her, shopping in the artisans' market.

'Oh, be careful when you go downtown,' she warned, touching my hand. 'Many thieves. And be sure to bargain in the market. Those *inditos*, the little Indians, they will trick you and over-charge you. Go with a Guatemalan, someone who knows their tricks.'

Just then, the skies opened up and the rain came pounding down, drumming on the roof and splattering the garden where the gardener pressed himself against the wall of the little concrete shed that served as the maid's quarters. Suddenly, Ingrid cried out and the maid came running into the room. Ingrid was pointing outside. 'Oh, María, how could you be so stupid? Poor Oscar!'

Immediately, María ran outside to the white cage; the gardener came dashing over, and together they scooted the cage to the door and into the room. The bird squawked and ruffled itself dry while Ingrid made kissing sounds and spoke to it in a baby voice. 'Ah, poor birdie, poor little birdie,' cooed the ladies. The maid brought a mop to clean up the water dripping off the cage.

'María, it doesn't do any good to mop when you are soaking wet yourself,' said Ingrid angrily. 'Look at the water dripping off you. Now go change your clothes. You're embarrassing me. And make some more coffee – with this rain, it has become chilly in here.'

Hours later – after endless cups of coffee and servings of

sweets, after gossip and rumours and speculation about the president's relationship with a female minister, after discussion of shopping trips to Miami and bank accounts in the Bahamas and *quinceañera* parties to celebrate the fifteenth birthdays of the daughters of club members – I stood at the door, brushing my cheek against Ingrid's. She held my hand, and told me how glad she was that I'd taken the time to visit her.

I passed through the wire-topped gate and into the flooded street, where the armed guard continued to patrol the neighbourhood, rifle at the ready. Half a block ahead of me, a maid swished along in her polychromatic skirt, a basket of tortillas balanced on her head, the guard watching her every movement. When she passed a gate – a gate she must have passed every day as she went about her chores – a large dog was sent into a frenzy of snarling and barking. Thirty seconds later, when I passed the same gate, a total stranger, the dog looked at me, sniffed the air, then wagged its tail. In Guatemala, even the dogs held prejudices.

CHAPTER 16

The Mayan movement

THROUGH a friend at the university, I had arranged interviews with two representatives of Mayan organisations in Antigua Guatemala, the old capital, located about fifty kilometres from Guatemala City – an easy drive along a smooth four-lane highway. Because I had taken the direct route to Antigua many, many times, I decided to follow a more roundabout course, descending southward out of the capital toward the Pacific Ocean, then doubling back north at a small market town called Palín. It was at least twice the distance of the main road, but I wanted to see the famous silk-cotton tree in Palín. Besides, the longer route, as is so often the case, was the more scenic; it was also, as I should have known by now, the more uncertain.

The road dropped immediately as the bus left the capital, 300 metres in twenty kilometres, following a series of switchbacks and sharp turns. Near Lake Amatitlán, the road levelled out for a few kilometres, and the bus raced along past fields of steaming hot springs. Agua's perfect volcanic cone towered to our right; on the left, the irregular summit of Pacaya sent up a plume of ash. The little town of Palín sat in the shadow of the two volcanoes. Just outside the town, the highway began its final precipitous drop toward the coastal plain, losing 800 metres in thirty kilometres. Situated halfway between the coast and the sierra, Palín was the meeting place for farmers from the highlands and tropical lowlands. Everything from apples to sugarcane was for sale.

Guatemala's markets are famously picturesque, and Palín's is held to be one of the best. At its centre stands a giant silk-cotton or *ceiba* tree, sacred to the Maya. In Mayan cosmology, the *ceiba* is the 'World Tree', the axis of the world and centre of the sky. The trees provide paths of communication between the temporal and the eternal worlds. I'd come across the image of the *ceiba* as World Tree everywhere in the Mundo Maya: carved in the stelae of Copán, painted on pots in the archaeological museums, woven into the elaborate designs on *huipiles* that the women still wear today. They are indeed unusual trees, spreading their branches very broadly, their trunks studded with spikes, and only rarely blossoming – sometimes only once in a decade.

The specimen in Palín plaza spread its lush and massive boughs over the crowded market scene. Squatting vendors took up every available space within its shade, some sitting on the huge roots that buttressed the distinctive bulging trunk. I walked around the market, taking an informal inventory of the goods for sale. As was usual in Indian markets, vendors of like products congregated in the same area; despite the immediate presence of their competitors, they sat passively awaiting sales. Almost no one called out offers to passers-by, and if a shopper stopped to barter, neighbouring vendors never undercut an agreed-upon price. It was almost as if the traders belonged to a guild or cartel – an interesting dynamic, given that the abundance of competition should, according to the principles of market capitalism, have worked against the vendors.

I passed through the spice and herb section, where chillies, cinnamon, annatto, cardamom, oregano, marjoram, *epazote* leaves, cacao and cilantro were carefully displayed in burlap sacks, their rims neatly rolled down to form thick rings. A chaos of scents filled the air. Nearby, kneeling women sold packets of incense, holy *pom* and *copal*, ready for burning before altars in the church.

Leaving the spices behind, I passed into the bread section to peruse wide, blanket-lined baskets chock-full of loaves. Next came the flower section, with its colourful arrangements. Then vegetables and fruits, also carefully and aesthetically arranged in piles and bunches: corn, beans, cabbages, carrots, onions, tomatoes, breadfruit, melons, plums, bananas, mangoes, papayas. I had to ask the women for the names of unfamiliar produce: *anona, cassava, chayote, tomatillo, huicoy, nance, pacaya.* '*Pruébelo, joven,*' the women called out to me, their hair decorated with ribbons coiled like bright red snakes. Give it a try, youngster.

The dry-goods stalls sold yarn, thread, pottery, plastic jugs, cookware, utensils, watches, straw hats, shoes, radios, cassettes, toys. These were some of the most crowded stalls. Near the outskirts of the market, I found stacks of rickety furniture, and further off still I came upon the meat market, where the animals, both alive and butchered, created a congress of stinks.

After making several circuits of the market, I stopped on the steps of the church for a final view of the plaza. Looking over the scene, it seemed to me that the concept of a World Tree, with the *ceiba* standing at the centre of the earth, made sense. Here in Palín, on market day, it looked as though all the world – the people who lived on it, the bounty it produced – was pushing toward the centre, gravitating toward this colossal, awe-inspiring tree. The *ceiba* itself seemed to extend its branches to encompass it all, gathering everything together under its canopy.

❁

As I made my way around the market, I asked for information about travelling directly to Antigua from Palín. I got several conflicting reports on just when a bus might leave for Antigua, or even whether such a bus existed. Some people told me I'd have to go back to the capital; others told me to just start walking, that eventually a bus or truck would come along that I could try to flag down. Finally, someone pointed out a man from Antigua who supposedly had a taxi and might be willing to give me a ride.

'Sure,' the driver agreed when I approached him with my request. 'Just help me with these coconuts.'

The driver, Jorge, had come to Palín to buy fruit from the Pacific coast, tropical fruit being much cheaper here than in Antigua. Now and then Jorge made a little money by driving to

Palín, buying a load of fruit and hauling it back to the market in Antigua, where his relations had a stall. The car was a 1970s model Dodge, many times repainted, most recently in a luminous lime green. And indeed the word 'Taxi' had been painted on both sides in banana yellow (alongside the silver silhouette of a reclining, volcano-breasted woman). Loaded down with a multi-coloured mix of produce, the Dodge looked like a float in a fruit parade.

I helped Jorge carry several dozen coconuts, which we stuck into whatever space remained in the car. The back seat was crammed with pineapples, plantains, oranges and coconuts; the trunk was full of sugarcane. Jorge had made such a good deal on the coconuts that he wanted to squeeze in as many as he could. Unfortunately, I was now taking up space in the passenger seat, space that could have held still more coconuts, so he asked me to hold a few of them for him. He brought some over, and passed them to me through the window; I arranged the coconuts on the floor around my feet. He brought more, and I filled in the spaces on either side of me. He brought more, and I wedged them on the dash against the windshield. He brought more, and still more. By the time we got started, I had a dozen coconuts balanced on my lap, their fibrous husks scratching my belly and thighs.

With the car finally full of fruit, Jorge climbed in through the window – the driver's door didn't open – and took out a pack of cigarettes. He was about to light up when he paused.

'You're not *evangélico*?'

'No. Catholic,' I replied.

Relieved, Jorge lit the cigarette. 'Too many goddamn evangelical missionaries in Guatemala,' he said. 'And too many of their goddamn rules – no drinking, no smoking, no women. That's why I'm a devout Catholic.'

He pointed to a little statue of the Virgin on the dash – a coconut had knocked her slightly askew – and crossed himself. Before I could discuss the religious issue further, Jorge started the car. The lime green fruitmobile had no muffler, and our conversation came to a hasty end.

Under the close observation of the market crowd, Jorge back-fired us around the dusty parking lot – people jumping out of our path – and we turned tail on Palín, getting in a few parting shots, the explosions causing the chassis to shudder as we roared off. Jorge gunned it and the car bounded off the choppy pavement and onto the choppier dirt track that would, God willing, take us to Antigua. After a kilometre, I realised that the fruitmobile seemed to lack not only a muffler but also an entire exhaust system. The smell of gasoline invaded the car, an odour that competed with the dust pouring in the windows, Jorge's cigarette smoke and the tropical fruit market we were hauling.

Muffler or no, Jorge tried to carry on the conversation by shouting at me. I had no idea what he was saying, but I nodded anyway and shouted back, '*Sí . . . sí . . . sí.*' Periodically, he waved with his cigarette at something in the landscape, and I was left to wonder what he'd wanted me to see. A cornfield? An Indian hoe-ing? Cows? A wall made of lava rock?

We were skirting the slopes of Agua, but clouds obscured the cone. In fact, the skies had darkened considerably with the usual afternoon thunderheads, and I worried that a rainstorm would force us to roll up the windows, thus trapping the noxious fumes inside the car. I would much rather have gone on breathing road dust.

But I had a more immediate problem: shifting fruit. With each bump in the road, the rattling chassis produced subtle and not-so-subtle shifts in the arrangement of the coconuts on my lap. I could feel bruises growing on my thighs, chafe marks on my skin. Worst of all, the mutant nuts were squishing mine and sending shooting pains through my groin.

And then the storm clouds broke. My earlier fears about trapped fumes proved unwarranted: the fruitmobile's windows didn't roll up. The windshield wipers didn't work, either. Jorge slowed to a crawl on the inundated track, the hard rain pelting me through the open window and turning the layer of dust I wore to mud.

Just when I was wondering if we would ever reach Antigua, we crossed from cattle pasture into the shaded coffee plantations that surrounded the old capital. Then it was Antigua's cobblestoned streets, the muddy bus stop at the rear of the market, and a lurching, backfiring halt next to the market's redolent middens. When we finally extricated ourselves from the fruitmobile – several coconuts falling into a puddle when I shook open the door – Jorge hit me for gas money.

'*Muy cara la gasolina,*' he explained soberly. Very expensive. I gave him a blue note, twenty *quetzales*, which must have been good enough because Jorge pumped my hand and told me to give him a call if I needed a taxi for sightseeing. He handed me his card. '*Servicios Turísticos,*' the card read. 'Jorge Godoy . . . *Guía Oficial.*'

❂

Jorge was certainly not the only Antigueño trying to cash in on the tourism business. The colonial capital of Guatemala had become one of the most popular tourist sites along the Ruta Maya, and it was easy to see why: cobblestoned streets, colonial Spanish buildings (some still in ruined heaps from an earthquake over 200 years ago), Indian handicrafts at bargain prices and stunning volcanoes towering over it all. To use guidebook prose, the place was quaint and picturesque to the core.

In fact, Antigua was one of the hubs on the Ruta. Centrally located, with all the tourist amenities at hand, it was the favoured base for tourists visiting Guatemala's highlands. Over the years, foreigners had bought up much of the property, starting businesses that catered to other foreigners, and in the process introducing a whole new social order. Property costs were comparable to San Francisco, one of the most expensive cities in the States. Antigua had thus become an enclave for foreigners, a tourist town full of language schools, yoghurt shops and expensive restaurants serving *haute cuisine*.

This time, however, I had not come to Antigua to participate in the tourist carnival. I was stopping only for my prearranged meetings with the Mayan activists, who I hoped would give me a

Mayan perspective on this concept of a tourist trail across Mayan lands.

I spoke first with Solomon Alvarez, the author of a memoir about growing up as a Maya in a society dominated by the elite and Westernised Maya, or *ladinos*. Solomon Alvarez was the first Maya I'd met who could be called, in the Western sense, an 'intellectual'. A university graduate and now a professor at a private university in the capital, he was one of a growing number of Maya who had received a Western-style education but who maintained a distinctly Mayan outlook. These Mayan scholars, working in the US and in Guatemala, were actively promoting Mayan ethnic resurgence and empowerment. I met him at a small research library housed in a beautiful colonial mansion with a courtyard and fountain at its centre.

Solomon Alvarez was eager to talk about the Movimiento Maya, a movement that was attempting to unite the different Mayan groups to construct a pan-Mayan ideology, 'built of Mayan values from the ancestors'.

Solomon argued that a unified ideology was necessary because of the widespread misunderstanding of the Maya. To illustrate, he discussed the interpretation of a carved figure found at the Mexican site of Palenque, a reclining figure apparently gazing at the stars and apparently helmeted. In the popular imagination, this figure was called 'the Astronaut', an interpretation, Solomon Alvarez told me, that allows outsiders to detract from the accomplishments of the Maya. It was too hard for some people to believe that a 'primitive' people like the Maya constructed such amazing things, so they chose to believe that extraterrestrials were responsible.

In Guatemala, Solomon continued, misinterpretations like this were even more insidious, because they supported the notion that the Maya disappeared a thousand years ago. And that was precisely what the government and *ladinos* preferred to think – that the Maya did not exist today as a viable cultural group. 'But we do exist and now we are talking. Before we could only listen in silence. That is what the Movimiento Maya is all about – raising our voices and recovering our ideology from all the misinterpretations.'

It was interesting that Solomon spoke of raising voices, because, like most of the Maya I had met, he had a serene, contemplative demeanour – very different from the stereotype of the sullen Indian – and he spoke a clear, lucid Spanish. He was polite and insightful, but without the brashness and egotism common among Western scholars.

As for the Ruta Maya concept, Solomon Alvarez thought it could be successful if tourists learned who the Maya *really* were, instead of falling for ancient astronaut legends and Mayan prophecy frauds. Of course, the concept was not acceptable if it led to further exploitation: the Maya had to participate in the decision-making. They already knew from previous experience that tourism wasn't necessarily a good thing for the Maya.

The hour planned for the interview passed much too quickly. I still had questions I would have liked to have asked him, but Solomon had to leave for his classes in the capital. We agreed to meet the next evening at a restaurant in Antigua.

❂

My second interview was with Josefina González, a young anthropology student and a member of a group of Mayan women who have professional careers.

Are there many professional women among the Maya? I asked.

'Very few. But all the time there are more.'

Josefina told me that Mayan women in particular have had a hard time overcoming the stereotypes, prevalent among Guatemala's European population, of the stupid, lazy, dirty Indian. For her, the problem had been compounded because she continued to wear her *traje*.

Outside Guatemala, she observed, Mayan weaving was world famous and was often used to signify the beauty and artistry of the country; Miss Guatemala, for example, was often dressed in stylised *traje*. But in Guatemala itself, those who wore *traje* were subject to abuse because, as Josefina González explained, the assumption was made that only uneducated, ignorant Indians clung to traditional culture. Historically, an Indian who managed to get an education had by definition become Westernised. Inside Guatemala, therefore, *traje* signified backwardness and ignorance.

Josefina González had experienced this prejudice her whole life. When she wore her *traje*, she was sworn at, pushed, given orders, ignored in stores and generally subjected to abuse that was both subtle and direct. But when she put on jeans and high heels, she was treated with more respect. She told me that the majority of Mayan women, including those going to university, still wore their *traje* in spite of the abuses. This trend was part of a new phenomenon in Guatemala – Maya who studied and became professionals were choosing to stay culturally Mayan. 'The Movimiento Maya is trying to reclaim ancestral Mayan teachings,' Josefina González emphasised. 'Rather than becoming "ladinized", educated Maya are becoming more Mayan.'

Antigua was a prime example of what anthropologists call 'a contact zone' – a place where a dominant culture and an indigenous subculture come into contact. As a contact zone, Antigua was also a hot spot for cultural tourism. This term, like 'ecotourism', had won currency of late as a label for new types of tourism that were supposed to create meaningful cross-cultural encounters and thereby promote awareness among tourists, while providing sources of income for indigenous people. Was this happening in Antigua? I wanted to know.

Josefina didn't know what the tourists gained from the encounter, but for the Maya, especially the Mayan women, the tourist trade was a mixed blessing. 'Yes, the women can earn some money for their work, and this money helps supplement the family income. And for the widows of the violence, maybe selling to the tourists is the only income. But at the same time the relationship is not equal. There are too many vendors. The buyers control the transaction.'

What Josefina said was true. The glut in supply was very much in evidence as I walked around Antigua. Everywhere I saw Mayan women holding piles of hand-woven shirts, trailing after tourists. They held up samples of their wares, but most of the time the tourists brushed past them, only occasionally deigning to look, and then warily, as though suspecting a scam. Even little girls carried bundles of clothing for sale. The prices were ridiculously low, given the amount of work that went into producing the articles. Every tourist who bothered to think about the matter was thus faced with a quandary: were you contributing to exploitation when you bought at the going rate? I asked Josefina for her view.

'You mean that you as the tourist feel guilty because you pay so little. So it is.'

'All right. Let's say a well-meaning tourist wants to buy a nice example of *traje*, but he wants the artisan to get a fair deal. What can the tourist do? Are the cooperatives an option?'

'I think that maybe the cooperatives are good, but not always so good. Many are the operations of the government and evangelical churches and foreign organisations like the Peace Corps. They have the interests of the women in mind, but outsiders are still in control. There is a cooperative very close. Do you want to see?'

We walked down the cobblestoned street, across the plaza and up another street to the cooperative store. The owner, Josefina told me, was from France. For nearly an hour, we strolled through the store while she drew my attention to the distinctive patterns the different villages gave to their weaving. The sophistication was impressive: each article required months of physically painful work on a backstrap loom, the weaver kneeling on the ground for hours at a time. The prices, I noted, were much higher than elsewhere in town.

'But who gets the money?' I asked Josefina. 'Does the owner really give the artisan a fair share?'

'Good question,' said Josefina. 'Here, I want to show you something.'

She led me to a display of framed photographs, the work of the cooperative's owner. They were beautiful portraits of the weavers at work.

'Very nice,' I remarked.

'Yes, but look at the price. You see? Perhaps the owner gives these women more of the profits, but still he values his own work more than theirs. He charges more for a picture of the women at work than he does for what the women produce. So now I ask: What is a fair price?'

❂

A cold drizzle was falling when I met Solomon Alvarez for dinner. The clouds were low and dense, sealing off the valley and obscuring the volcanoes. Our table by the window gave us a good view of the passing foot traffic. American college students in tight, boisterous clusters of four and five clumped down the sidewalks, the thudding of their hiking boots echoing off the old colonial walls. When one cluster met up with another, they paused to compare notes on restaurants and events around town. It was evident from their appearance that the fashionable traveller had to wear some article of Mayan clothing – a shirt, a blouse, a belt, a dress. But when vendors of the articles approached, the tourists ignored them and continued to discuss the latest scoop. Perhaps a hike up one of the volcanoes was being organised, or a mountain-bike tour out to one of the Indian villages.

The young Americans typically moved in groups. Young Europeans, in contrast, walked alone or in pairs. Dressed head to foot in Mayan-made clothing, they carried enormous backpacks that forced other pedestrians off the sidewalks and into the streets. While the Americans relied on hot tips from other travellers, the Europeans all seemed to carry thick, well-thumbed guidebooks, which they consulted periodically as they wandered the streets in search of rock-bottom meals and accommodation.

Solomon ordered a local speciality for us and while we waited for the food to arrive, I asked him what he thought of the peace accords that had recently been signed by the government and the guerrillas. The accords were supposed to have put an end to Central America's longest civil war, a war that had devastated the highlands for thirty-five years and left at least 150,000 people dead. The accords called for the UN to monitor respect for human rights in Guatemala; for radical reforms to limit the functions of the Army; and for the practical, not just theoretical, recognition of the rights of Guatemala's indigenous majority (sixty per cent of the population) in the educational, judicial and political systems.

Solomon was of the opinion that the accords sounded good, but that right now 'peace was still just a concept on paper'. And there were flaws. The accords did not provide for the punishment of war-related crimes committed during the civil war; in fact, the accords gave amnesty to those guilty of such crimes. Because of this impunity, the peace was hollow and would perhaps be short-lived.

But beyond the amnesty question, Solomon felt that the accords had other serious shortcomings. For one thing, while the accords acknowledged that poverty was a serious problem in Guatemala – the country had one of the highest poverty rates in Latin America – they did not address issues of land reform and the lack of employment. These problems had contributed to the origin and perpetuation of the civil war in the first place. The accords offered hope in that they had been signed at all, but whether the signatories were seriously committed to the high-minded words was another matter.

If the peace held, I suggested, then tourism, which was already substantial in Guatemala, would most likely increase. What effect, I wanted to know, would efforts to promote the Ruta Maya have on the Maya themselves?

'First you need to understand our history since the conquest,' Solomon told me. 'For five centuries we have suffered the loss of our lands. Poverty has forced some Maya to migrate to the coffee, sugar and banana plantations in search of work.'

The civil war, which had divided Mayan communities and destroyed entire villages, forced many Indians into exile, Solomon went on to explain; others were driven into the concentration camps that the Army called 'model villages'. In some places, corn, the very substance of life in Mayan religion, had lost

197

out to export crops, heavily promoted by the US Agency for International Development. Finally, many young Indians had gone to work in factories that had been set up in the highlands to take advantage of inexpensive labour; these young Maya were learning values quite different from those of their heritage. All of these factors had affected the relationship the Maya had with their world.

'Now, the biggest problem with the concept of the Ruta Maya is that the Maya and the outsiders interested in its development have very different attitudes toward the land. In the first world, land is property and wealth is acquired by developing the land. For the Maya, however, land is sacred. You cannot develop the land. You cannot exploit it for the creation of wealth. The culture that does this, in the Mayan view, cannot survive. *Bueno*, perhaps the promoters of the Ruta do not mean to exploit. But even positive development has serious consequences. You have to understand that development is not equal, because the money for the development comes from the outside. You can already see the result in Antigua. Here, the profits do not go to the Maya. *Ladinos* and foreigners are the owners, while the Maya supply the labour.'

Given outside ownership of the tourism infrastructure, and given the resulting imbalance in capital transfer, Solomon argued that the Ruta Maya promoted in the Maya an external orientation (such as producing handicrafts for sale to foreigners rather than solely for domestic use) that had significant consequences in social relations and cultural production. These consequences were already apparent along the Ruta Maya in places like Panajachel and Antigua, where the Maya were left with trickle-down jobs and low incomes, while the profits went to foreigners.

To illustrate the point, he reminded me that the waiters in the restaurant were Indians dressed up in stylised Mayan costumes. 'Like clowns,' Solomon said bitterly. 'It is a travesty of our culture, all for the benefit of tourists.

'What I believe is this,' he concluded. 'The benefits that promoters of the concept see in the Ruta are not always benefits from the Mayan point of view. The Ruta is the product of Western thinking, and the Western way has not always been so good for indigenous culture.'

In the courtyard of the hotel across the street, a marimba band dressed in Mayan uniform was hard at it, playing show tunes familiar to the restaurant's clientele – an older and wealthier class of tourists visiting Guatemala on an all-inclusive tour. Outside the restaurant, a shrivelled old woman hunched over two sorry-looking pomegranates she had displayed on a scrap of newspaper. Abruptly, the evening's drizzle turned to a hard rain, and the American kids hurriedly donned their forest green and burgundy rain gear. The pomegranate vendor pressed herself up against the window of the restaurant, a pane of glass separating us from her. Her long grey hair hung in tangles, caught up in the ragged shawl she had wrapped around her shoulders. She was so thin she looked mummified.

Seeing her in the window and recognising the vulgar distraction her appearance must have been creating for the restaurant's clientele, one of the clown-suited waiters rushed to the door and spoke to her in Cakchiquel. Slowly, she stooped to pick up the pomegranates, one by one, her gnarled hands grasping them with difficulty. Then she disappeared into the night mist, barefoot on the wet cobblestones.

The Ruta Maya:
Chiapas, 1997

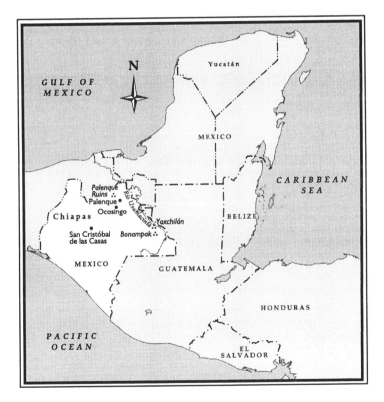

CHAPTER 17

Bus to the border

THE bus, bound for the Mexican border, was a cast-off Greyhound. Having ended its career in the States, it was now pressed into service on Guatemala's mountain roads. But with its new assignment came enhanced status: in the US it had been a rattletrap; here, the old bus had become first class – first class meaning that my ticket guaranteed me a seat. The service was called Express: no stops. Not five klicks outside the capital, however, the bus rattled to a halt to bring on board an old man, along with his obligatory burlap burden. He stood in the aisle. Before long the aisle was filled with passengers who clutched the overhead storage rack and leaned into the seated passengers each time the road curved. And of course several of the standing passengers were elderly women, so it wasn't long before I felt guilty and surrendered my seat.

In joining the aisle riders, I'd become part of a game. It seemed that it was illegal for the bus to operate with passengers standing in the aisle, but this illegality merely provided the police with opportunities for shakedowns: if the driver was caught, he would have to pay a bribe. So every time we approached a town with its police station, the driver's assistant waved those of us in the aisle into a squatting position.

'What will happen if I refuse to squat?' I asked the young man beside me, who was wearing a Michael Jordan shirt.

'You will have a long walk,' he told me.

'They'll send me off the bus?'

'Of course.'

'What if we all refuse?'

'Then we will all have a long walk.'

Clearly, the idea of the power in numbers had not taken root in local consciousness, a fact of Guatemalan life that had chagrined would-be revolutionaries for years.

So it went all the way across the highlands, a non-stop squat-and-stand exercise. The bus followed the region's oldest highway, the Pan-American, which runs down the spine of the isthmus. Each bend in the road, each climb to a summit, provided long, dizzying views across undulating hills and valleys hemmed in by perfectly conical volcanoes. The hamlets clustered on hillsides in the near distance looked idyllic and peaceful – if one didn't know any better – with their whitewashed churches and adobe houses.

Near Chimaltenango, the road passed several *maquilas*, the new style of factory that assembled clothing for export. Owned by Americans and Koreans, these huge, airless concrete buildings – as big as football pitches – had been built in a new free export zone along the Pan-American. Out here, the foreign manufacturers could take better advantage of a cheap labour force made up of Mayan adolescents who worked twelve-hour days, six days a week, for a few dollars.

The presence of the *maquilas* was a sign that new forces were shaping Guatemala's highlands. There were other signs as well: the land along the highway no longer belonged to the Maya; gone were the subsistence plots of traditional agriculture. Taken over by agribusiness, the land was now planted not with corn – the most significant crop in Mayan culture – but with products more suitable to the global economy, such as snow peas and broccoli. The Maya now worked the fields as hired hands, migrants in their own land; most of the produce they farmed was for export. I saw them marching through the fields spraying pesticide from canisters carried on their backs. These pesticide packs were everywhere. Boys riding bicycles on the highway wore them, the nozzles dangling from their sides and dripping poison on the road. At one point, the bus stopped to pick up a man who carried one of the canisters; the oily, noxious smell soon filled the bus, and it lingered long after the man had left us, only a few kilometres further on.

Near San Andrés Semetabaj, we passed a *mirador*, a scenic viewpoint. There are numerous *miradores* along the Pan-American, places with such a stunning view that a rest stop has been created to afford tourists the opportunity to snap a picture and buy souvenirs from the vendors who have staked out the spot. I remembered this *mirador*. Several hundred metres below and a few kilometres away was the shimmering mirror of Lake Atitlán, a strong candidate for the title of World's Most Beautiful Lake. Three volcanoes rose above the waters, sheer cliffs rimmed much of the shoreline and a dozen picturesque villages nestled between cliff and shore. Even a dour, jaded traveller had to admit that the sight was breathtaking.

But by taking the direct bus to the border, I was purposefully avoiding the lake. More precisely, I was avoiding Panajachel, the tourist town on the lake. Panajachel was unattractive and overrun by outsiders, especially by a hippie set that had transformed the once Indian town into a Woodstock-era hang-out. I had been to Pana many times before and was not interested in its 'scene': it was one of the blighted places on the Ruta Maya, a place where Solomon Alvarez's fears had been realised.

But the fleeting glimpse of the lake and the volcanoes awoke in me a desire to take the scenic road after all. I could feel myself being drawn to the lake, its allure was that strong. Why not stop for a couple of nights in Pana, cross the lake to beautiful Santiago, make a side trip up to nearby Chichicastenango, the famous market town? Pana was ugly and touristy, to be sure, but there were some good restaurants, some nice hotels, and plenty of shopping bargains. In a few moments, the bus would stop at Los Encuentros, the crossroads where I could catch a bus down to the lake. It would be easy, the sirens sang, why not? Why not?

Sure enough, the bus stopped for fuel in Los Encuentros, and I stood by the side of the road amidst the hubbub, weighing up my options. Second-class buses rumbled past, spewing clouds of smoke and filled to overflowing with passengers and burlap sacks and farm animals. Vendors hustled back and forth, holding up bags of fruit and nuts to the windows of stalled vehicles. Trotting right through the middle of the dust-blown Texaco came a bleating herd of goats, following a stick-swishing Mayan boy dressed in the red pinstriped outfit of the nearby village of Solalá.

Big, sleek tour buses with polarised windows sped past on their way to the tourist towns. Today, most were headed up to Chichi for the Sunday market, an event that brought in thousands of tourists. The plaza in Chichi would be crammed with tent-covered stalls selling handicrafts and trinkets – masks, dresses, blouses, dolls, statues of saints, jewellery, wooden animals, hats, blankets, baskets, bags. The tourists would be cooing over their purchases, taking photos, comparing prices; the tired vendors, having left home at two or three in the morning, would be calling out some of the English phrases they had learned: 'Good price for you!' 'What I give you, my friend?'

At least the infiltration of Chichi was limited to market days. But down in Panajachel, the invasion was more permanent. The hundreds of gringos who had moved into Pana – now jokingly called Gringotenango – had bought up property and opened businesses catering to other foreigners, completely altering the culture of the town, even more so than in Antigua. Refugees from the first world in search of a new spiritual home, they believed they had found authenticity – and a cure for their own disaffection – on the shores of Lake Atitlán. In setting up artisan shops, adventure tour agencies and New Age shops, the foreigners had appropriated the Maya and Mayan culture for their own profit and benefit. The Maya were waiters and cooks and dishwashers, reduced to servants in a service economy, chasing after trickle-down dollars. The Maya made the handicrafts that the foreigners sold. Mayan villages and sacred places were the objects of the trips that the tour agencies arranged. Along with moon drops and aromatherapy and 'vortex energy access sites', the New Age shops were selling Mayan tarot cards and books on Mayan prophecies and 'Mayan horoscopes interpreted by Mayan priests'.

As beautiful and inspiring as the moody lake was, the pretentious carnival atmosphere of Panajachel had always fatigued me, and I was glad to slip past. Despite the temptation, I ignored the sirens' song and reboarded the bus.

❂

As the bus got rolling again and passed the turn for Panajachel, I remembered the last time I had gone down that road. It was several years before, when I was driving with some Guatemalan colleagues to a conference in Quetzaltenango. We'd detoured to Sololá so I could see the church there, but somewhere on the outskirts of the village we were forced to a halt: a huge tour bus was blocking the way. The coach, on its way down to Panajachel, had come across a Quiché procession for Saint Anthony. Garlanded with piles of flowers, the saint stood on a bier supported by members of the village brotherhood, the *cofradía*, who were dressed in elaborate outfits – sashes and bandannas and finely woven ponchos. The tour guide left the bus to speak to the leader of the *cofradía*. After a brief negotiation, they shook hands and the tour guide waved to the bus. Instantly, a score of tourists laden with cameras burst onto the road and began shooting the procession. When they had finished, they each presented the leader with a crumpled *quetzal* note and climbed back on board. The bus then continued down to Panajachel, and the procession continued on its way to the church.

It had been the quintessential Ruta Maya encounter: a culture-for-cash exchange. But the true value of the encounter remained difficult to assess.

❂

The highway twisted away from Los Encuentros and rose into the mountains, the temperature dropping as clouds swirled over the road. Above the tree line, the fields turned rocky and barren; herds of sheep and goats wandered in the mist, barefoot children trailing after them. But the road was surprisingly good; in fact, throughout most of Guatemala the roads were in better condition than those in other Central American countries. It was difficult to explain why this should be so, as Guatemala's tax rate was the lowest in the hemisphere, leaving the government with little to spend on infrastructure. And the money it did have was often lost to corruption. So why the decent roads? An aide in the US Embassy later gave me an explanation. Back in the 1930s, the dictator of the day, Jorge Ubico, had loved to ride on his motorcycle, and so he'd made road building the pet project of his brutal governance, using unpaid Indian labour and the expertise of US engineers. That effort had laid the foundation; subsequent military dictatorships, particularly in the 1970s and 1980s, had expanded the road system and improved the existing infrastructure as part of counterinsurgency campaigns. The existence of good roads, like so many other things in Guatemala, was overshadowed by a history of violence and oppression.

The Pan-American Highway climbed to a tableland, then descended to another junction: Cuatro Caminos, where an intersecting road branched off to Quetzaltenango, the second largest city in Guatemala. The Pan-American veered toward another mountain range, the curves in the road adding to the rigours of the journey for those of us standing in the aisle. My neck ached from the strain of bending down to look out the window, but the view was too good to ignore. On a bluff above the highway, the white colonial church of San Francisco El Alto seemed to float on the mist clinging to the mountainside. In the distance, the Santa María and Zunil volcanoes thrust their black cones through scudding clouds. Guatemala, quite simply, is one of the world's most beautiful countries; as the anthropologist Oliver La Farge once remarked, it's a country so beautiful it hurts.

Eventually, the road levelled off as we entered a plateau and the town of Huehuetenango. It was cool and damp, with the Cuchumatanes, Central America's highest mountains, looming to the north. The Pan-American skirted the sierra, before plunging off the plateau to follow a long, precipitous descent through the narrow defile of the Selagua River. It was then at last that we came to the clutter of the border – the carters-for-hire, the money-changers, the touts and the myriad authorities in their bewildering array of uniforms.

The Spanish equivalent of 'out of the frying pan and into the fire' is *salir de Guatemala y entrar Guatepeor*. It's a pun on *mala*, the Spanish word for 'bad', and it means 'to get out of Guate-bad only to enter Guate-worse'.

I was on my way out of the frying pan of Guatemala. What awaited me was the fire of Chiapas.

CHAPTER 18

Encounters in San Cristóbal

R AIN in San Cristóbal de Las Casas, an unending, cold, mountain rain. Such was my introduction to a place I had long
wanted to visit. I arrived in the evening and spent several hours in
search of lodging, slipping on slick sidewalks and getting
drenched. After two backbreaking bus rides and a tedious border
crossing, I'd anticipated a fine evening in the colonial town,
drinking Mexican beer and eating *tacos al pastor*. But every hotel
I tried was full up, and I had to put my plans for taco nirvana on
hold.

At 2100 metres, nestled in a valley of pines and surrounded by
mountains and Indian villages, San Cristóbal has long been a
favourite stop on the gringo trail. Young travellers like the place
for its colonial look and Indian spirit, its cheap prices and supply
of magic mushrooms. As in other popular places along the Ruta
Maya, an infrastructure of vegetarian restaurants and book shops
and handicraft markets supports the gringo presence. San
Cristóbal is laid-back – even if an Indian rebellion has in recent
years increased tensions in Chiapas, Mexico's poorest (and most
Indian) state, and introduced a nervous military presence to the
town's environs. The conflict, however, doesn't seem to bother
the gringo trail's hard-core travellers, and San Cristóbal continues
to be a popular destination, a highlight on the Ruta Maya.

It was almost midnight before I finally found a place with a
vacancy. It was dingy and cold, the sheets damp with mildew, but
there was a reward of sorts in store. I asked the young man at the

front desk if he knew of a good place for *tacos al pastor* nearby. His eyes lit up. Of course! This was San Cristóbal, he declared proudly. Here were the best tacos in Mexico! He drew a map for me and marked several places I simply had to try; all were within four blocks of the hotel. It seemed I had stumbled upon a Golden Triangle for taco joints, and the only price I had to pay was to pass a restless night in a clammy room.

The taco places turned out to be the highlight of my stay in San Cristóbal. Their fare held restorative powers much greater, to my mind, than the herbs and potions sold in the New Age shops here and elsewhere on the gringo trail. Nothing better, in fact, on a rainy evening in cold Chiapas, than to step off the slick sidewalks into the warmth of a small *taquería*, a three-table place heated by the rotisserie flame. The cook sliced meat from the flame-enveloped rack and folded the slices with a piece of pineapple into a just-made, still-hot corn tortilla. He served it with an assortment of hot sauces, and the waiter carefully explained the roster for me: this red one was called Volcano, the green called Desperado, and the blood-black sauce was the local favourite, Gringo Killer. My eyes filled with water, my sinuses blew open, my throat raged with the conflagration – an ecstasy that required many beers to quell.

❂

When you travel a much-publicised circuit like the Ruta Maya, it is inevitable that you run into the same tourists again and again as you make your way from place to place. Even travelling against the normal north–south flow on the Ruta, I had met up with the same characters in each town I'd come to. In San Cristóbal, I saw once again the German traveller I had dubbed the Steppenwolf.

I had first seen him at La Mesilla, on the Guatemala–Mexico border. He was an imposing sight, not so much for his height as for his bulk, itself largely the result of his olive-drab greatcoat and the huge, deeply soiled backpack he carried. He had a fanatical appearance – bristly hair cropped short, a thin face with sharp

jawbones, a permanent scowl – and he walked very quickly, taking long, deliberate strides that let you know he was hell-bent on
getting to his destination. At the border, I had watched him
advance down the street on the Guatemalan side, pushing his way
through the crowd of porters and money-changers and freelance
document processors who are found on every border in Central
America. Two money-changers, both short and portly, manoeuvred in front of him, flashing their calculators. 'Change money,
change money,' they shouted up at him. He knocked them aside
and barrelled into the Guatemalan *migración* post.

I had joined a group of foreign travellers to ride to the Mexican
immigration post in a Volkswagen bus. The group needed a few
more people to fill the bus and cut down on the cost, so when the
German came out into the street, an Irish woman invited him to
join us. He glowered at our little group and then said in deliberate, accented English, 'I go solo. With no one, no one.' Then he
strode off in the direction of Mexico. Several hundred metres
down the road, we passed him and his enormous backpack. He
was hot, sweaty and dusty, but alone as he had wished, alone as
the Steppenwolf.

Now, in San Cristóbal, I was in line at a bank waiting to
change money when he approached me. 'Here to change money?'
he demanded. His scowl had not altered since I'd seen him at the
border.

'Yes.'

'You are American?'

'Yes.'

'I do not like the Americans. The Americans are ignorants.
You know nothing and control everything. Look at Mexico. The
Americans control. They rule the world and destroy everything.
The Americans are too ignorants. Look, I have the perfect
English. Do you have the German?'

'No.'

'You see? Ignorants.'

I said nothing. There wasn't any point in arguing, and anyway
I wasn't patriotic enough to care about the criticism. But when a

bank guard came over and told us in Spanish that the person who handled money exchanges was at lunch for another hour, I realised that the Steppenwolf did not understand. I neglected to translate for him and left him standing in line. I might have been ignorant, but at least I had the Spanish.

I had a less confrontational but more disturbing encounter in one of San Cristóbal's numerous gringo-oriented vegetarian restaurants. While I was trying to chew my way through something soy-based, a little Mayan girl appeared at my side. Her head barely reached table level. She had long, neatly braided brown hair and the largest eyes I had ever seen. From her shawl, she slowly withdrew, one by one, the tiny clay figurines of an entire menagerie. With great care she placed each figurine on the table and announced their names: Rabbit, Fox, Snake, Armadillo, Puma, Deer, Turtle. I did not want to buy the figurines, but I was powerless to stop the girl – her voice, her eyes were too enchanting. And the figurines themselves had a certain charm.

'Who made them?' I asked.

'My auntie.'

'How much are they?'

'Ten pesos.'

I could probably get them for less than that, but there was no sense resisting: I paid full price for the lot.

'Why, what a darling little girl!' exclaimed a woman behind me. She was dressed in one of the white blouses embroidered with Mayan designs that fashionable gringas favour, while her companion was evidently a photographer: he wore a khaki vest bulging with film canisters and was busy cleaning the lenses of his several cameras.

'Honey, look, you'll just have to take her picture. Oh, what's that you've bought?' The woman came over to study the animal figurines. Meanwhile, the photographer had finally taken notice of the girl. 'Oh, yes,' he agreed, 'let's get a shot of her.'

The staccato clicking of the camera startled the girl. She didn't know what to make of this bushy-bearded man who squatted to aim the camera at her. And yet she endured the scrutiny with remarkable poise, waiting patiently until the photographer was done and the woman hunted in her purse for a ten-peso bill. Then the girl scurried from the restaurant, leaving the woman to twitter, 'Oh, honey, that's one that will be selected, I can just feel it.' She turned to me. 'I know about these things. My husband Michael's a photographer, and I just have this sense about which pictures magazine editors will choose. That girl's a keeper.'

The woman went on to tell me that Michael was on assignment for a major travel magazine, which was planning a special issue on Mexico, and that Michael had been commissioned to take pictures and write a story on Chiapas.

Michael interrupted to say they had better hurry up and order if they didn't want to be late for their next appointment.

'Michael's meeting with the mayor this afternoon,' the woman told me with evident pride.

For the rest of the day, the episode weighed on me. It had me depressed. I felt stabs of jealousy when I thought of Michael, with his equipment, his contract, his prearranged meetings with important people, while I stumbled along, leaving everything to chance and ending up with no publishable photos, no interviews, just a set of idiosyncratic notes. Long into the night, I lay awake taking inventory of my journalistic shortcomings. Leading the list, I decided, was my reserve, a passivity that made me shirk from opportunities to speak with people. In the dead of the Chiapas night, with the interminable chilly drizzle falling outside the *pensión*, I made a resolution: I would be more assertive, approach people, interact more.

❂

I soon had the chance to test that resolution. The next afternoon another downpour sent me scampering for shelter in San Cristóbal's central plaza, the *zócalo*, where there was a pavilion whose open-sided upper deck served as an outdoor cafe. A group of vendors were pressed against the wall with me; one held up a blanket, hoping for a soggy sale.

It looked like the rain had set in, so I climbed the steps to the cafe level and ordered a beer. Another gringo was already there, sipping coffee and studying maps at the table next to mine – an obvious opportunity to interact that I would normally have let slip. Steeled with the previous night's resolution and a beer, I plunged in, albeit with a rather feeble gambit.

'This rain's really something.'

The gringo looked up from his map, and glanced out at the rain as though he hadn't until now noticed the heavy downpour. He was balding on top, but had grown his hair long and combed it back into a feeble pony-tail. He took a sip of coffee and studied the rain.

'Stay here long enough,' he said, 'and you get used to it.'

'How long have you been here?'

'Five years, more or less, doing this and that. I'm trying to get a business started, an alternative tours kind of thing for people who want something a little different. Customised travel, off-beat adventures – horseback riding at the Montebello Lakes, hiking, rock climbing down at Sumidero Canyon, that sort of thing. I had one guy, wanted to hang-glide off of different cliffs. We made arrangements with the Indian villages for him. You have to be careful here, go about it the right way. The Indians get pretty defensive about their lands. That's why we always work through a local contact.'

'How's business?'

'Not too bad. Getting the word out is the hard part, along with scraping together the capital to get equipment. This place has loads of potential and it's totally virgin territory. Plus, Chiapas has things nowhere else does. Like right now, I've got this group from California that wants to come down to meet with native shamans and go on mushroom hunts in the forests. Not many places give you those options.'

'I would think that the political situation would prove a hin-drance.'

'What do you mean?'

'With the Zapatistas.' After all, it couldn't be easy arranging tours around the activities of a band of rebels who had seized several towns and villages in the highlands.

'Oh, them. No, they're not a problem. Well, maybe the negative publicity keeps some people from coming down. But we haven't had any hassles. You had hassles?'

'No.'

'You see? Actually, the Mexican army's the bigger problem. They've got patrols and roadblocks all over. I've learned you have to factor bribes into your operational costs. Just part of doing business here.'

While we talked, a couple of the pedlars from the *zócalo* climbed the stairs in the hope of hawking their wares – a familiar sight on the Ruta Maya. Any time a foreigner paused to sit or study a map or tie a shoe, a peripatetic vendor or two would approach to unfold a blanket or blouse or hammock for the foreigner's inspection. Responses varied: some gringos ignored them, some murmured *no gracias*, some took a closer look or asked the pedlar to dig out some other samples. To most travellers on the Ruta Maya, the presence of pedlars was a mixed blessing: they loved the handicrafts and low prices, but they loathed the 'hassle' of always having to fend off the vendors.

One small girl wanted me to buy a blouse. The price she started with was low enough, but in response to my silence she lowered it three times. If I'd bargained, I could probably have persuaded her to sell the blouse for little more than the cost of the materials, all the labour that had gone into making the garment netting only pennies. To me, this was the uncomfortable reality of the Ruta Maya: I felt bad about my privileged position, but then I didn't exactly want to surrender it – not at the expense of losing out on seeing the wonders of the Mundo Maya, anyway. I convinced myself that I was somehow superior to other tourists, that I genuinely cared about the Maya, that I was not a crass consumer of their goods and services, and that my presence would benefit them in some undefined way.

It turned out that the ecotour entrepreneur had similar thoughts. When I told him that Mayan intellectuals had raised questions about tourism's negative impact on indigenous peoples, he readily agreed.

'They're absolutely right. What you see around here can be pretty nauseating, what with all the fat cat tourists crawling all over the place, buying up their tacky souvenirs. That's what we're trying to get away from. We take only small groups. We try to emphasise the education side of things, learning about the ecology of the place, the cultures, that sort of thing. We make sure our clients' contact with the place is authentic.'

'But aren't your clients pretty much wealthy fat cats, too?'

'Well, I guess you could say that. But it's a different class of people interested in our options. They're into the learning experience aspect of it. They go home and support causes – rainforest, social justice, et cetera. It's positive tourism.'

'Is it any more beneficial to the Maya than conventional tourism?'

'I would have to say yes. Hell, yes. Absolutely. Look, your average group comes down for a backpacking trip to the Montebello Lakes. All right, so that's eight people, spending maybe a couple of thousand dollars each on goods and services. That sixteen thousand bucks has a real ripple effect in these communities. A little extra money circulating here has a big impact. I have to hire an entire team – you got your guides, your cooks, your porters, drivers, staff. All that happening from one little tour. The ripple effect. How can it not be beneficial? Look at it this way. What if there were no tourism? A lot of these communities would be the poorer for it. I mean, we're talking about a significant amount of money pumped into the local economy.'

'But how is that any different from regular tourism?'

'The attitude. The attitude's what's different. We stress that good tourism is a learning experience. We hire anthropologists, ornithologists, biologists. People go home changed. And because we value what's here, because we depend on it staying like it is, we have to act to, you know, preserve the land and the cultures. That's responsible, sustainable business.'

'Sounds like you're doing a world of good.'

217

'I'd like to think so. Hey, you should invest in a tour, see what it's all about. Here, let me give you my card. You want to try a tour, let me know. I'll work you in with a group. Check us out, maybe you'll want to invest in the company. I got a bunch of clients already done that. It's a real good opportunity.'

❂

In between doses of Gringo Killer and chance encounters with other travellers, I visited San Cristóbal's sightseeing speciality – its churches. The cathedral featured a plaque dedicated to St Christopher, patron both of travellers and the city. All travellers were welcome in the cathedral, the plaque proclaimed, to receive special blessing and dispensation. With this encouragement, I entered to light a candle to the saint and ask for my traveller's blessing. But inside I couldn't find St Christopher anywhere. When I asked the porter, a wizened mushroom of a man, he led me to the altar and pointed to an upper niche of the *retablo*. St Christopher was too high up to receive candles; it appeared I would have to continue my journey without heaven's protection.

The patron saint's image didn't appear much around town – he was too peaceable a saint, perhaps, for the *coletos*, the residents of European descent. They preferred the warrior image of Santiago – St James, killer of Moors and, in the New World, killer of Indians. It was militant Santiago and not mild San Cristóbal who was depicted on the central relief of the facade in the town's cathedral.

In fact, San Cristóbal de Las Casas seemed misnamed all around. If St Christopher did not suit the citizens, the town's other namesake, Bartolomé de Las Casas, was even more of a mismatch. True, Las Casas had been bishop of the town in 1545, but for 400 years the powers-that-be in Chiapas had roundly rejected his preaching, for he had been the Defender of the Indians, the man who had most eloquently argued for the humane treatment of the New World's aborigines. According to legend, Bartolomé de Las Casas had cursed the city from a hilltop – an apocryphal story that had the ring of truth. It seemed strange that a town where, until the middle of the twentieth century, Indians hadn't been allowed to use the sidewalks should be named for the great defender of indigenous rights.

❂

An Indian crafts market had taken over the raised forecourt outside the Church of Santo Domingo. Under the dour and corroded gaze of the saints perched in the elaborate facade – St Hyacinth, St Peter Martyr, St Dominic, St Catherine and St Rose among them – Indians from the outlying village hawked their handicrafts, including handmade dolls of the Zapatista rebels with their trademark black ski masks. When I passed, little children came up to me offering handmade trucks with three or four Zapatistas riding in the bed. 'Comandante Marcos,' they shouted. *'Guerrilleros!'*

Apparently, in the eyes of some gringo travellers, the rebels possessed a certain élan. Named for Emiliano Zapata, a hero of the Mexican Revolution, the Zapatista National Liberation Army (EZLN) had first achieved international attention on 1 January 1994, when it had led groups of Indians in an orchestrated revolt that resulted in the short-lived seizure of several towns and villages in the highlands. The rebels had taken government officials prisoner and ransacked their offices. San Cristóbal itself had been surrounded, before Mexican troops regained control.

In the mountains, fighting had lasted only two weeks, but the suppression of the uprising left a toll of somewhere between 150 and 400 lives, depending on who did the counting. The Zapatistas subsequently retreated, and since then they have locked the government in an ideological stalemate in which the Zapatista leader, a mysterious man known only as Subcomandante Marcos, has resorted to letters-to-the-editor and Internet postings as his main weapons. In his manifestos, Marcos has demanded land reform, economic support for peasants, greater educational opportunities and autonomy for Chiapas.

The government, meanwhile, has fought back with its own publicity campaign, hoping to undermine the rebel's romantic image and expose him as a fraud. According to the government, the mysterious 'subcomandante' is merely the upper-middle-class scion of a furniture family. But Marcos has continued to nurture the mystery behind the mask, describing himself to journalists as 'owner of the night, lord of the mountain, man without a face and with no tomorrow'.

Marcos has a proclivity for such pseudo-mystical pronouncements. At times he sounds like a cross between a schoolboy poet and a cult leader. In one promotional video, Marcos smokes a pipe through his black balaclava, pink-and-white scarf knotted around his neck, bandoleer slung over his shoulder. 'In the night we were born,' he tells the camera. 'We live in the night and we'll die in the night. But in the morning will come light for all the rest, for all who cry throughout the night, for all who are denied day, for all to whom death is a gift. For each, for all, the light!'

This kind of talk has won Marcos and the Zapatistas a goodly number of admirers throughout Mexico and the first world, where his rebel charisma and esoteric mystique play very well among the disaffected cadres. And it's true that there's something appealing in the image of the Zapatistas, who show up for peace talks with the government carrying vintage rifles and wearing black woollen ponchos, multicoloured Indian belts, ski masks and Chicago Bulls caps. Given that sense of style and panache, who wouldn't want a Zapatista doll?

❂

Next to Santo Domingo stood La Caridad, a church with an odd history. In 1712, the Indians of the small village of Cancuc claimed that the Virgin had miraculously appeared amongst them. A cult subsequently spread throughout the highlands, but rather than being pleased that the Indians had taken to Christianity, the Spanish religious authorities refused to recognise the cult and persecuted its leaders. The highland Maya revolted (the Zapatista movement of the 1990s is merely the latest in a long history of Mayan rebellions in Chiapas) and carried the insurgency right up to the gates of San Cristóbal. Only reinforcements from Guatemala and Tabasco enabled the *coletos* to quash the rebels. Curiously, the *coletos* chose to believe that the Virgin had miraculously come to *their* aid: they organised processions in her honour, and the bishop vowed to build a church dedicated to her, the church that is now La Caridad. Although the building was dedicated to the Virgin in her Lady of Charity guise, the figure that stood in the centre niche of the *retablo* was outfitted with the military sash of a Spanish general. Locals called her La Generala, preferring to honour her miraculous military achievements in saving the city rather than her image as the Lady of Charity.

Inside La Caridad I took a look at La Generala, before going to the chapel to see the wooden statue of a mounted Santiago, killer of Moors and Indians. The statue, which looked like something off a merry-go-round, already had visitors: an Indian couple, he in Western clothes, she in a blue traditional blouse and black skirt. They prayed and lit candles and rubbed incense on the wooden horse and its sainted rider, seemingly unimpressed by the saint's reputation as a killer of their kind.

Outside La Caridad, I came across a row of kiosks lining the sidewalk. A large group of gringos swarmed around one kiosk which, I saw, was peddling Zapatista memorabilia – key chains, watches, cigarette lighters, playing cards, posters, T-shirts, even swizzle sticks, all with the image of Subcomandante Marcos and the EZLN logo. A large, bejewelled *coleto* presided over the sales.

At the adjoining kiosk, another *coleto* sold cheap watches. They were displayed in rows on a board, and young Mayan men were staring at them and whispering. The two groups of shoppers jostled past one another, the foreign tourists occupying most of the sidewalk, laughing and taking pictures and throwing money at the commodified revolution, while the diminutive Indian men gazed longingly at the imported baubles.

CHAPTER 19

Native lands

THE mountains around San Cristóbal shelter scores of small Mayan villages, the so-called *pueblos de indios* where the Spanish built mission churches in an attempt to bring the scattered Indians under centralised control. When I visited several of these villages, I was surprised to find them relatively unaffected by tourism. The villages of the Chiapas Maya had resisted infiltration by outsiders, establishing rules that prohibited photography and allowing entry into the church only with special permission. And in Chiapas the rules were enforced. Officials wielding club-like staffs made their rounds on the lookout for disobedient tourists; the officials were not afraid to administer beatings if necessary.

My first stop was San Juan Chamula, where a Coca-Cola sign dominated the plaza, its huge red letters announcing that the soft drink would endure *siempre*, forever. The message was repeated on every wall in town. I tried to look past these foreign signs and focus on things Chamulan, starting with its church. The simple facade was whitewashed and trimmed with bright yellow, turquoise and blue. The arcaded entrance was decorated with crosses and flowers. Clay pots adorned the steps, and the niches of the facade were painted with elongated faces. The Spanish had built this mission church centuries ago, but it was clear, compared with the baroque structures back in San Cristóbal, that an altogether different vision had produced these designs.

Inside the church, the contrast was even more startling. The saints were there, arranged in the glass boxes that lined the walls, but little else seemed to derive from the dire and sumptuous Spanish version of the faith favoured in San Cristóbal. Here, it was all far simpler. The church was warm with candlelight, redolent with flowers and rich in the sound of human voices – an assault on the senses that was voluptuous, but not garish.

I stood at the back of the church and watched the Chamulans fill the nave, where tourists were not allowed to go. There were no pews or seats; the families sat and knelt on the blue tile floor. Pine needles were strewn everywhere; piles of flowers, palm branches and pine boughs surrounded the saints and large crosses leaned against the wall. The hundreds of candles placed on the floor created a dazzling effect, especially as the light reflected off the saints' glass boxes. The families sat among the candles and made little mounds with the eggs they had brought. The men sprayed mouthfuls of cane alcohol over the candles to excite the flames. In their shawls, the women cradled live chickens and bottles of Coca-Cola.

A man in a white tunic patrolled the back of the church, wielding his large staff to keep the more curious tourists from pushing into the nave. He spotted me writing and came over; he wagged a finger at my notebook and whispered, 'Better to pray for your soul.' Then he smiled and winked as he walked off.

The presence of Coca-Cola in the church both disappointed and intrigued me. Every family group seemed to have two or three bottles of the stuff, which they passed around to one another, sharing it like communion wine. This foreign intrusion bothered me, until I remembered that anthropologists had documented the Mayan people's religious flexibility, their capacity to absorb disparate notions and artefacts into their world-view without compromising their core values. In Chamula, they had incorporated Coca-Cola in much the same way that three centuries earlier they incorporated a crucified deity. In Santiago Atitlán, back in Guatemala, the Maximón cult used aerosol sprays in its ceremonies. In a chapel in Zinacantán, just up the road from Chamula, I saw an altar bordered with blinking Christmas lights, while behind the altar a noise box produced an unending electronic bird tweet. And everywhere in the highlands of Guatemala and Chiapas I saw church interiors decorated with neon lights and coloured light bulbs. To people like me, these imports were abominations; to the Maya, they merely enhanced the sacredness of their holy places.

❂

Every year in Chamula, the world is destroyed: for five days, chaos reigns before the new world is created and a new year begins. The five days of misrule are called the *ch'ah k'in*, the lost days, the evil days, in the month of Crazy February, when the world is lost between years. The concept goes back to the ancient Maya, who observed a five-day period called the *uayeb*, omen-filled days when time fell into a profound sleep. According to one of the Maya's two ways of counting time, the solar year was divided into eighteen months of twenty days each. The remaining five days, the *uayeb*, marked the transition from one year to the next. They were considered unlucky and chaotic days, when strange and evil things happened.

In Chamula, this five-day period is still observed in a huge fiesta, now somewhat Christianised, called K'in Tahimol, the Festival of Games. Virtually everyone in the village is involved in one way or another. The festival officials dress like Spanish lords in red velvet suits, while other men take the part of monkeys wearing high-pointed and beribboned hats. Musicians throng the plaza playing home-made flutes and beat-up brass trumpets, and the boys of the village shoot off skyrockets and lob petards into the crowds gathered to see the processions.

For hours on end, day after day, the velvet-robed headmen parade flower-printed cloth banners around the village on turquoise poles tipped with silver and wrapped with rainbow ribbons. Scented smoke from hand-held braziers billows up to the banners, purifying them, feeding them. Sometimes the headmen break into a trot and run the banners around the square, or dance them around clay drums filled with water. At night, they haul the banners up the steep hillsides surrounding the village, and the crowds follow to pass a cold night in the mountains beneath the stellar scorpion's curled tail and the glittery trails of exploding skyrockets.

The embodiment of misrule, and bane of the banner cult, are the primeval monkeys who roam Chamula for the five days, spreading mischief, playing tricks, rapping people across the head, cracking bull penis whips. The height of the festivities belongs to them. Amidst the explosions and the discordant music and the blowing of conch shells, they usher in the evil days, leading the forces of destruction, tearing down the orderly world and heralding the tyranny of chaos.

The monkeys are anachronisms from an earlier, evil incarnation, from before Time. At one point during the festival, a headman reads a letter that reminds Chamulans of the invasions they've suffered, the wars, the rebellions, the interventions of foreigners. To the Chamulans, the monkeys are the embodiment of these foreigners, these agents of chaos.

The headmen must dance and dance and dance to hold back these forces of evil, but the monkeys' misrule eventually gets out of hand: they set fire to the pine needles covering the plaza, scorching the sacred earth. Thick clouds of smoke fill the air. It falls to the headmen to quell this evil: they must run with their banners through the flames, through the smoke. With the whole village watching, they run, trampling the flames, bearing the banners of Christ the Sun. They run to restore order. They run to re-create the world. They run to usher in a new cycle of time.

❂

I was sitting on the bus waiting to leave Chamula, when a small entourage emerged from the *municipio* building. It was Michael, the photojournalist, shadowing me – or was I the one in shadows here? Several of the village headmen escorted Michael and his silver-haired wife. Though it was not a fiesta day, four Chamulans had donned ceremonial outfits – one was dressed as a *ch'ah k'in* monkey – and brought out a banner from the Festival of Games.

Michael was carrying a tripod, and two cameras dangled from his neck. Photography was forbidden in the village, but Michael had somehow secured permission – his contract with the major travel magazine was probably enough to persuade the Chamulans to grant dispensation. Once again, Michael had the privileged position, while I watched from afar. The headmen led Michael to the atrium outside the church, where he set up his tripod and motioned the costumed Chamulans into a posed arrangement, as though they were models at a photo shoot. Off to the side, his wife was beaming; I could imagine her announcing to the entourage that this one was a keeper.

❂

Several different Mayan languages are spoken in the Chiapas highlands, two of which predominate: Tzotzil, common primarily in villages to the north-west of San Cristóbal (such as San Juan Chamula), and Tzeltal, more common to the north-east of the city. From Chamula, I headed for Tzeltal country and the village of Tenejapa, thirty kilometres from San Cristóbal.

The ride aboard the second-class local was difficult. The road rose sharply, curving up and around hill after hill. Soon it entered the clouds, and I caught only an occasional glimpse of ravines and pine forests and maize fields in between billows of mist. It was evident that the road had caused erosion on the hills, as deep gullies trailed away from the embankment. In places, half the road had collapsed into the ravine, and the bus was forced to rock slowly over the rough patches. Another time, we were brought to a dead halt when a herd of sheep loomed suddenly in the mist. Their shepherdess wore a brilliant turquoise poncho, and her jet black hair stood out against the white cloud-veil swirling around her and the herd.

The road passed through a place called Romerillo, where the fences were made of tree branches and the porches of the houses were fringed with ears of corn. A grove of tall crosses stood in a field, emerging from the clouds as we drew near. At their feet, a lone woman dressed in black arranged flowers in the dust.

After the turn-off for Tenejapa, the pavement gave way to dirt and the last few kilometres were a tedious crawl, the bus grinding gears as it churned over ruts. Then, far below, the town came into sight: silver-roofed shacks, an orange and dun church, a white plaza. More twists and turns and bumps brought us slowly down the mountain and into Tenejapa.

At the plaza, the other passengers scuttled off down side streets, leaving me to contemplate the little square alone, with its pergola of green and white ironwork, its black benches and its fenced polygons of shrubbery. The lampposts were connected by string, from which dangled squares of coloured paper cut into floral designs, along with clusters of Spanish moss. Opposite the church stood the Palacio Municipal and the adjoining Casa de Cultura. A new clock had been installed in the facade of the *palacio*, but it had been installed askew, so that the twelve was no longer at the top.

Abruptly, the empty plaza began to fill with men, only men, three or four at a time, until over the course of twenty minutes some thirty or forty had congregated next to the pergola. Their black woollen tunics covered white long-sleeved shirts, and medallions and crosses and coloured beads dangled to their waists. They wore cowboy hats decorated with coloured tassels. Some wore work boots, others wore sandals, and one younger man wore red high-top basketball shoes. They all carried walking sticks.

Feeling conspicuous, I walked over to the portico of the Casa de Cultura and peered through the windows. In one room, I saw a man kneeling in prayer before a cross decorated with pine boughs. Pine needles were scattered on the floor, and a single candle burned before the cross. On a table in the middle of the room were eight crates of Coca-Cola and four bottles of home-made cane alcohol. Through a second window I saw a room full of home-made instruments – guitars, harps, violins.

I was caught looking in the windows by a young man who came out of the *palacio* and approached me. He wore a denim jacket, jeans and a white hat, and while he appeared genial enough, I felt momentarily nervous – it was entirely possible that I had overstepped the bounds and transgressed in some way – but of course my fears were misplaced. The young man simply greeted me and asked if he could be of help.

His name was Alejandro López, and he was the director of the Casa de Cultura. Alejandro explained that special prayers were offered before the cross at this time of the month, prayers that lasted for three days. During that time, true believers, or 'those whose hearts were in it', as Alejandro put it, fast and ingest a special mixture of tobacco and garlic. This was the reason the *regidores*, the village officers, had gathered in the plaza.

'What are the *regidores*' responsibilities?' I asked.

'They are responsible for the care of the community. They help solve problems, for example marital disputes and conflict between neighbours.'

In answer to my questions, Alejandro went on to tell me that the *regidores* served for a year; they were elected by their fellows, and it was a great honour to be chosen, but also a costly one because the *regidores* lost a lot of working time in their fields.

Then I asked him about the ceremonial outfits the *regidores* wore – the hats, the sashes, the adornments. He was patient and generous in responding, but after a while it became clear that he thought my questions were foolish.

'Why do they wear a chain of coins?'

'It is part of the outfit.'

'What do the coins symbolise?'

'They are part of the outfit.'

I decided not to push matters. Instead, I asked Alejandro if I could visit the church.

Inside the church, several biers rested on the floor, ready for an imminent procession. The smaller biers supported crosses draped with flowers; others bore grey-faced saints holding beribboned staffs. Bunches of pine needles and dried plants adorned them, and, as always, scores of small candles burned on the church floor. The altar, off limits and blurred by candlelight, was shrouded in darkness, but closer to me was another altar, just a small table really; on it had been placed a picture of the agonised Christ in his crown of thorns. Bundles of pine needles, burning candles and dried wildflowers encircled the picture. Approaching the altar, I saw that the picture was three-dimensional, a religious novelty that anywhere else would have suggested spurious piety, but not, somehow, in Tenejapa. As I passed, the eyes of Jesus opened and closed, his death throes eternally repeated.

Outside, the constant drizzle of the Chiapas highlands had begun anew. The *regidores* were now sitting on benches, passing bottles of *posh*, the clear, home-made liquor that lubricated Mayan rituals. They ignored the rain and drank, one at a time, from a small cup that an old man filled and passed to each in turn. The wind and the rain swished through the pine trees. A boy passed carrying firewood on his back. A young woman appeared in the portico. She carried a baby wrapped in a black shawl decorated with magenta pom-poms.

To me, this experience in Tenejapa was just another in an ever-growing list of odd travel moments and incidents that didn't make sense, largely because I never hung around long enough for the logic in the scene to reveal itself. But this is what travel so often amounts to – abrupt arrivals and departures, random encounters, mysterious and inexplicable moments. There's a paradox in travel: it connects you to the world, yes; but at the same time, its nature keeps you at a remove from the things you encounter. You glimpse things only in passing, and what you see are but fleeting surfaces, exteriors, outlines, shadows. Thus, the travel experience is often endowed with a surreal quality – I don't know what else to make of my three hours in Tenejapa.

Only one thing – besides me – seemed out of place: on a dirt road just off the plaza, a Coca-Cola delivery truck blocked the right of way. The driver had his handcart out, and was wheeling crates of soft drink into a small store. The truck may have been out of place, but for me it represented an opportunity. Alejandro had told me that the next bus back to San Cristóbal didn't leave until evening, and he had advised me to hitch a ride back to the main road where more buses would pass. I decided to try to hitch a ride with the Coca-Cola man.

I explained my situation to him; he found it amusing, but he was accommodating. He could give me a ride not just back to the main road, but all the way to San Cristóbal, if I liked.

His name was Marco, a ruddy, gregarious man of mixed Spanish and Indian descent, or *mestizo*, who for some reason known only to himself found everything laughable – except the condition of the national *fútbol* squad, which he found scandalous. Marco couldn't contain himself; as the big red and white truck roared up and down the mountains, he indicated things that caught his attention, and then broke into a boisterous laugh. What exactly was so risible in what he saw wasn't always clear, but it soon became apparent that it was the Indians that amused him most.

'Look at this boy with his goats! He can't catch them, stupid Indian!'

'You see the old women with their buckets of water? All their life they go to the river, they don't know the government put in a well with a pump! Ah, these Chamulitos!'

'In this place I deliver too much Coca – these Chamulitos suck it down like elephants! They think it's medicine, can you believe it?'

'Lookee here, you see the road is so bad? It's because now the government is run by the Indians!'

And so it went all the way back to San Cristóbal. I was sitting pretty, high above the deteriorating road, but forced to listen to Marco's running commentary on life in the highlands, his amused denigration of the Maya. He always referred to them as 'Chamulitos', when in fact there were no Chamulans in this area, for we were in Tzeltal country, but Marco made no distinction. As for his notion that Indians ran the government, that was the most absurd of his beliefs about the highlands' problems. I supposed his attitude was typical: blame the Indians for everything, credit them with nothing. It was easy to understand why Chiapas was such a volatile state.

As we neared San Cristóbal, it occurred to me to ask him about the Zapatistas. I wanted to know if he found the rebellion as funny as everything else and, of course, he did.

'Subcomandante Marcos! What a joke, with that pipe of his! You know he's only in it for the Indian women. He starts a revolution and now they all sit on his lap. He doesn't know the Indian women all fuck for nothing. They're always on their hands and knees! Look how many babies!'

CHAPTER 20

Merle's place

THE downbound bus from San Cristóbal to Palenque plunged through clouds and pine forests, mile after mile of roller-coaster turns and dips that unsettled my stomach, leaving me exhausted and exasperated in expectation of an end that didn't come but seemed to recede, vanish, then reappear, until I'd abandoned all hope of arrival and surrendered to the unceasing motion, the endless swaying, the harrowing rush down, down, down, through frond thicket and canebrake, over a careening track, aboard a dismal, tetchy, hurtling rattletrap – the downbound bus, San Cristóbal to Palenque, metaphor for a lifetime's travels.

But worse than that – worse even than the whining of the motor, the grinding of the gears, the seeping smell of gasoline and the macho driver's swerving that sent waves of panic through my gut – was the non-stop chatter and giddiness and unselfconscious hyperactivity of the American college kids – ten all told – who occupied the seats in front of me and who could not for the life of them refrain from commenting on everything they saw ('Oh, look at the donkey!') or inarticulately squealing and giggling as they leaned into one another on every curve.

These loud products of shopping malls and orthodontics were not even aware that they were the centre of attention for the peasant Indians on board, the Indians being for the college kids the colourful background to their adventure in Mayaland. For several hours, they cooed over souvenir purchases, opened bags and bags of snacks, consulted with one another on how to ask a question in

Spanish, and commented on the suspect sanitation of the *sanitario* at the back of the bus (whose door banged open on the sharpest curves, contributing still more pungent emissions to the bus's foul interior).

One brawny youth held a map open on his lap and announced the names of the towns we passed through. He wore a black muscle shirt, a red bandanna on his head and a golden ring in each of his pierced ears – an outfit that occasioned much discussion between the two Mexicans seated behind me. They referred to the young man alternately as the pirate and the butterfly – the latter a slang judgement on the gringo's sexual orientation. A heavy-set girl, meanwhile, read aloud from her guidebook: 'Oh wow, this town is famous for its yellow cheese,' she told the group.

At Ocosingo, where Zapatista activity had been heavy, the bus was forced to stop at a military checkpoint. A tank was parked for show at the roadside, and a score of sleepy soldiers stared up at us from a concrete bunker.

'Oh, wow, look at the soldiers,' said the American students, and they reached into their backpacks for cameras. They were loaded and ready to shoot when the driver's aide noticed them lowering the windows and gave a cry of alarm. 'No, no, no,' he shouted, dashing down the aisle to raise the windows, jabbering and gesticulating emphatically.

'What's he saying?' the students wanted to know.

'No pictures, I guess.'

'Gaw, talk about sensitive!'

But the aide had not acted quickly enough. A lieutenant had spotted the flurry of activity on the bus, and he boarded to see what was amiss. He advanced slowly down the aisle, his eyes shaded by mirrored sunglasses. The driver's aide stammered an explanation; the lieutenant stared down at the college kids, nodding. One of the girls had long blonde, almost white, hair, and the lieutenant stepped over to her, reached out and lightly touched his fingertips to a stray wisp.

'*Muy bonito el pelo,*' he muttered. Very beautiful hair. Then he turned and strode off, and the bus was waved on its way.

For several kilometres, the students sat in silence, so stunned by the episode that they stopped chattering.

Then the blonde girl confided that the experience had left her 'totally freaked'.

'That was pretty weird,' another girl mused. 'Wasn't that weird?'

'Yeah,' the butterfly pirate said, 'that was freaky.'

❂

I had intended, while at Palenque, to visit two nearby Mayan sites – Bonampak and Yaxchilán. These remote ruins, 150 kilometres from Palenque, were accessible only by dirt road, a jungle hike and – for Yaxchilán – a boat trip on the Usumacinta River, Mexico's border with Guatemala. But I arrived in Palenque just as the news broke that a Canadian and five Mexican archaeologists had been reported missing after an altercation with local villagers near a small Mayan site on the Usumacinta. There were all sorts of rumours, the most prevalent of which held that a radical Mayan group had taken the archaeologists hostage.

After several days, the missing scientists turned up with a bizarre story to tell. At a press conference, they related the circumstances of their disappearance. The trouble had begun when the archaeologists attempted to recover a Mayan altar at a remote archaeological site halfway between Yaxchilán and Palenque on the Usumacinta. The team believed they had the permission of local authorities to proceed with the excavation; residents of the nearby villages, however, had not agreed with the plan to remove the altar by helicopter. A machete and stick-bearing crowd surrounded the scientists and threatened them. After two days of tense negotiations, the team was forced to surrender their equipment, their footwear, their money and their documents. Told to leave the village, they made their way through the jungle to the banks of the river, where they attempted to locate canoes for their escape. But a large mob followed and overtook them, attacking the scientists with rifle butts and machetes; one suffered a broken jaw, and another was wounded severely in the spleen. They managed to escape by diving into the river and swimming to the Guatemalan side. They then hiked all night, barefoot, in an intense downpour, and it was two days before they managed to find a boatman to take them upriver, where eventually they met up with a Mexican patrol boat searching for them.

During the press conference, the archaeologists were careful to point out that they had secured permission from local authorities to remove the altar. Their motive had been to preserve it from looters – a very big problem in the Mayan jungles – by taking it to a secure location in the nearest large village. In their opinion, this case had nothing to do with cultural sovereignty because they had obtained permission from the proper authorities. The attackers, they asserted, had been motivated by simple thuggery.

The incident raised broader questions concerning the intrusion of outsiders in the so-called Mundo Maya. Whether the outsiders were authorised scientists or simply curious tourists, some Maya had become increasingly sensitive to the intrusions. Moreover, the incident pointed to potential problems along the Ruta, as the number of these intrusions increased with the tourist traffic. In fact, the archaeologists' showdown had taken place only a few kilometres from the tourist site of Yaxchilán; it wasn't impossible that a discontented mob could turn their wrath on tourists instead of archaeologists.

The threat was real enough, anyway, to make tour operators in Palenque skittish about trips to the Usumacinta region while tensions were still high. A few operators said they could make the trip, but their blithe optimism raised doubts in my mind – especially when most agencies were being cautious despite facing losses in revenue. For the time being, the site at Palenque would have to suffice.

❂

The ancient Mayan site of Palenque flourished from 600 to 800 AD. By 1000 it had been abandoned, lying dormant and all but unknown beneath jungle vegetation until the nineteenth century, when first amateur and then professional archaeologists had rescued it from oblivion. Palenque was now flourishing again as one of the more frequently visited sites along the Ruta Maya. Its temples and palaces were built on a flat shelf halfway up the low foothills of the mountain range that dominates the Chiapas highlands. Some of the temples were built into hillsides now dense with rainforest vegetation. From the top of the temples, I could see far out over the broad coastal plain that bordered the Gulf of Mexico. This view, and the dramatic contrast of the ancient stones rising from the jungle growth, made Palenque a particularly compelling site to visit, the more so with parrots squawking and a morning mist burning off the grassy plaza thirty metres below my pyramid perch.

While visiting Palenque, I made a discovery of my own when I climbed to the top of the Temple of the Cross. A tour group was listening to their guide's description of the bas-relief sculptures on the panels inside the temple. It was readily apparent that this group was different from the many other clusters of tourists following guides around the site. Their guide was a small and aged woman leaning on a cane. She looked so frail that I thought she must have been carried to the top of the pyramid, yet her speech was full of energy and passion as she explained the symbolism of the panels to her note-taking audience. From the clarity and thoroughness of her explanation, I knew she was no ordinary guide. And indeed I learned from a man who had stepped aside to take a picture that he was part of a group of college professors and that their guide was none other than Merle Greene Robertson, the renowned art historian and doyenne of Palenque. There wasn't anyone alive who knew the place in greater detail. I knew I'd never have an opportunity like this again, so I decided to follow at a distance and eavesdrop.

Robertson's apparent frailty was misleading. She had white hair, thick glasses and a hearing problem. She used a cane to get around. Yet she bustled from building to building, climbing steep steps and flouting the heat and humidity. She seemed to draw energy from the stones of Palenque. She had spent most of her life there, and the place was her passion. Her contribution to the field of Mayan studies was vast; among other things, she had organised the Palenque Round Tables, at which many significant advances in the deciphering of Mayan glyphs had been announced. She had also produced multiple volumes of drawings detailing the artwork of Mayan sites.

For her, each stone told a story. 'Now over here,' she began, pointing with her cane to one of the piers atop the Temple of Inscriptions, 'we have a wonderful depiction of a ruler transformed into a supernatural being. This is the ruler Chan-Balum as a child, being held by his parents and ancestors . . . here as he transforms into God K, who we now know was called K'awil. We have to understand the public nature of these events. These piers, you see, were designed so the public could view them from the plaza down there. When it was all painted, why you could probably see the whole business from a hundred metres away.'

As she walked from building to building, Robertson paused to decipher a panel or a tablet. 'Now here on this pier we have evidence of the snake dance at Palenque. This dancing figure, probably the ruler Pakal, you see, dances with an axe in one hand and this snake fellow in another. And this second person, well we don't know who it is because there's no glyph, but it's a woman we think because of the net costume, which is usually female. So maybe it's Pakal's wife or mother, and she's grabbing hold of the snake. They're wearing the costume of the first father and the first mother.'

Robertson knew the stones so well because she had drawn and photographed and made rubbings of the depictions on each one of them – a lifetime of work. She even knew in minute detail the murals that no longer existed, time and the elements having erased the images. Resting near the wall of a building in the Palace complex, she described the rows of painted flowers that once decorated the wall, some with birds or maize or deer hanging from the blossom. Now only a few streaks of red remained. The paint had gradually faded in the years since archaeologists had exposed the building. Worse still, the eruption of a nearby volcano in 1982 had coated Palenque in ash: when rain had fallen, the mixture of water and ash had turned into a scouring powder that had finished off the remnants of the mural. Robertson had finished her drawings just in time.

The old lady gazed at the wall, transfixed, her eyes moving back and forth, reading a text that only she could see. The rest of us were left to look at bare stone and wonder.

❁

As long as I stayed near Merle Greene Robertson, Palenque made some sense. Through her tutelage, I could see designs in the jumbled contours and convoluted lines, I could read the signs that the Maya left behind twelve hundred years ago. There was the celestial bird atop the foliating World Tree; there, hoary God L smoking a cigar; there, the Nine Lords of the Night; there, the beautiful Maize God; there, the snaggletoothed God N; there, the dilatory jester god whose name means 'Not Right Now'; and there, the weird God K, with a smoking axe embedded in a mirror affixed to his forehead, and a leg that was simultaneously transforming into a snake.

But once I was on my own, the images vanished before me; they dissolved back into vague etchings and inscrutable scrawls, the gods and beasts receding into the stones. And I reverted once more to the mystified stranger, the puzzled Westerner raised on rationalism, unable to decipher the sketchy signs or find design in the cluttered cartouches.

In Palenque, I experienced the same confusion that I had felt at Copán and Tikal and other Mayan sites. I was confounded by this culture – by its Long Count calendar that tracked cycles of time in millions of years; by its architecture that transformed buildings into open-jawed monsters; by its religion, which considered blood-letting and self-mutilation acts of piety; by its public ceremonies, which scholars could name – 'the fish-in-hand ritual', 'the flapstaff event', 'the shell-kin event' – but could not explain.

But in truth, I was drawn to the Mayan sites in part because of that sense of confusion. I found Mayan culture so compelling precisely because it seemed so incomprehensible. My thoughts kept returning to the Mayan Vision Quest, the central act of the culture. The celebrant would puncture his penis, draw a thorn-studded cord through the wound, and then dance around so as to bleed more profusely, thereby bringing on a trance that would allow him to enter into communication with the Other World. How could such an act be understood? The concept was too alien, too remote from my way of thinking. But that is what a journey is all about. We travel not to see things we already understand; we travel to contemplate the incomprehensible, to encounter the ineffable, the bizarre, the strange.

❁

Leaving Palenque, I ran into Michael, the photojournalist who had cast a shadow over my journey. He was in the main plaza, setting up his tripod when I passed, his wife and one of the park guards standing nearby. Once again, I felt a little stab of envy when I saw Michael at work, taking notes and photos for a story guaranteed to be published.

But then I overheard the guard talking to Michael's wife. 'Down inside the *templo*,' he explained, 'they find, how you say, where is he dead?'

'Tomb?'

'Yes, tomb. And there they find really big, how you say, stone on top of this tomb . . .'

As I left Palenque, I felt a rush of triumph: finally, I was one up on this guy and his commissioned article. I was the one lucky enough to stumble upon Merle Greene Robertson, the best guide one could hope for in Palenque. Michael was stuck with a government tout. For once, I was the one who'd gotten the scoop.

❁

I hadn't expected much from the town of Palenque. Situated seven kilometres from the ruins, with tourism as its sole reason for existence, Santo Domingo de Palenque promised to be a dirty, hot dump overrun with tourists. It turned out to be all these things; but for some reason, I liked the town. I liked especially to walk its few streets in the evening after a long day at the ruins, streets that offered the sort of rich imagery that makes Mexico such a sensuous, visceral experience.

A statue of a Mayan chieftain's head marked the crossroads where the highway from San Cristóbal met the road into Palenque. The kilometre walk from the crossroads to the town's central park took me past pretty much everything Palenque had to offer. Just beyond the chieftain's head, a gleaming, government-operated Pemex filling station faced a rather run-down, dreary-looking government-operated hospital. Further down, a tour agency with posters promoting the 'Mundo Maya' stood next to a butcher shop displaying three pigs' heads in the window. A dwarf shack – one had to duck to enter the tiny doorway – housed a haberdashery. In a fried-chicken joint with walls made of bamboo stalks, a television blared in competition with the distorted noise of a jukebox, while the cook's three children swung in a hammock slung from the rafters and chickens patrolled the floor for leftovers.

Many more bicycles and tricycles than cars crowded Palenque's streets, especially in the evening when the tricycle vendors were most active. These vendors pedalled up and down the streets on three-wheeled vehicles (the two-wheeled front supporting a large metal basket) hawking their goods – bread, fruit drinks, rice-milk, ice cream. The sidewalks, meanwhile, were crowded with stationary vendors, who displayed boots or cassettes or religious charms on plywood tables under plastic tents. Others simply sold their goods from a basket plopped on the sidewalk. Shrimp, chillies, mangoes, onions – everything imaginable was for sale.

School children in blue uniforms sauntered home. Peripatetic vendors hauled around stacks of straw hats or carried armloads of hammocks. Tourists paused before restaurant windows trying to determine if the establishment looked 'safe': these were the images of Palenque, a hot, jammed, lively, makeshift town that provided an entertaining contrast to the imposing grandeur of its dead and abandoned namesake a few kilometres away.

❂

One afternoon, I waited for an hour and a half in a bank line to cash some traveller's cheques. When I finally reached the front of the queue, I presented my paperwork; the teller glanced at it and disappeared. Five minutes later, she returned to give me back my passport. Then she disappeared again. Five more minutes passed without a sign of her. At last a manager came to the counter. '*Depósitos,*' he called out. 'Anyone have deposits?' Those who did were moved to the front of the line. I asked the manager (was I mistaken, or did he bear a resemblance to the Mayan god 'Not Right Now'?) for an explanation. 'We are out of money,' he explained. 'When we get enough deposits, we will continue changing cheques.'

The other gringos in line had grown extremely impatient, to the point of hostility. When I relayed the explanation, they erupted in hoots and howls. 'A bank out of money? That's incredible. That's so like the Mexicans. These people are the most inefficient on earth. What kind of bank doesn't have money?'

Almost everyone gave up and left. I, however, was stuck because the teller had taken my cheques. As the deposits trickled in, I reflected on the little incident. The other gringos were right – this sort of thing typified Mexican culture. The unusual circumstances didn't seem to faze the Mexicans waiting in line; for the gringos, on the other hand, it was a great indignity and a farcical confirmation of their stereotypes.

But there was something else that the gringos had overlooked, something equally representative of the culture. A television set had been placed to one side of the queue for the entertainment of the clients while they waited in line. For an hour, the screen had shown images of the Mexican landscape, the sea and its people, while a narrator recited the poetry of renowned Mexican poets such as Octavio Paz. The presentation wasn't noticed by the tourists, but many of the Mexicans watched – and listened. Maybe it was true that a bank running out of money was typically Mexican, something that would never happen in the United States. But when in the US would a bank – or any place for that matter, including public television – entertain customers with poetry readings? What American would listen to poetry for more than three minutes? Bank inefficiency was one thing about Mexico; a love of poetry was another.

❂

It was my last night in Palenque and everybody in town was at the Restaurant Maya, just off the corner of the plaza. And, of course, when I entered I saw, seated at different tables, not only Michael and his wife, but also several of the American college kids who had joined me on the bus from San Cristóbal and, as an added bonus, the Steppenwolf. The coincidence unnerved me – was this some 'Twilight Zone' episode? – until I remembered that there were only so many restaurants in town. Besides, my guidebook recommended this place above all others, and everyone it seemed was carrying the same book.

The German, I saw, had not lost his Steppenwolf scowl. First he scowled at the menu – no doubt he thought the prices were too high. Then he scowled at the table of college kids, ugly Americans who had erupted in a new round of laughter and excited chatter. He tossed the menu on the table and marched out of the restaurant, muttering to himself.

Before I could take a table, Michael's wife hallooed me. 'Hey there,' she called. 'Don't we know you from somewhere?'

I considered feigning ignorance, but it probably wouldn't have been any use; no doubt, Michael's wife was the kind of person who remembered every conversation she'd ever had.

'San Cristóbal,' I said.

'Oh, right, I remember. The veggie restaurant. That little girl. Oh, what a precious angel she was! Well, why don't you join us? Here's a seat. Let Michael buy you a beer. He can afford it. He's getting his expenses paid. You can afford it, can't you Michael?'

Michael grunted some sort of confirmation while he busied himself with an array of lenses. Reluctantly, I sat down, dreading the usual traveller small talk. But as the waiter brought first one Dos Equis, then a second and a third, I loosened up. Michael and his wife – Crystal – weren't so bad. They related a funny story about a friend who got set up with some pot and was hauled off a bus in Costa Rica. At least, it was funny after three rounds of beer. I trotted out my Amazon boat-wreck story for yet another round, winning a flurry of flirtatious giggles from Crystal.

Eventually, the conversation came around to our Palenque visits. Michael was not pleased with the fruits of their visit. He thought his pictures would turn out all right, but he felt he'd failed to capture something, that he hadn't got the best story. For one thing, the park guard who guided them had spoken poor English, and they'd had a hard time getting any information out of him.

As Michael spoke, a thought germinated in my head. I tried to suppress it, but it grew and grew until finally I let it go: it was time to make peace with my nemesis. I told Michael about Merle Greene Robertson.

I gave away my one scoop. But it was all right, really. More people needed to know about Merle Greene Robertson and her incredible work. And with an audience far bigger than any I could ever find, it was only right that Michael should tell Merle's story. Maybe then, tourists would learn about the wonders that once decorated Palenque's walls. Maybe then, visitors to Palenque would know why the town had a street called Calle Merle Greene.

The Ruta Maya:
Yucatán, 1997

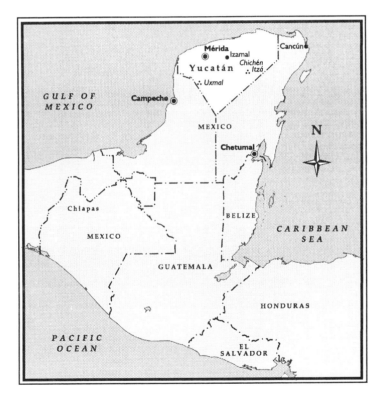

Interlude

A nightmare of a night train crawls from Palenque to Mérida in the Yucatán – eleven hours according to the deluded chalk-board sign in the Palenque station; twenty hours, in reality, if the train doesn't break down or derail and leave you stranded in some derelict town, lost on a dead-end side-track. With luck on your side, you'll make it in twenty.

That's twenty hours of lurching and screeching. And at each hot stop, the insects invade the cramped second-class carriage, along with hawkers bearing baskets of beer and banana-leaf *tamales* and pork rinds and fried grubs. Rainforest gives way first to scrublands and then to unbroken swamps; a slow, surreal progress through Mexico's nether lands, to the burning-oil twilight of Campeche, the Spanish city huddled behind walls thrown up to fight off the vast thorn and nettle wasteland that the Maya called 'place of the snake and tick'.

But even nightmares have their peculiar allure; when you awaken, safe from dreamt dangers, the bizarre and unexpected phantasmagoria lurking in your mind takes on a certain fascination. What an intriguing dream, you think. So it is with bad travel; once the dread has passed, once the ordeal is done, you realise, with some surprise, just how stimulating, just how quickening it has been to cut so close to the unknown edge, to push the envelope – even if only the envelope of discomfort and tedium.

And on the long train trip across the Yucatán, there are moments when the discomfort and the tedium yield to something pure and enchanting, something that cuts to the quick. For two hours as the train crosses the forbidding region known as Sal Si Puedes, a peasant family – and some of their farm animals – have you pinned against the window, your ass numb on the wooden seat, your legs cramped. Then the train stalls in the middle of nowhere and vendors suddenly appear, invading the already jammed aisles with their bulky baskets and shrill voices and reeking foods. The family buys some *pulque*, sacred drink of the Aztecs, the sappy brew scooped from a stone urn by the vendor. The old man of the group unexpectedly passes the cup to you with two gnarled hands, and the little girl gives you some tortillas for your hunger. There in the dark stuffy carriage, stalled in the dead of night in some all but uninhabitable place, you come to understand the meaning of communion.

Near dawn, you push open the rear door of the carriage and stand on the platform in the fresh air. The train slowly sways and rocks along through the branches and fronds slapping up against the carriages. The sun rises, a great glowing orange fireball that suffuses everything – landscape, train, your hands – with vivid, vital colour. And when the train comes lurching at last into the outskirts of just-waking Mérida, you think, 'What a ride that was, what a wild and wonderful ride.'

CHAPTER 21

The white city

A white city, built on the deconstructed Mayan centre of Tihó (of which no evidence remained, every stone having been undone for the building of Spanish cathedrals and plazas and houses), Mérida was one of those places that seemed to offer little of interest to the traveller, but turned out to be rather enjoyable precisely because it lacked attractions. It was a sensuous town of heat and colour and pungency, of long, slow hours spent at sidewalk cafes, taking it all in. On humid evenings, under the plaza's arcade, huge moths beat against fluorescent tubes overhead and white-suited waiters delivered dripping dishes of sherbet, while over one, two, three sweaty bottles of León you waited out the persistence of hammock hawkers, strolling mariachis, one-trick magicians and children proffering sandalwood fans.

But little in Mérida was Mayan. The tourist infrastructure kept alive the imagery of the vanished Maya, the noble savages who had raised pyramids and kept an accurate calendar: Mayan glyphs appeared on corporate logos; Mayan heads decorated labels; Mayan processions danced across T-shirts celebrating the 'Mundo Maya'. The living Maya, meanwhile, were pushed aside, kept in attendance if needed for cheap labour. Tourists only saw them waiting – waiting on the sides of the plaza with their stacks of straw hats; waiting at the entrances of hotels with piles of embroidered blouses; waiting at the third-class terminal for the third-class buses to take them back to their outlying villages of mud and wattle.

✿

For me, the big event in Mérida was a press conference held by the Mundo Maya Touristic Programme, a government agency which, according to its promotional material, spearheaded the development of a 'singular, unified tourism product' in the region. 'The Mundo Maya product', the handout read, 'combines world-class beach resorts with jungle shrouded ruins, and grand Old World colonial cities with unspoiled natural settings rich in exotic flora and fauna'.

The press conference was held at the Mérida Chamber of Commerce. The speaker, Alejandra Zorilla, the National Co-ordinator of the Mundo Maya programme, was immediately on the defensive. A few weeks previously, the Third International Congress of Mayanists had met in Chetumal on the Belize–Mexico border. Representatives at the Congress had criticised government agencies, the Mundo Maya programme in particular, for policies that could lead to the spoiling of the region's archaeological sites and environment. The representatives had claimed that outsiders were taking most of the profits, and that the trend could only lead to the destruction of indigenous culture and heritage: in short, the needs of tourists were taking precedence over indigenous needs.

Zorilla was emphatic in rebutting the criticism: 'The Mundo Maya is a tourist project that in no way intends to destroy the cultural and historical legacy.' The National Institute of Anthropology and History (INAH) supervised and evaluated the programme, she stipulated, 'and no report indicates that the Mayan people or their culture are afflicted.' Nor, for that matter, she maintained, did the programme destroy either the environment or the efforts of popular artisans.

She also used the occasion to announce that fifteen thousand colour brochures promoting the Mundo Maya had been prepared for distribution in Europe, Canada and the US. Beyond the boundaries of the Mundo Maya, the purple prose of those brochures might resonate with tourists who liked the idea of the beach resort–jungle ruins–unspoiled natural settings combination that the tourism ministry was promoting. But within the Mundo, there were growing numbers of doubters, particularly among Mayan activists.

If the Mundo Maya project had a credibility problem, it might have been because the agency had a tendency to refer to the Maya as a 'product'. Then, too, the co-ordinator's faith in INAH's supervisory role did not sit well with Mayanists, who argued that INAH had a history of supporting reconstruction – sometimes unscientific reconstruction at that – for touristic development rather than for archaeological inquiry. Finally, the Mexican government had a long pattern of making lofty statements and then doing the opposite. In the 1950s, for example, leaders had insisted that 'tourist activities . . . respect our customs and ethical principles', in the words of one president. In the early 1960s, PRI, the ruling party ever since 1910, had maintained a policy that sounded quite similar to today's eco-programme: nature, cross-cultural understanding and 'Mexicanness' over coarse commercialisation and profiteering. But before the decade was over, the same PRI had begun building Cancún and four other mega-resorts. Another PRI president, skilled in sophistry, had argued that the influx of tourists (and capital) had reinforced Mexican cultural identity, apparently because the influx spurred the poor into handicraft production. Such barefaced reversals left many advocates for indigenous people suspicious of government pronouncements. A showdown over the Mundo Maya seemed imminent; the press conference was an early skirmish presaging battles to come.

❂

Portions of the Yucatán Peninsula, especially in the south, are as wild as anywhere in the Americas. Lacking a reliable water supply and covered with nearly impenetrable thicket, the Yucatán has been, until the twentieth century, an unknown land. Nevertheless, some of the best developed sections of the Ruta Maya, and some of its most heavily visited sites, are in the Yucatán. The reason is simple: the huge holiday resort of Cancún that sprawls on the eastern coast of the peninsula. The highway connecting Cancún with Mérida crosses the northern portion of the peninsula and gives tourists easy access to the restored ruins of Chichén Itzá and Uxmal.

I found travel in Yucatán fairly monotonous, given the flat landscape and poor, thin soil that allowed nothing but small trees and scrub to grow on the limestone bedrock. The one topographical variation was in the region around Uxmal, a range of low karst hills known as the Puuc. After travelling through fifty kilometres of scrublands, the road began to wind and climb into the rolling hills, reaching heights of around a hundred metres, just high enough to grant a view of the vast, featureless thicket, unbroken except for patches of exposed limestone where slash-and-burn agriculture had left the land barren.

The Mayan site of Uxmal lies in a valley just south of the hills. It was an odd place to build a city of any size, since there is no evidence of a natural water supply anywhere in the area. Archaeologists have unearthed artificial cisterns, built for the capture of rain water; even with these cisterns, however, the need for water must have been a constant concern for the inhabitants of the region. And yet the Maya built one of their most beautiful cities here, renowned for its clean and precise architecture.

Uxmal is representative of what archaeologists call the Puuc Style, a style that flourished in the Late Classic period, from 600 to 900 AD, when Mayan civilisation had reached its peak. The standard opinion holds that it was here that the Maya produced their finest architectural work: buildings of symmetry and grandeur decorated with intricate, finely realised facades.

The aesthetics of the work speak across centuries and cultural boundaries. And yet, while it is easy to appreciate the site's beauty and artistry, the cosmic vision that inspired the aesthetic programme remains elusive. Scholars have been unable to determine the function of many of the buildings at Uxmal. An example is the so-called Nunnery Quadrangle. An early Spanish explorer of the Yucatán fancied that nuns had lived in the complex's seventy-four rooms; and while his guess seems most unlikely, given the oversized phallus symbols decorating the facade, no certain solution has ever presented itself. The building is still called the Nunnery Quadrangle in scholarly studies.

Whatever they were used for, these buildings remain magnificent structures. Despite the massive scale of their construction, they possess crystalline precision and an appealing simplicity. The Palace of the Governors, for example, is nearly a hundred metres long. More than twenty thousand large sculptured pieces make up its facade, and yet, as a whole, the building seems simple and clean-lined. One scholar has called it 'an edifice of striking harmony and repose'.

Ultimately, however, these buildings intrigued me not because of their familiarity, but because of the estrangement they inspired. One source of that estrangement was the mosaic artwork adorning their facades. Beautiful as the artwork was, it was also baffling, even troubling. While interpretation of the mosaics' iconography has been open to much speculation – words like 'probable' and 'possible' pepper scholarly writings on the ancient Maya – scholars believe the designs on Uxmal's buildings were not purely decorative, but were imbued with important religious and cultural meanings. A latticework of crisscrossed stones, for example, represented certain mats that in Mayan eyes symbolised authority. Serrated designs suggested serpents or reptiles. Stylised owls had underworld connotations.

But by far the most prominent image one sees at Uxmal is that of a masked face, its teeth bared, grim eyes glaring and its long snout curled up like an elephant's trunk. Scholars have determined that this is the rain god Chac. Living in a region where water was scarce, the Maya of Uxmal were obsessed with the rain god; stucco images of Chac adorned every facade in the city, and stacks of Chac masks formed the cornices of buildings, adding a macabre note to the otherwise clean architecture.

But to see this exceptional architecture as the Maya had conceived it, I had to look past the restoration – at times fanciful, at times utilitarian – imposed on the site by archaeologists. This reconstruction had been undertaken by the Mexican government through its cultural heritage agency INAH, the basic goal being to give tourists something impressive to look at and photograph at a site that was accessible and convenient to visit. This policy meant that foreign materials, such as cement, had been used in the reconstruction, and that ancient buildings were rebuilt quickly and inaccurately. Many archaeologists had questioned the commercial intentions of this policy, particularly when those intentions had inhibited further enquiry into sites like Uxmal.

At Uxmal, I spoke with an archaeologist whose request for permission to excavate a structure at the site had been turned down because his proposed excavation required three seasons to complete; INAH would fund only those projects that could be completed in one season. 'They're completely results oriented at INAH,' complained the archaeologist, who refrained from telling me his name, fearing that his criticism would harm his chances of future funding. 'They want visual results, something for tourists to look at. They're not interested in learning more about a place like Uxmal; they're only interested in uncovering and rebuilding the things that can be incorporated into the existing restored sites. The problem with my proposal is that the building is not close to the central area, meaning it's not accessible to tourists. INAH just works building by building, with no sense of context. It's not archaeology, really – it's engineering.'

He went on to give me two examples of what he called INAH's 'questionable commitment to science'. First, they had allowed stones 'left over' from reconstruction to be carted off and used in the building of the tourist hotel at Uxmal. Second, buildings like the Templo Mayor had been 'hastily and unscientifically' reconstructed to aid the sound and light show put on for tourists. No attempt had been made to recover and study the motifs and designs that had fallen from the facade – a difficult and time-consuming task, but necessary in order to discover something about the purpose and function of the building. Instead, the tops had been left blank, so that the show might go on.

❂

After steeling myself with a few bottles of León, I gritted my teeth and took in Uxmal's sound and light show. Having proven popular with tourists, these shows are staged at various sites around Mexico, and the Uxmal version lived up to its billing – lots of sound, lots of light, but not much insight. Tourists were led by flashlight into the interior courtyard of the Nunnery Quadrangle, where a row of plastic chairs had been set up. The show began with a whorl of coloured lights – red, green and blue – shooting across the sky and over the face of the looming structures. As some of the tourists gasped and squealed, the lights focused on the courtyard below them, where darting colours highlighted features of the facade – owls, crocodiles, snakes, long-nosed Chac. All the while, moody, ethereal music, reminiscent more of Egypt than of Mexico, increased in volume until, following a crescendo of cymbals and drums, a baritone voice invited me to journey to the past, to the world of the mysterious Maya. The lights faded, the timpani rolled, and the narrator intoned, 'Come, let us go now to that vanished world.' It was at just about this point that I was wondering whether I'd had one beer too many or one too few.

For the next forty-five minutes or so, the show took me on a bizarre trip through a Disneyesque Mayaland with a cliché-ridden script and a soundtrack straight out of Cecil B. De Mille. I heard a dialogue between elder astronomers and their apprentices. I was overwhelmed by an ear-splitting chant to the rain god, cries of 'Chac! Chac!' swelling until I didn't know whether to cover my ears or laugh. A swamp full of frogs erupted in belches and croaks, while thunder crashed and the lights simulated lightning. By the end, there was no doubt about it: I should have had that extra beer.

❂

The next day, before leaving Uxmal, I took one last tour of the site. Before I could complete the circuit, a sudden thunderstorm, a true sound and light show, came crashing with terrific violence. From the south side of the Nunnery Quadrangle, I watched as tourists scurried toward the porticoes of the ancient buildings. The wind blew leaves and twigs and trash across the grounds; a hard rain pelted the stones and turned the paths to mud. A great bolt of lightning blazed overhead and a huge branch came crashing to the ground, prompting screams from tourists sheltering nearby. I heard some voices moaning, softly at first but becoming louder: 'Chac! Chac! Chac!' The voices, I discovered, came from a musty room coated in bird shit: a group of American college students, now breaking up in laughter over their mock chant.

CHAPTER 22

In search of Bishop Landa

THE Yucatán Peninsula was so rich in historical places that it was easy to overlook sites that did not feature grand attractions. A place like Izamal, for example, with its large, yellow sixteenth-century Spanish monastery and huge pyramid remnant from Mayan times, would be a principal tourist site in most other regions – but in the Yucatán, it went almost unnoticed.

Maní was another unknown place on the peninsula. Even though some of the greatest events in the Yucatán's history had occurred there, only a true wayfarer ever passed through the tiny village. It wasn't on a main road and guidebooks didn't mention it; there wasn't anything scenic or picturesque to contemplate. None of that mattered to me. Crossing the peninsula by bus, I left the tourist trail between the Mayan ruins of Uxmal and Chichén Itzá to take a beat-up third-class bus to Maní. I was not about to forgo the chance to see the place where in 1562 Diego de Landa had staged a great auto-da-fé and burned a valuable store of Mayan manuscripts, in effect obliterating Mayan literature.

The bus dropped me at the market. I asked a fruit vendor for directions to the church. 'Do you want to buy my *chirimoya*?' she asked.

'No,' I said. 'I want to know where the church is.'

She smiled at me from across a table covered with green, scaly fruit, her full smile making the flesh of her face jiggle. 'Have you ever tried *chirimoya*?' she said.

I admitted that I hadn't.

'Then how do you know you don't want it?'

When I hesitated, she snatched a plump green bulb and sliced it open to reveal the fruit's white pulp and black seeds. 'My *chirimoya* is the best in all Mexico.'

I tasted the offered piece, and nodded. It was very good.

She laughed. 'Now I will tell you how to arrive at the church.'

Following her directions, a bag of *chirimoya* crooked in my arm, I walked down the dusty road toward the church.

When the Spaniards arrived in the Yucatán, in 1519, Maní was the most important of some twenty city states on the peninsula. After twenty hard-fought years, the Maya finally capitulated when the lord of Maní, Ah Kukum, surrendered to Francisco Montejo and converted to Christianity. The Spaniards then built a monastery in Maní to facilitate the mass conversion of the Mayan people.

But the conversion was only superficial. Early in 1562, two Indian boys told Maní's friars that they knew where idols and human skulls were hidden in caves outside the village. The surprised and disturbed friars collected the idols, then brought some local Indians in for interrogation. The friars were even more surprised when the suspects openly admitted to praying to the idols for rain and good crops. All the Indians in the region, they said, did the same. With this news, the friars widened the investigation and brought in more Indians for questioning. At one point, the town jail, the hospital and several other buildings were filled with detainees.

Then the tortures began. During an interrogation, the friars would tie the prisoner's wrists together and hoist him from the ground until he confessed his idolatry and admitted where the idols were located. If the Indian did not confess to a sufficient number of idols, heavy stones were fixed to his feet, and he was left to contemplate his insolence for a while. If the friars remained unsatisfied, they resorted to flogging and the pouring of burning wax on the recalcitrant heathen. A pile of idols, turned in by penitent Indians, began to accumulate outside the church.

The first auto-da-fé was held in the atrium in front of the mission church. The penitents were marched in, roped together by the neck, bearing the idols in their hands. On this occasion, the ceremony concluded with a stern sermon and the mass lashing of the penitents.

When I arrived at this atrium, now a peaceful grassy plaza in front of an old, decrepit church, I found it difficult to believe that anything of great moment had happened at such a place. The day was completely still in the harsh sunlight of a Yucatán afternoon. The only sound came from inside the almost ruined monastery – the shrill cries of children. I crossed the atrium and entered the building, moving from the hot glare to the mildewed dimness of the nave.

Like other mission churches in the Yucatán, the church of San Miguel in Maní had a primitive, tunnel-like quality. The gloom of the interior contributed to the effect, as did the prevalent iconography depicted on the altars and *retablos*: Christ's gory passion, Our Lady of Sorrows, a saint with eerie bloodshot eyes, wooden sculptures of gaunt Franciscans, and everywhere clouds of severed heads supporting the unearthly feet of Virgins and saints.

It was a relief to leave the dark nave for the open air of the cloistered courtyard, where I found a collection of bicycles. The children of the village had come for their catechism, taught in a room off the courtyard. The shouting I had heard had died down, giving way to murmured prayers. As I climbed a wide stone staircase to the monastery's second storey, I thought about how proud – and justified – Diego de Landa would have felt to have heard these pious voices, the voices of the descendants of the Indians he had tortured in the name of God.

One of the more enigmatic figures in the history of the conquest, Diego de Landa first came to the Yucatán in 1549, at the age of twenty-five, in response to a call for Franciscans to assist in the work of Christianising the New World. According to the historian Inga Clendinnen, Landa was a man of 'endless volcanic energy, both physical and mental'. Having learned to speak Mayan, he translated the catechism into the native language and revised the grammar the friars had been using. Not content to remain in the tranquil surroundings of the monastery at Izamal, where the Indians had been pacified, he ventured alone into the unknown heart of the peninsula, an area whose inhabitants had recently revolted against the Spaniards. During these years of wandering missionary work, Landa came to know the peninsula better than any European. He also achieved a remarkable intimacy with a people his compatriots considered sinister and volatile. Or so it would appear, judging from Landa's *Account of the Things of Yucatán*, written in Spain after he was forced to return to his homeland, exiled from his exile. The book, a precursor of latter-day ethnographies, included a wealth of details on domestic life and the Mayan world-view that could only be gathered by someone who was accepted into that society. The single most telling sign of that acceptance was the Mayan elders' revelation to the young friar of the secret, sacred books kept in the possession of the ruling lineages. These accordion-like books were made of beaten-bark paper and covered with a thin layer of plaster. Some were almanacs for the timing of ritual; others presumably recorded legends of the gods and ancestors. It was an unusual action on the part of the guarded elders to defy tradition by taking the outsider into their confidence, an action that can only suggest that Landa had attained an intimacy with the Indians.

By 1561 Landa was made Provincial, the head of the order in the Yucatán. A year later, the troubles began in Maní, and several weeks after the first auto-da-fé, Landa arrived in the village to assume supervision of the inquisition. He set up his court under the trees outside the monastery, and there, for the next three months, Landa interrogated and tortured more than 4500 Indians, including people whom he had befriended during his missionary days. At least 158 Indians died during the interrogations.

Upstairs in that same monastery, I wandered through the dusty cells where the monks had lived out their days in a hostile exile. Looking out a window on the north side of the monastery, I spotted a little arbour of banana and avocado trees. I imagined Landa holding court right there, in the tropical shade, under the glistening fruit trees. I imagined him contemplating the fruits of paradise dangling over his head as he awaited the arrival of another miserable backslider. On the patio nearby there was a working mule-powered well with two large creaking gears for drawing up the buckets; the device looked ancient enough to have been functioning since Landa's time. I imagined the mule continuing on its endless rounds while the tortured humans dangled from the hoist a few metres away. And I imagined the buckets being hauled up, spilling cool water, so that the inquisitor might soothe his parched throat in between interrogations.

I continued making my way through the cells until I entered a long room, some sort of gathering place. I took several steps into the room, the floorboards groaning, before I noticed a sign warning against entry: Danger – unstable floor. The sign was positioned where it couldn't be read until the trespasser had passed well into the room. It occurred to me that the Maya must have felt this way in their relations with Landa: the warning signs had appeared too late for them.

I gingerly backed out of the room and tried a narrow stairway that led to the belfry, only to run into a padlocked screen that prevented passage onto the roof. I was disappointed: I remembered reading how John Lloyd Stephens, the great American traveller and explorer of Mayan ruins, had stepped out onto this roof more than 150 years before and beheld a 'boundless view of the great region'. I peered through the screen at the same view, toward the distant line of the Puuc Hills and the surrounding villages. There, lingering on the horizon, I could see the first signs of an afternoon storm.

As I looked down on the grassy atrium fronting the church, I was struck once again by the contrast between its present tranquillity and its violent past. On 12 July 1562, this square had been the scene of pomp and pageantry and persecution, a strange occasion that defied the imagination. Landa had decided to stage his own auto-da-fé, a ceremony more elaborate and more terrible in its display of the Church's supremacy than any previous pogroms in the Yucatán.

Preparations for the great event required contributions from the entire community. Indian women dyed cloth for the making of painted banners, and prepared yellow scapulars painted with bright red St Andrew's crosses – the sanbenitos that penitents would wear in the ceremony. The friars supervised the construction of crosses that were to be shrouded in black cloth. A large wooden platform was built in the square for the Spanish dignitaries in attendance.

On that July day in 1562, beneath a broiling Yucatán sun, the Franciscan friars of Maní proceeded into the plaza, bearing black-shrouded crosses. The friars intoned their litanies while the Indians selected for penance followed in their yellow and red garments. A mounted guard rode behind them, the Spanish soldiers dressed in armour despite the sweltering heat.

All around the atrium, thousands of Indians were gathered to witness the macabre rituals. What went through their minds that day, I wondered, as they gazed upon the colourful assembly of friars and penitents, and upon the huge heaps of masks, wooden statues, pottery vessels and jewelled human skulls – the 'idols' that had so horrified the priests. The Indians listened as Landa delivered a sermon in Mayan. They heard the proclamation of the sentences imposed on the confessed idolaters. They watched as their kinsmen, already debilitated from torture, were tied to posts and lashed; watched as blood added its rich hue to the spectrum of the day; watched as streaked backs burned in the hot sun and the stained stones of the plaza seethed. And then, after the ceremonies, the sermons and the punishments, they watched as Landa set fire to the heap of so-called idols the friars had collected from the tortured penitents – some five thousand objects in all. Before the bonfire died down, Landa pitched in twenty-seven hieroglyphic rolls, the precious folding codices made of beaten-bark paper and deerskin covers that contained the sacred writing of the Maya. With that, Landa transformed a bonfire into a holocaust equal in devastation to the Alexandrine conflagration. What amounted to a sacred Mayan library was lost.

No record was made of the Indian reaction to all this, other than Landa's own words. From his perspective on the viewing platform, Landa thought 'they all showed much repentance and readiness to be good Christians'. He did note, however, with some surprise, that 'they regretted to an amazing degree' the burning of the codices, 'which caused them great affliction'. Landa recorded these observations in his remarkable book, *Relación de las cosas de Yucatán* (Account of the Things of Yucatán), which he wrote in the mid-1560s in his home monastery in Toledo, Spain. After conflicts with the Bishop of Yucatán over the treatment of the Indians, Landa returned to Spain to drum up support for his position (and to defend his actions at Maní before the Council of the Indies). While in Toledo, he wrote the *Relación*, a short but informative report that covered the geography of the peninsula, the cultural practices of the Yucatán Maya and the history of the Spanish presence in the territory. Curiously, his own book disappeared from record until it was discovered in a Paris archive vault 300 years after he'd written it.

Ironies and paradoxes abounded in Landa's story, the most obvious of which was that the man who had worked so hard to destroy Mayan culture was the same man who had diligently recorded details of that culture and who left the world such a wealth of information that one scholar has stated that 'ninety-nine per cent of what we today know of the Mayas, we know as the result either of what Landa has told us . . . or have learned in the use and study of what he told'. And yet Landa's book was important largely because he himself had destroyed the very texts that would have been an even greater source of information had they been spared the flames. At first glance, the enigmatic and contradictory Landa seems characteristically medieval – cruel, bigoted, dogmatic; a destroyer of things alien to his narrow-minded view of truth. At the same time, however, he is a model modern, the precursor of so many Europeans who followed him into 'primitive' lands: all the scientists, anthropologists, ethnographers, colonists, writers and naturalists who made exacting records of the cultures and environments that their own enterprise was in the process of making available and accessible for destruction.

In the few moments I'd taken to muse over the scene of the great auto-da-fé, the storm clouds had grown bigger and darker. Thunder rumbled and the wind picked up. The storm soon came upon Maní and unleashed a driving rain – just another afternoon shower, typical of the region in the rainy season. In July, such storms could be expected daily; I wondered if a storm blew up on that July day in 1562. Did Landa, knowing the likelihood of rain, plan the ceremony for the morning hours? Did they rush to get through the lengthy proceedings as the storm clouds began building on the horizon? And did the rain, when it came at last, quench the smouldering ashes of the pyre? Did the Indians watch the sky, hoping that Chac, their god of rain, would interrupt the event, or at the very least send cleansing showers to wash away its stains? Or did the storm clouds hold off that day, the sky remaining a clear, shimmering, empty and remorseless blue, like the eyes of the Spaniard gazing upon the spectacle from the makeshift stage?

The rain kept me cloistered in the monastery for nearly an hour. I sat on a bench under the arcade of the interior courtyard and drifted into a light sleep while listening to the thunder, to the water running off the roof, and to the voices of Indian children reciting the catechism, the hard lessons repeated over and over until learned by rote.

The rain finally diminished to a drizzle, and I took my groggy leave of Maní. At the door to the church, a tiny old man sidled from the shadows to intercept me. He dragged a deformed leg behind him, the wizened leather of his boot scraping on the floor and echoing in the cavernous church. He drew quite near and brushed against me, appearing like some cave creature emerging from the depths. But as usual, the first impression deceived. A soft, clear voice belied the man's grotesque appearance.

'Do you like our old church?' he enquired. He nodded when I told him I did. 'Yes, it is an interesting place with an interesting history.' He was, he informed me, the doorman of the church and the custodian; he rattled a ring of keys on his belt as confirmation of his status. Did I see everything, he wanted to know? The well? The stone cross? The painting of Santa Lucía? In his opinion, the carvings on the *retablos* here at Maní were the best in all of Mexico. It was a shame more people did not come to see it. If tourists would come, then there might be money for the preservation of the church. But tourists did not come. 'It's not in good condition,' he said with a sigh.

I told him I had come because of Maní's place in the history of the Yucatán. I had come to see the scene of Landa's great auto-da-fé. But I wondered why there was no marker, nothing to commemorate that history.

The doorkeeper looked up at me with a sad, wry smile. 'Ah, well, that is another matter. How do you say *odio* in your language?'

Hatred, I replied.

'Well, you see,' he explained, 'here we have much *odio* for Diego de Landa. No, there can be no memorial to Landa in Maní.'

CHAPTER 23

Mayaland

MY last stop on the Ruta Maya was Chichén Itzá – Mexico's most popular Mayan site. I steeled myself, knowing that I was about to risk tourism overload.

Each day I crossed the large car park filled with tour buses to reach the entrance complex, called the 'Unidad de Servicios', the Unity of Services. Here, the rampant commercialisation of the site was concentrated, amidst the crush and babel of tourist groups all trying to get to the same place. In the stalls outside the main building, vendors proffered examples of Mexican kitsch – fake obsidian pyramids, straw sombreros, lurid masks. The tour guides, on a tight schedule to get through the ruins and back on the Cancún bus in a few hours, herded their groups and tried to keep some sense of order. 'OK, please, everybody listen please,' I heard one exasperated guide say to a group of Americans all shouting at once about when and where their bus would depart. 'I know there are many mentalities in this group but we must stay together please.'

Out on the main plaza, in between the Castillo and the Principal Ball Court, there was more room but hardly less confusion. The huge groups collided and jostled for space in the shade and for prime viewing locations. I walked around, dazed by the moiling crowds.

But given their tight schedules – arriving at eleven in the morning and departing by three in the afternoon – most groups didn't venture far from the main plaza. They made the rounds from the

Ball Court to the Temple of the Jaguars to the Pyramid of Kukulcán to the Temple of the Warriors and the Group of the Thousand Columns, with quick side trips to take in the Sacred Well and the Caracol, the unusual round observatory where the Maya marked the appearance of stars and planets. When the crowd was concentrated in one area, it was possible to head down side paths and win some quiet moments away from the frenzy. During prime time, I wandered down these paths to look at some of the smaller, lesser-known structures.

At one such structure, the Bonehouse, I came upon a restoration project in process. Ancient stone blocks were arranged in rows on the ground. A crew of locals worked at fitting and cementing the stones into one of the pyramid's walls. Their presence served as a reminder to those of us walking around the dead city that its builders, the Maya, were still alive. A reminder should not have been necessary – after all, more than a million Maya lived in the Yucatán and visitors passed through their villages en route to the ruins from Mérida or Cancún. But tourists rarely came into contact with these people, except as waiters or vendors – roles that removed the Maya from their own culture and thrust them into the artificial environment created for tourist comfort.

At the Bonehouse, the Maya workers were at least doing something meaningful. But as I looked at the incised markings on the stones and listened to the workmen speaking their soft, guttural language, it occurred to me just how odd their endeavour was. At the base of the temple lay the remnants of a dead language recorded in stone; above, on the temple platform, the speakers of a descendant language worked at restoring the stones to meaningful order. Perhaps the ancestors of these same men worked on the original construction of the temple they were now reconstructing. The Maya believe history is cyclical: here was good evidence. In the past, however, the temples had been built for the perpetuation of a culture; now they were being rebuilt for the restoration of a culture, or rather the remnants of that culture. And the restoration in this case was being done not for themselves or even for their own elite, but for a foreign elite, a leisured class who had come to enjoy the fruits of native labour. The workmen, however, were probably glad to have the job. But what was the ultimate price, especially if one believed, like Mayanist Michael Coe, that 'the frantic development of tourism over the last twenty-five years has managed to spell the doom of Maya culture' in the Yucatán?

❊

Back in the main plaza of Chichén Itzá, it was readily apparent that the Maya had been appropriated – and commodified – in a number of ways: by those travellers, now legion, for whom the empty materialism of their own civilisation had palled and who were searching for alternative visions of reality; by more sybaritic tourists who had no interest in the sacred and symbolic but who bought into the commercialised spectacle; and of course by those entrepreneurs who recognised a good product and were now prof-iting from the marketing of the Maya. This was perhaps what Michael Coe meant.

All of these appropriations come together in a single event in a single location – the Castillo at Chichén Itzá – where once a year, on the spring equinox, tens of thousands of visitors gather to watch a shadow serpent slither down the balustrades of the pyra-mid. The serpent is created by triangles of light that appear on the otherwise dark northern face of the Castillo precisely at the moment of the equinox. The triangles join to form a body twenty-five metres long that slithers down the pyramid to where the open-jawed stone head of the snake completes the illusion. The elaborate architectural trick simulates a theophany, for the serpent represents Kukulcán, the feathered serpent god, making his descent to the underworld.

Whatever the manifestation meant to its creators, today it has become the signature event of the Mundo Maya. To the entrepre-neurs it means a major marketing ploy, a pseudo-event of the first order. To the sunbathing tourists from Cancún, it means a brief diversion from their beach vacation. And to the New Age seekers, it means – well, I don't know what they think it means, but it brings them out by the thousands. They beat brass gongs, chant (never mind that the chants are from Far Eastern religions), strum guitars, burn incense, raise crystals to the sky and sprinkle each other with ointments.

❁

During prime time, I found it difficult, if not impossible, to see the Castillo for what it once had been. But if I arrived early enough in the day, it was still possible to climb up alone and relish a few moments of solitude twenty-five metres up, with the Mundo Maya and the vast, flat Yucatán spread out below me.

On my last day at Chichén Itzá, my last day on the Ruta Maya, I passed through the empty Unity of Services complex and entered the ruins just after sunrise. Alone on top of the Castillo, I took in the grand view. It seemed even grander in the early-morning light, long beams of sunlight streaming over the dead city, touching fire to the rubble and causing the depictions of warriors on the lintels of the temple to stand out with startling clarity. To the south, the luxury hotels and the seedy tourist town of Pisté interrupted the scrub that overran the Yucatán. In the distance I could make out the long line of steel towers, running from horizon to horizon, that carried the power line from Mérida to Cancún. The power line paralleled the same highway I'd be taking to Cancún for my flight back to the States – a trip I didn't really want to make, but my time was running out. I descended and left Chichén Itzá just as the first tour buses pulled into the car park.

Even though I had a head start, all those buses – and some that hadn't even arrived yet – would beat me back to Cancún. By the time I hitched into Pisté, flagged down a bus and rode a score of slow kilometres, the tourists had made their rounds at the ruins and were speeding back to Cancún. Meanwhile, the slow second-class bus I rode stopped at every small village and churned along muffler-less; by the late afternoon, we were still struggling over the newly paved macadam while the sleek coaches sailed past with a blast of the horn, spewing gravel pellets into our spider-webbed windshield. Cheesy salsa music blared from a distorted stereo. A figurine of the Virgin, looking more like Barbie than Mary, jiggled on the dashboard. And I, having boarded the bus mid-journey, was forced to stand, clinging to the overhead rail, all the way into Ciudad Cancún, the service centre for the huge island resort just across the lagoon.

The hotel and restaurant workers lived in Ciudad Cancún and took the bus over the bridge to the island every day. I didn't even bother to cross over to the Zona Turística, opting instead for a more reasonably priced room on the mainland. By the time I checked in, darkness had fallen. Exhausted from the bus ride and incurious about the government-built town, I fell asleep in my room.

❁

I woke a little after midnight, disturbed by the traffic and the hot diesel smell that drifted into the room through the air-conditioning vent. I opened the curtain for the first time and looked out the window. There, spread out against the horizon, was the glitter and dazzle of the hotel strip, a long row of towers all lit up and glowing in the night. The cylindrical beams of spotlights roved the sky, calling attention to some spurious attraction or another.

No doubt the festivities were in high gear over in Cancún. The revellers, wearing their goofy souvenir T-shirts ('One Tequila, Two Tequila, Three Tequila . . . Floor'), would be dancing and drinking after a day of snorkelling, sunbathing or fishing. There'd be theme restaurants and stripteases and gaudy floor shows that culminated in staged Mayan sacrifices.

I envisioned the Cancún festivities as a weird version of the *ch'ah k'in* carnival in Chamula, the festival that occurs during the lost and evil days between one year's end and the next year's beginning. The monkeys of misrule – foreigners, invaders – wreak havoc and spread disorder throughout the land, celebrating the triumph of chaos. In Cancún, the party was going great guns, while the Maya waited out the misrule of these invader monkeys.

Sitting at the window, looking across the water to the carnival lights, I was certain that I had seen this view, or one very much like it, somewhere before. Over there, a row of lit-up towers jutting into the night sky; here, on this side, a jammed, noisy, stinking clutter. Then I remembered: it was the same arrangement as on the US–Mexican border, in San Diego and El Paso and Brownsville, where the rich, over-built US leaned over impoverished, underdeveloped Mexico. I had made it back to the border; or rather, the border had come to me. The US had pushed across the gulf and set up a new frontier just off the Mexican coast, a border zone where the dollar was the currency, where English was the language, and where the great *ch'ah k'in* carnival was in full swing, a festival of evil days bringing the millennium to its close.

Epilogue

'The demands placed on ecosystems and natural resources from increased tourism can destroy the very attractions that draw people.'
– Elizabeth Boo, World Wildlife Fund

'A jungle hike is merely nature-oriented tourism. It becomes ecotourism only when the resources generated by the tourist's presence are used to improve and protect the natural resource base.'
– Claude Larreur, Organisation of American States

'Green tourism is not always and inevitably considerate, optimizing, controlled, planned, and under local control. This may be the ideal scenario but is not always realism, and there is little if any evidence that it could always remain so, if the tourism industry grows.'
– R. W. Butler, University of Western Ontario

In Latin America, ecotourism is being touted as a near-perfect industry – one that attracts foreign currency, boosts the economies of remote regions and preserves fragile areas. The president of Brazil's national tourism board has summarised the hopes of the region's governments: 'Ecotourism is ideal because it can substitute a few of the more predatory activities, such as agriculture, cattle-raising, and mining, yet it allows an area to develop at the same time'.

That, at least, is the way ecotourism appears in government reports. But out in the wilds, things are quite different. In my travels, it became apparent to me that without some sort of regulation,

271

ecotourism itself would pose a serious threat to the ecosystems that support it. One of the biggest problems is the increase in numbers of nature-oriented tourists. Ecotourism is trendy and therefore lucrative, and where money can be made, opportunists quickly set up shop. Responsible ecotour operators must keep their tours small – the opportunists simply provide services for those visitors who can't be accommodated.

Moreover, the opportunists have recognised that most holiday-makers who say they want nature-oriented tours are in fact only interested in vicarious experiences – that is, they like rustic lodging in the jungle, but they like electricity, hot showers, restaurants and boardwalks even more. Certainly, I found many more operators in Iquitos and Costa Rica promoting comfort than those promoting environmental ethics. These 'soft tour' operators do very little to keep the rainforest pristine, nor do they put much of their profits into its preservation.

With thousands of tourists pouring into the rainforest, and with little infrastructure to handle the flood, the governments in the region may find that ecotourism only hastens what it intends to deter. Given this threat, various international organisations have proposed guidelines for ecotour operators that emphasise resource-sustainable tourism, sensitivity to other cultures, environmentally sound waste disposal and enriching educational experiences. But, of course, adherence to these guidelines is voluntary, and for every operator who conducts business in a responsible and sustainable manner, there are dozens of unregulated and unscrupulous companies which ignore the guidelines and entice travellers with lower prices than their ethical competitors. And at one-fourth the price, they find plenty of takers.

Enforcement of guidelines or of governmental regulations presents yet another problem. Even in the US, enforcement is difficult. Peter Berle, president of the Audubon Society, notes that the US Fish and Wildlife Service finds it 'difficult to make a case against operators' who break the law. In poorer countries, enforcement is even more difficult. With limited funds, a lack of infrastructure, and apathetic justice systems, the countries of

Latin America have no immediate realistic hope of implementing and enforcing regulations.

Yet even a carefully monitored environment like the Galapagos Islands has been damaged by so-called ecotourism. In 1981, Ecuador established a limit of twenty-five thousand tourists a year to the fragile Galapagos. But the islands have proven enormously popular with foreign tourists, and that means big money. By 1990, the government was pressured into allowing over sixty thousand tourists to visit the islands. As a consequence, water pollution and the flourishing of non-native species on the once pristine islands are now evident.

What has happened in the Galapagos could well foreshadow the fate of Latin America, particularly of Amazonia and Costa Rica – namely, hordes of tourists trampling fragile areas, turning wild natural systems into tame playgrounds. My own experiences have taught me how easily it can happen, how well-meaning people such as Bruce, Heather and I can connect with a González and wreak a little havoc.

❂

Back home, I watch the news for developments in Latin America, but information is hard to come by; the region rarely warrants coverage in the United States. Occasionally, images flicker across the screen – a few seconds of a natural disaster or a civil war or drug trade violence. Crucial details are lacking, and the reporters themselves seem uncertain about which country they've parachuted into and unconvinced that the elided details ultimately matter.

Nevertheless, through alternative media sources and serendipity, I gather bits of information that give me some idea of the latest developments. Every few weeks, I receive 'rainforest updates' in the mail – slick, glossy brochures and booklets (much more sophisticated than those I once collected *in situ*) that detail countless opportunities for a 'once in a lifetime journey' and 'high adventure' in Amazonia. The outfits seem to be vying with one another, pushing deeper and deeper into 'unexplored regions' in order to claim that they go 'where other companies simply don't go'. The brochures entice me with photographs of endangered species and descriptions of canopy exploration. I am invited to join 'rugged camping adventures' – one week for $2400, airfare not included.

From these sources, I discover that Iquitos has grown into its role as a base for these elaborate eco-adventures. A new airport, first-class hotels and souvenir stores have all opened up in recent years; the number of tourist arrivals increases annually. Near Francisco de Orellana, a large private biological station now hosts ecotourists interested in learning more about the rainforest canopy. More such camps are scheduled to open in the near future. Yet the huge state of Loreto, of which Iquitos is capital, still has no roads.

✪

I find news of Costa Rica posted on the Internet: the government announces that deforestation has been brought under control and that the country is now a net reforester, planting more trees that it is losing. Almost immediately, the cyberspace claim is answered by cyber-environmental groups who charge that in fact the opposite is true, that more trees are being felled during this logging season than in the last several seasons.

For weeks, I follow the issue on my computer screen. The government announces 'landmark legislation' in the form of a new Forestry Law that bans land-use changes in natural forests. Environmental activists argue that the well-meaning legislation has too many loopholes, and that the logging industry lobby has undermined the legislation by throwing money at legislators.

Also on the Internet, I find information concerning a dispute between the author of a guidebook on Costa Rica and the corporate developer of a large beach resort. The writer gave the resort a bad review on the grounds that the developer's ecological practices were wanton. The corporation, claiming that these claims were false and that in fact the corporation was a model of environmental concern, threatened to sue. The offending material was removed from the guidebook, so the writer has now gone to war on the World Wide Web.

✪

A Guatemalan friend sends me an update from her country. While in Guatemala, I noticed only scattered references to ecotourism – certainly nothing remotely like Costa Rica, where the term appeared everywhere. Now, my friend tells me, Guatemalans have discovered that the concept of ecotourism can be lucrative. A university in the capital has started a degree programme in the subject, and the ministry of tourism, INGUAT, is promoting what's left of Guatemala's rainforests.

My friend includes a copy of an INGUAT publication, a magazine that is placed in every room of finer hotels around the country. Called *Discover Guatemala*, the magazine speaks of the 'major potential for ecotourism' and of the 'great efforts made to protect the country's remaining natural areas' (note the use of the word 'remaining'). INGUAT concludes that Guatemala is 'a treasure trove for ecotourists who crave a return to nature'. As an example, the magazine cites the opportunities for 'authenticity and richness' in Sayaxché, a jungle town in the Petén, where 'you will find speed boats, telephone, and radio' and 'three inns offering hot water and television'.

✪

The mail also brings me a newsletter promoting investment opportunities in Mexico. I will no doubt want to invest in their development projects, the newsletter suggests, when I learn that twenty-two million tourists visited Mexico last year, and that the number is growing by six per cent a year. Indeed, tourism is Mexico's number two product after oil. The newsletter specifically refers to 'the ground-breaking tourism and regional development initiative known as Maya World'. Chiapas is touted as an especially good opportunity, given the newly opened airports in Palenque and San Cristóbal. A new highway under construction near the Guatemalan border will open up remote archaeological sites such as Bonampak and Yaxchilán – the very area where Mayan villagers recently attacked a team of archaeologists. The newsletter boasts that 'visitors to such indigenous communities as San Juan Chamula increased by a total of fifty per cent'. The bottom line: 'ecotourism opportunities are seeing visitor numbers on the up' and the smart investor will get in on the game. The newsletter does not mention the Zapatistas.

❁

Bit by bit, news trickles in from south of the border. But over the years, I have heard virtually nothing about the Mosquitia. The place achieved some fame in the 1980s when Paul Theroux published his novel *The Mosquito Coast*, and shortly thereafter Harrison Ford starred in the film version. I read the book: a good novel, an interesting and entertaining story. I found it difficult, however, to recognise the Mosquitia that I knew in the one that Theroux depicted. The descriptions were beautiful and no doubt accurate, but Theroux wrote mainly about the Garífuna people and the interior of the Mosquitia. My experience, on the other hand, was with the Miskito Indians on the easternmost coast.

The Miskito did make the news in the mid-1980s when Ronald Reagan, in his obsession with ridding the Western hemisphere of the Sandinista plague, adopted the Miskitos as his cause célèbre. The Nicaraguan Miskitos, it seemed, suffered mistreatment at the hands of the Sandinistas (mostly by way of a misguided policy that attempted to relocate the Miskitos out of conflict zones where Reagan's Contras had set up for business). Some Miskitos fled Nicaragua for refugee camps in Honduras.

But in the brief flurry of news coming out of the region, I never heard mention of Brus Laguna or the biosphere. The place remained unmarked on maps, unknown, isolated, frozen in time. I came to regard it as my own private reserve. No one else I knew had ever been there, and I revelled in that knowledge.

Then, the other day, I went to the bookstore. As is my habit, I browsed the travel section, checking out the new titles. The Latin American shelf has grown substantially in the last few years, with Mexico and Costa Rica leading the way. A good number of titles reflect the growing interest in ecotourism: *Adventure Guide to Central America*; *Guatemala: A Natural Destination*; *Adventuring in Costa Rica*.

On this visit, I came across a slim white volume I had never seen before, and its title gave me a sudden pang: *La Mosquitia: A Guide to the Savannas, Rain Forests, and Turtle Hunters*. Flicking through the pages, I learned that several ecotour operators had set up shop in Tegucigalpa, San Pedro Sula, La Ceiba and even in Brus Laguna. Ecotourists could now have jungle treks and canoeing and birdwatching arranged for them in the once untrammelled wilds of the Mosquitia.

One section of the book concerned Brus Laguna; another provided details on visiting the biosphere. My Brus Laguna. My biosphere. I stared at the map on the page, trying to find some evidence of the places I knew. There were similarities, but it was clear that Brus Laguna had undergone some changes: a restaurant, some stores, a few hotels. All pretty basic, according to the guidebook, but certainly more than I found twenty years ago.

I learned that the World Heritage Committee has placed the biosphere on its List of World Heritage in Danger. Cattle ranching has reduced the forest area, and illegal lumber operations have extracted the precious hardwood. Commercial hunting, often under the guise of ecotourism, is hastening the extermination of endangered species. Just as the biosphere is being discovered, it is vanishing.

And then I read a section on what the book referred to as 'Cannon Key', a small island in the lagoon where buccaneer cannons and an old fort had been uncovered. It was, I had no doubt, the same island I had visited with Old Mr Goff and Pastor Mark. A sportfishing camp has been built there. 'Caribbean Adventure Tours', I learned, takes tourists by launch on deep-sea fishing excursions and on photo sessions around the lagoon. Three hundred dollars a night, inclusive. Electrical generators, hot water, North American food, a fully stocked bar.

The place was now forever lost to me.

The jungle doesn't exist. I know. I've been there.

LONELY PLANET JOURNEYS

JOURNEYS is a unique collection of travel writing – published by the company that understands travel better than anyone else.

It is a series for anyone who has ever experienced – or dreamed of – the magical moment when they encountered a strange culture or saw a place for the first time. They are tales to read while you're planning a trip, while you're on the road or while you're in an armchair, in front of a fire.

These outstanding titles explore our planet through the eyes of a diverse group of international writers. JOURNEYS books catch the spirit of a place, illuminate a culture, recount an adventure, or introduce a fascinating way of life. They always entertain, and always enrich the experience of travel.

'Lively, intelligent and varied . . . an important contribution to travel literature' – *Age (Melbourne)*

BRIEF ENCOUNTERS
Stories of Love, Sex & Travel
edited by Michelle de Kretser

Love affairs on the road, passionate holiday flings, disastrous pick-ups, erotic encounters . . . In this seductive collection of stories, 22 authors from around the world write about travel romances. A tourist in Peru falls for her handsome guide; a writer explores the ambiguities of his relationship with a Japanese woman; a beautiful young man on a train proposes marriage . . . Combining fiction and reportage, *Brief Encounters* is must-have reading – for everyone who has dreamt of escape with that perfect stranger.

Includes stories by Pico Iyer, Mary Morris, Emily Perkins, Mona Simpson, Lisa St Aubin de Terán, Paul Theroux and Sara Wheeler.

DRIVE THRU AMERICA
Sean Condon

If you've ever wanted to drive across the US but couldn't find the time (or afford the gas), *Drive Thru America* is perfect for you.

In his search for American myths and realities – along with comfort, cable TV and good, reasonably priced coffee – Sean Condon paints a hilarious road-portrait of the USA.

'entertaining and laugh-out-loud funny'
– Alex Wilber, Travel editor, Amazon.com

SEAN & DAVID'S LONG DRIVE
Sean Condon

Sean and David are young townies who have rarely strayed beyond city limits. One day, for no good reason, they set out to discover their homeland, and what follows is a wildly entertaining adventure that covers half of Australia.

'a hilariously detailed log of two burned out friends' *– Rolling Stone*

'a definitive Generation X road epic . . . a wonderful read' *– Globe & Mail*

FULL CIRCLE
A South American Journey
Luis Sepúlveda (translated by Chris Andrews)

'A journey without a fixed itinerary' in the company of Chilean writer Luis Sepúlveda. Extravagant characters and extraordinary situations are memorably evoked: gauchos organising a tournament of lies, a scheming heiress on the lookout for a husband, a pilot with a corpse on board his plane . . . Part autobiography, part travel memoir, *Full Circle* brings us the distinctive voice of one of South America's most compelling writers.

WINNER 1996 Astrolabe – Etonnants Voyageurs award for the best work of travel literature published in France.

IN RAJASTHAN
Royina Grewal

As she writes of her travels through Rajasthan, Indian writer Royina Grewal takes us behind the exotic facade of this fabled destination: here is an insider's perceptive account of India's most colourful state, conveying the excitement and challenges of a region in transition.

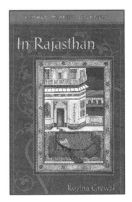

'a vibrant portrait of the state of princes, snake charmers and astologers' – *Tatler*

THE GATES OF DAMASCUS
Lieve Joris (translated by Sam Garrett)

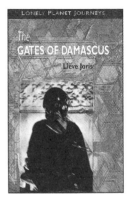

This best-selling book is a beautifully drawn portrait of day-to-day life in modern Syria. Through her intimate contact with local people, Lieve Joris draws us into the fascinating world that lies behind the gates of Damascus. Hala's husband is a political prisoner, jailed for his opposition to the Assad regime; through the author's friendship with Hala we see how Syrian politics impacts on the lives of ordinary people.

'she has expanded the boundaries of travel writing'
– Times Literary Supplement

LOST JAPAN
Alex Kerr

Lost Japan draws on the author's personal experiences of Japan over thirty years. Alex Kerr takes his readers on a backstage tour, exploring different facets of his involvement with the country: friendships with Kabuki actors, buying and selling art, studying calligraphy, exploring rarely visited temples and shrines.

'one of the finest books about Japan written in decades' *– Insight Japan*

KINGDOM OF THE FILM STARS
Journey into Jordan
Annie Caulfield

Kingdom of the Film Stars is a travel book and a love story. With honesty and humour, Annie Caulfield writes of travelling in Jordan and falling in love with a Bedouin with film-star looks.

She offers fascinating insights into the country – from the tent life of traditional women to the hustle of downtown Amman – and unpicks tight-woven Western myths about the Arab world.

'part travelogue, part love story – and always compelling'
– Mademoiselle

THE OLIVE GROVE
Travels in Greece
Katherine Kizilos

Katherine Kizilos travels to fabled islands, troubled border zones and her family's village deep in the mountains. She vividly evokes breathtaking landscapes, generous people and passionate politics, capturing the complexities of a country she loves.

The Olive Grove tells of other journeys too: the life-changing journey made by the author's emigrant father; the migration of young Greeks to cities; and the tremendous impact of tourism on Greek society.

'beautifully captures the real tensions of Greece'
– Sunday Times

SONGS TO AN AFRICAN SUNSET
A Zimbabwean Story
Sekai Nzenza-Shand

Songs to an African Sunset braids
vividly personal stories into an intimate
picture of contemporary Zimbabwe.
Returning to her family's village after
many years in the West, Sekai Nzenza-
Shand discovers a world where ancestor
worship, polygamy and witchcraft still
govern the rhythms of daily life – and
where drought, deforestation and AIDS
have wrought devastating changes. With
insight and affection, she explores a culture torn between respect for the old
ways and the irresistible pull of the new.

THE RAINBIRD
A Central African Journey
Jan Brokken (translated by Sam Garrett)

The Rainbird is a classic travel story.
Following in the footsteps of famous
Europeans such as Albert Schweitzer
and H.M. Stanley, Jan Brokken jour-
neyed to Gabon in central Africa. A
kaleidoscope of adventures and anecdotes, *The Rainbird* brilliantly chroni-
cles the encounter between Africa and
Europe as it was acted out on a side-
street of history. It is also the compelling, immensely readable account of
the author's own travels in one of the
most remote and mysterious regions of
Africa.

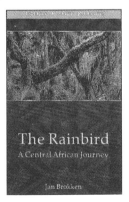

PLANET TALK
Lonely Planet's FREE quarterly newsletter

Every issue of PLANET TALK is packed with up-to-date travel news and advice including:

- a letter from Lonely Planet founders Tony and Maureen Wheeler
- travel diary from a Lonely Planet author
- find out what it's really like out on the road
- feature article on an important and topical travel issue
- a selection of recent letters from our readers
- the latest travel news from all over the world
- details on Lonely Planet's new and forthcoming releases

To join our mailing list contact any Lonely Planet office.

LONELY PLANET OFFICES

Australia: PO Box 617, Hawthorn 3122, Victoria
tel: (03) 9819 1877 fax: (03) 9819 6459
e-mail: talk2us@lonelyplanet.com.au

USA: 150 Linden St, Oakland, CA 94607
tel: (510) 893 8555 TOLL FREE: 800 275-8555
fax: (510) 893 8572
e-mail: info@lonelyplanet.com

UK: 10a Spring Place, London NW5 3BH
tel: (0171) 428 4800 fax: (0171) 428 4828
e-mail: go@lonelyplanet.co.uk

France: 71 bis rue du Cardinal Lemoine, 75005 Paris
tel: (01) 44 32 06 20 fax: (01) 46 34 72 55
e-mail: bip@lonelyplanet.fr

www.lonelyplanet.com

THE LONELY PLANET STORY

Lonely Planet published its first book in 1973 in response to the numerous 'How did you do it?' questions Maureen and Tony Wheeler were asked after driving, busing, hitching, sailing and railing their way from England to Australia.

Written at a kitchen table and hand collated, trimmed and stapled, *Across Asia on the Cheap* became an instant local bestseller, inspiring thoughts of another book.

Eighteen months in South-East Asia resulted in their second guide, *South-East Asia on a shoestring*, which they put together in a backstreet Chinese hotel in Singapore in 1975. The 'yellow bible', as it quickly became known to backpackers around the world, soon became *the* guide to the region. It has sold well over half a million copies and is now in its 9th edition, still retaining its familiar yellow cover.

Today there are over 240 titles, including travel guides, walking guides, language kits & phrasebooks, travel atlases and travel literature. The company is the largest independent travel publisher in the world. Although Lonely Planet initially specialised in guides to Asia, today there are few corners of the globe that have not been covered.

The emphasis continues to be on travel for independent travellers. Tony and Maureen still travel for several months of each year and play an active part in the writing, updating and quality control of Lonely Planet's guides.

They have been joined by over 70 authors and 170 staff at our offices in Melbourne (Australia), Oakland (USA), London (UK) and Paris (France). Travellers themselves also make a valuable contribution to the guides through the feedback we receive in thousands of letters each year and on our web site.

The people at Lonely Planet strongly believe that travellers can make a positive contribution to the countries they visit, both through their appreciation of the countries' culture, wildlife and natural features, and through the money they spend. In addition, the company makes a direct contribution to the countries and regions it covers. Since 1986 a percentage of the income from each book has been donated to ventures such as famine relief in Africa; aid projects in India; agricultural projects in Central America; Greenpeace's efforts to halt French nuclear testing in the Pacific; and Amnesty International.

'I hope we send people out with the right attitude about travel. You realise when you travel that there are so many different perspectives about the world, so we hope these books will make people more interested in what they see.'

– Tony Wheeler